to Molly –

Joseph Dudonolay

TO LIVE
WITH
HOPE,
TO DIE
WITH
DIGNITY

TO LIVE WITH HOPE, TO DIE WITH DIGNITY

SPIRITUAL RESISTANCE IN THE GHETTOS AND CAMPS

JOSEPH RUDAVSKY

JASON ARONSON INC.
Northvale, New Jersey
Jerusalem

Library of Congress Cataloging-in-Publication Data

Rudavsky, Joseph, 1922–
    To live with hope, to die with dignity : spiritual resistance in
the ghettos and camps / by Joseph Rudavsky.
        p. cm.
    Previously published: Lanham : University Press of America, c1987.
    Includes bibliographical references.
    ISBN 1–56821–940–7 (alk. paper)
    1. Holocaust, Jewish (1939-1945) 2. World War, 1939-1945—Jewish
resistance. 3. Jews—Poland—Warsaw—Intellectual life. 4. Jews—
Lithuania—Vilnius—Intellectual life. 5. Jews—Poland—Lódz—
Intellectual life. 6. Jews—Lithuania—Kaunas—Intellectual life.
7. Poland—Intellectual life—1918-1945. 8. Lithuania—Intellectual
life. I. Title.
D804.3.R83   1997
940.53'18—dc20   96–340

Manufactured in the United States of America. Jason Aronson Inc. offers books and cassettes. For information and catalog write to Jason Aronson Inc., 230 Livingston Street, Northvale, NJ 07647.

Dedicated to the Memory of
Dr. Karl Heinz Neisser
(1907-1981)

Devoted friend, ardent Jew,
committed to his people's survival

Contents

Introduction

A study of Jewish history and thought reveals a number of basic Jewish concepts that have helped the Jewish people survive two millenia of homelessness and persecution. Among others, these concepts include monotheism, messianism, reward and punishment, sin and repentance, *Shivat Tziyon* - return to Zion, *Kiddush Hashem* - sanctification of God's name, *Tzedakah* (the application to life of righteousness and justice), *Talmud Torah* (the obligation to study Biblical and Rabbinic writings), and *Zechut Avot* (the merit of the Fathers). [1]

During the Holocaust Period yet another concept was perceived to be crucial for Jewish survival under almost intolerable conditions. This concept, *Kiddush Hahayyim*, stressed the sanctification of God by living, not surrendering, in the face of oppression. It was distinct from *Kiddush Hashem*, which required martyrdom as the way to sanctify the Divine Name.

Nathan Eck, an historian of the Holocaust Period and a Warsaw ghetto survivor, relates that he was present at a secret meeting of Warsaw's Zionist leadership early in 1940. The meeting, held at the home of Rabbi Isaac Nissenbaum (1868-1942), was convened to deal with the question of *Aliyah* (immigration to Palestine) which was still possible at that time. At this gathering the term *Kiddush Hahayyim* was first applied to describe how Jews should respond to the impending catastrophe. It was an epigram of Rabbi Nissenbaum, who at age 72 could look back over four decades of Jewish communal and religious leadership in Poland, Latvia, and Lithuania. He was an individual who stood at the forefront of Jewish life as an outstanding Rabbi and *Darshan* (preacher) at Warsaw's Ohel Moshe Synagogue, as an editor and Hebrew writer, and as a molder of Mizrachi, the Religious Zionist Party. Rabbi Nissenbaum characterized the nature of the response pattern of the Jew as an individual and as a member of the community confronting Hitlerism and Nazism. He told the gathering:

> "It is a time for *Kiddush Hahayyim*, the sanctification of life, and not *Kiddush Hashem*, the holiness of martyrdom. In the past the enemies of the Jews sought the soul of the Jew, and so it was proper for the Jew to sanctify the name of God by sacrificing his body in Martyrdom, in that manner preserving what the enemy sought to take from him. But now it is the *body* of the Jew that the oppressor demands. For this reason it is up to the Jew to defend his body, to preserve his life . . ." [2]

Eck concluded his report by observing that the will to live not only physically, but of equal importance spiritually, surfaced among ghetto inhabitants with an almost mystical vigor unequalled in normal times.

In more modern terms, *Kiddush Hahayyim* might best be described as "the affirmation of life," in contrast to mere physical survival. *Kiddush Hahayyim* refers to the sanctity of the Jewish individual, to his daily life, and to the validity of Judaism as a way of life no matter what the external circumstances.

Kiddush Hahayyim, the late historian Shaul Esh wrote in the early Sixties:

> "... explains the enormous will to live that was emphasized at all times and in all places, in the midst of the basest degradation, a will best expressed by the Yiddish word that was on the lips of the majority of the survivors of the Holocaust — *iber-leyben*, to survive, to remain alive. The Jews of Eastern Europe felt, in fact, that victory over the enemy lay in their continued existence, for the enemy desired their extinction. 'However wretched existence may be, it is a *mitzvah* (religious duty) to exist." [3]

For Rabbi Nissenbaum, *Kiddush Hahayyim* was an authentic element in Jewish theology which reflected the Jewish will to live. It operated in historical terms to enable the Jew as an individual and as a member of the community to adapt to changing times and conditions. *Kiddush Hahayyim*, for Nissenbaum, stood in dynamic tension with *Kiddush Hashem*. In an early sermon on *Kedushah* (sanctification) published in 1911 Nissenbaum noted:

> ... But in the final analysis, the goal of *Kiddush Hashem* is not to die in the name of sanctity ... but rather to live in sanctity, to become holy through our way of life, 'because He (God) is holy' and we must adhere to His ways! *Kiddush Hashem* requires that we guard the people's sanctities ... this is our primary obligation ... If we fulfill *Kiddush Hashem* by the way we live we will not be impelled to sanctify the Divine Name through our death. We will live with sanctity and we shall be a sanctified people ... [4]

Kiddush Hahayyim, applied to the Holocaust, implied Jewish continuity and flexibility as responses to the external pressures which could have resulted in the complete breakdown and dissolution of the Jewish community. Instead, it inspired at least a goodly number of Jews trapped in the ghettos to try to reorganize their personal and communal lives in order not only to merely survive physically as long as possible, but also to make their survival spiritually meaningful. As distinct from the sacrifice of martyrdom, *Kiddush Hahayyim* implied that the sanctification of the Name of God results from acts that lead to worthy and dignified living. In the words of the Vilna poet Abraham Sutzkever:

> "Do not forget to survive for the sake of sanctifying the name of God, with stress on the word 'survive' " [5]

Isaiah Spiegel, a short story writer who survived the Lodz ghetto and the Auschwitz Death Camp, noted in an interview:

> "We are an optimistic people. Our Torah is a doctrine of life, not of death and of sacrifice. Ours is not to sanctify the name of

God by martyrdom, but rather by life itself." 6

As a basic Jewish concept, *Kiddush Hahayyim* is a normative frame of reference for Jewish life experiences. It must be understood not as an abstract principle but as an approach to life read out of Jewish thought, traditions, practices, moral imperatives, and movements that have developed within the community. Thus this work will begin with an overview of *Kiddush Hahayyim*, analyzing its development, its place, and its articulation in Judaism.

It also should be noted that this work recognizes that in fact relatively few survived the Holocaust. Thus it is not concerned with the measurement of the efficacy of *Kiddush Hahayyim* in terms of the number of Jews it may have helped to survive. Rather it deals with the unique quality of life that it encouraged in the eastern European ghettos during the Holocaust era.

This work describes a singular phenomenon: the creation and preservation of a life of high Jewish quality in the ghettos of Warsaw, Vilna, Lodz, and Kovno — a life that contrasts with the horrors of the physical living conditions in the ghettos. In retelling the Holocaust story in all its tragedy and horror this aspect is all too often obscured and lost. It is not intended to diminish in any way the enormity of the suffering, but rather to see the victims in a different light. Side by side with unspeakable persecution, suffering, and death, there were those who sought to rise above their calamitous situation. It is with this aspect that this work concerns itself. It is based on materials created and activities conducted by the victims themselves in several ghettos during the Holocaust years.

Originally, this book was written as a doctoral dissertation. At a very early stage it became clear that it was beyond the scope of this study to describe all the Holocaust ghettos, large and small, in terms of the object lessons they could provide in relation to *Kiddush Hahayyim*, the Jewish will to live with hope and, if necessary, to die with dignity. Therefore, the research reported here is limited to four of the largest ghettos that were established by the Nazis in Eastern Europe. The ghettos of Kovno, Vilna, Lodz, and Warsaw were selected because of what these communities represented historically in Jewish life. Kovno and Vilna, centers rich in Jewish tradition, known for their Yeshivot — Rabbinical academies and vital traditionalism. Lodz, the Manchester of Poland, where Jews actively participated in the fabric of the Polish economy. Warsaw, the Polish capital which boasted a cosmopolitan Jewish community that served as a national center for all Jewish life in Poland. These communities historically and in terms of the agony of the Holocaust period are most remembered and serve as archetypes of the hundreds of other ghettos.

There is yet another limitation that should be noted. It is the author's contention that although the concept *Kiddush Hahayyim* has the characteristic of a theological value, it has had in the past, as it has in the present, implications for Jewish secular life and thought. In reviewing the sources it seems clear that the extant secular materials justify an independent study.

The author, therefore, has limited himself to a religious and Zionist orientation with only a few allusions to secular material in the first part of this study.

It must be noted that this work would not have been completed without the generous help and advice of my dissertation advisors at New York University, Dr. Baruch Levine and Dr. David Rudavsky. In addition I also received invaluable assistance from Dr. Joseph Kermish, (former) Chief Archivist of Yad Vashem in Jerusalem, Shmuel Krakovski, his associate (now chief Archivist) as well as the staff of the library of Yad Vashem and its Director, Ora Alcalay. At other centers of Holocaust studies, particularly Beit Lochamai Hageta-ot, I greatly benefited from the meaningful help provided by its director, the late Tzvee Shner and its archivist Miriam Novitch, as well as from Shelomo Shazar of the Moreshet Archives at Givat Haviva. Gratefully, I refer to the good counsel offered me by Dr. Gershon Appel of Stern College, Yehiel Sheintuch of Mifaley Mendele at the Hebrew University, and Dr. Leonard Kravitz of the Hebrew Union College – Jewish Institute of Religion. I should like to acknowledge my editor, Gertrude Hirshler, for her exemplary efforts, as well as the work of volunteer typists Harriet Fishman and Julia Getzoff, two members of my congregation who helped prepare the original manuscript, as well as Elizabeth Schurer and Lee Ann Foley of Ramapo College of New Jersey.

I should like to acknowledge with thanks the cooperation afforded to me by the Art Museum of Yad Vashem, the Holocaust Martyrs' and Heroes' Remembrance Authority of Jerusalem as well as the Ghetto Fighters Kibbutz Museum. Both of these institutions allowed me to photograph their works of art for this book.

Finally, I also express my gratitude to the Memorial Foundation for Jewish Culture for the grant that enabled me to carry on the necessary research in Israel, and to the congregation of Temple Sholom of River Edge, New Jersey. It was during my tenure as its Rabbi that this project was completed with the congregation's understanding and encouragement.

---

1. George Foot Moore, *Judaism*, 2 vols. (Cambridge: Harvard University Press, 1932) Vol. 1, Monotheism, p. 360 ff; Repentance, pp. 507-534; Sin pp. 463-473; Merit of the Fathers p. 538 ff., p. 524 f.; Vol. 2, Messianism, pp. 323-376; Reward and Punishment p. 89 f.; Righteousness, p. 89; Study of Torah, pp. 18, 96, 239; 241, 245 f.
    See also:
    Louis Finkelstein, *The Jews*, 2 vols. (New York: Harper Brothers, 1949) Vol. 2, pp. 1327-1346 *passim*.

2. Nathan Eck, *Hato-eh B'darchay Hamavet* ("Wanderers on Death's Road") (Jerusalem: Yad Vashem, 1960) pp. 37, 244.

3. Shaul Esh, "The Dignity of the Destroyed," *Judaism Magazine*, Spring, 1962, p. 107.

4. Harav Yizchak Nissenbaum, *Hagut Halev* ("Thoughts of the Heart") (2nd ed.; Warsaw; n.p., 1911) pp. 33-34.

5. Hebrew University and The Institute of Contemporary Jewry, Oral History Division, Tape 2049 dated January 25, 1973. Interviewers: Rabbi Joseph Rudavsky and Mr. Yehiel Sheintuch. Interviewee: Abraham Sutzkever.

6. Hebrew University and The Institute of Contemporary Jewry, Oral History Division, Tape 2024 dated January 25, 1973. Interviewers: Rabbi Joseph Rudavsky and Mr. Yeheil Sheintuch. Interviewee: Isaiah Spiegel.

Part One
The Genesis of
the Jewish Concept
of *Kiddush Hahayyim*

Chapter One

Kiddush Hahayyim:
The Genesis of a Jewish Concept

Kiddush Hahayyim defines an authentic approach to life which flows through Jewish history, religion, practice, and culture. As a pivotal Jewish concept it can be identified and traced back to earliest Jewish sources.

Kiddush Hahayyim as a basic Jewish value rests on both Biblical and Rabbinic perceptions of God, His relationship to man, and the role of Israel in the Divine scheme of things. Both Biblical and Rabbinic sources view God not as the holy Other, detached from this worldly human life, but as a definitive force shaping and itself being shaped by human events. Hence, though Judaism is theocentric, God and man are interdependent, for it is through humankind that God is defined and realized in life. Thus Pesikta deRabbi Kahanah notes:

> Rabbi Simeon bar Yohai taught: 'If you are my witnesses I am God, but if you are not my witnesses, it is as if I am not God . . .[1]

In the Judaic value system, God, as the Creator and source of all existence, is actualized through the life and the experiences of humanity on earth. This is clearly expressed in the Zohar:

> . . . The unity of God, and the existence of the world that flows from it rests on man . . . The well-known introduction (part 2, page 1) explains the verse "Mee Barah et Aleh' ('Who created these'), not as a question, but as a declaration: The word *'Mee'* (Who) refers to God who is beyond questioning while the word *'Aleh'* (these) refers to the world, hence God, Who is beyond questioning, created the world. Continuing, the word 'Elohim' (God) is compounded from two words *'Mee'* and *'Aleh'* to indicate that 'until He created the world, His name was not God, for God is the One Who participates in the world . . .[2]

It is within this broader context that Israel the people exemplifies, reflects, and bring holiness into the world.

... for God is sanctified in His world through His relationship to mankind in general and Israel in particular ... Ezekiel observes " ... I bring you out from the peoples, and gather you out from the countries where you have been scattered; and I will be sanctified in you in the sight of the nations. And you shall know that I am the Lord when I bring you into the land of Israel ...' (20:41-42) ... The source of God's sanctity in His world is revealed in his revelation to mankind and to Israel.[3]

Clearly, the meaningfulness of human existence is based on humanity's relationship to God. Because God is holy, humanity too, through the pattern of life it develops, has the potential for holiness. Man achieves his holiness by incorporating into his life the essence of divinity as he seeks to emulate God in his own day-to-day life and conduct. This idea is expressed in numerous Midrashic homilies such as the *Mekilta deRabbi Ishmael*.

'And I shall glorify Him' ... Abba Saul says: 'O be like Him! Just as He is gracious and merciful, so you also shall be gracious and merciful ...[4]

Rabbinic homilies tend to focus on this world, rather than on the next, conceptualizing reward and punishment not primarily in terms of the hereafter, but at least equally in terms of earthly existence. The goal of Torah, the teachings of Judaism as set forth in Biblical law and Rabbinic tradition, is not specifically to prepare for the "World to Come" but primarily to enrich contemporary human life in concrete ways while one lives. Thus "salvation" in normative Judaism is not separate from life, but inextricably linked with human life and its worldly sanctity.

The specific obligation which the people of Israel assumed under the terms of the Covenant with God is to elevate all of humanity by exemplifying through its own conduct the role of God in human life. Israel's "chosenness" and its status as a "holy nation" simply implies that Israel is to live in the light of God. It does so by adhering to behavior patterns specified in Biblical law and explicated in Rabbinic tradition as conducive to a "life of holiness" in the here and now. Note the following verses of Scripture focusing on this role:

You Shall be My own treasure from among all the peoples. (Ex. 19:5) You shall be holy for I, the Lord your God, am holy. (Lev. 19:2) And you shall not profane My holy Name, but I will be hallowed among the children of Israel; I am the Lord Who hallows you, Who brought you out of the land of Egypt, to be your God. I am the Lord.[5]

These verses explicitly state Israel's duty to bear witness to God and to sanctify life. It is from these verses, too, that the architects of Rabbinic Judaism derived the concept of *Kiddush Hashem*, the "Sanctification of the Divine Name." Initially the concept of *Kiddush Hashem* required martyrdom as the valid response to a variety of situations. Yet since it is ". . . among the children of Israel. . ." that the name of God is to be sanctified, it was interpreted to mean that Israel is primarily expected to sanctify God by affirming life as it is lived for itself and all mankind. This naturally lead to the concept *Kiddish Hahayyim*, the Sanctification of Life. Dr. Ben-Zion Dinur, the historian and former Minister of Education and first president of the Yad Vashem Heroes' and Martyrs' Authority in Israel, points to the relationship between *Kiddush Hashem* and *Kiddush Hahayyim*:

> . . . *Kiddush Hashem*, the Sanctification of the Divine Name, may be defined primarily as *Kiddush Hahayyim*, the Sanctification of Life. It testifies to the sanctity of God, the Creator, and to Israel, which fulfills this task. Certainly the chosenness of Israel is a biblical concept from Abraham's time. As it was promised to him: 'I shall make you a great people, and through you the peoples of the earth shall be blessed' . . . The name 'Israel' is sacred. The role of Israel in the world is that of priests spreading sanctity in the world through their life before the nations as a community, as a people, and as individuals . . . Israel is obliged through its acts to testify to the sanctity of God and to proclaim it in the world . . .[6]

Both Biblical and Rabbinic tradition place a premium not only on the sanctification of God but also on the dignity and sanctity of human life as evidence of Divine Sanctity. The books of Leviticus and Deuteronomy are replete with what a later age would call "social legislation."[7] The Talmud expands at length Torah's social ethic with questions of human welfare and survival. For example, note such concerns as: If two people travel in the wilderness and they have between them only enough water to insure the survival of one of them, should the water be shared equally by the two with neither partner able to survive, or should it be consumed by one of them, in order that at least one will have a chance of survival?[8] If a woman is in difficult labor, may she be aborted to save her life, or must she die rather than forfeit the life of the fetus?[9] Jewish law forbids self-inflicted injury; under what circumstances may an individual transgress that law?[10] Is an individual's life less valuable than that of the group?[11]

Biblical and Rabbinic sources recognize the duality of human nature: sensuality and spirituality. Yet they deal with the human potential to develop a meaningful pattern of life without disparagement or denial of the sensual. What is most significant is the elevation, the sanctification of the sensual. The Midrash notes:

> (Humans) reflect two types of capacities: lower, animal-like and divine. Rabbi Yehoshua bar Nachman notes in the name of Rabbi Hanina bar Yitzchak and Rabbi Eliezer that humans were created with four capacities derived from the lower world and four from the divine sphere. The human being eats, drinks,

15

evacuates, reproduces, and dies like animals, while on the other hand he stands erect, speaks, comprehends, and sees like divine beings.[12]

The duality of the human being is broadened and conceptualized as *Yetzer Hatov* and *Yetzer Ha-rah*, the "good impulse" and the "evil impulse" respectively. The evil impulse which includes instinctual human drives is not a negative absolute, but is sublimated to the good impulse. In fact, evil impulses are potentially catalysts for the good. Thus man's task is not to deny his sensuality, but rather to sublimate it for the purposes of spirituality.

The Jewish sex ethic is illustrative of this approach. It is categorized as a function of *Yetzer Ha-rah*, yet it leads to human fulfillment and sanctity.

> Nachman said in Rabbi Samuel's name: 'Behold it was very good', refers to the *Yetzer Hatov* (the good impulse) while 'And Behold It Was Very Good', refers to the *Yetzer Ha-rah* (the evil impulse). Can then the Evil Impulse be very good? That would be extraordinary! But for the Evil Impulse, however, no man would build a house, take a wife, and beget children . . .[13]

In Judaism, human sexuality becomes a valid drive elevated and sanctified through *Kiddushin*, marriage which is not a concession to the demands of the flesh. Sex in marriage is sacred, fulfilling two primary human drives: procreation and sexual fulfillment. This is normative Judaism expressing the sanctity of the sexual experience in life. One can refer to the Moses Nachmanides (1195 – 1270) work, *Iggeret Hakodesh* (Epistle of Holiness), on this subject.[14]

Parenthetically, it is significant to note that the Talmud holds the individual accountable for all legitimate physical pleasures he denies himself in this world.[15] It also admonishes an ascetic not to add to the prohibitions and restrictions already in place.[16] Judaism deals here with what may be defined as the quality of life sanctifying rather than denigrating the physical. What is extrapolated is meaningful living which in essence is Jewish living, a function of *Kiddush Hahayyim*.

As already noted there is a continuum, polar in nature with *Kiddush Hahayyim* at one pole and *Kiddush Hashem*, that is to say martyrdom, at the other.

While the Jew is obliged to honor the concept *Kiddush Hashem*, as expressed in the readiness to suffer martyrdom rather than transgress the cardinal principles of Judaism, he is also commanded not to disregard the principle of *Pikuach Nefesh*, which provides that when life is in danger, saving life supersedes everything else.

In the book of Leviticus the warning against the pagan abominations of ancient Egypt and Canaan is followed by the verse (18:5), "You shall keep . . . My statutes and My ordinances, which, if a man do, he shall live by them." Rabbinic interpretation has singled out as the key phrase the words *Vachai Bahem* "he shall live by them". This means that God requires of man to live, not to die, as the result of obedience to His law. [17] Jewish law seeks to effect a balance between the preservation of the law and the preservation of human life. In matters of life and death, the law may be transgressed. If observance of the law is always given precedence over life itself, the logical consequence would be that the law itself would die since no one would be left to observe it. [18] Thus, the principle of *Picuach Nefesh* is life-affirming by its very nature. It operated to restrict overzealous adherence to the principle *Kiddush Hashem* as readiness to accept martyrdom without question.

In practice martyrdom as an operative option was severely limited by the second century Rabbinic authorities in Lydda (modern day Lod). It was ruled that the supreme sacrifice is required only when the choice is between survival and transgressing one or more of the three basic religious and moral prohibitions: idolatry, adultery, and murder. [19] Yet even in each of these three areas there are many complex and fine legal guidelines restricting the practice of martyrdom further. [20]

Kiddush Hashem as martyrdom was the last option for the Jew, not the first. Only in instances when it was existentially impossible to hallow God's name through one's everyday conduct did *Kiddush Hashem* as martyrdom supersede the principle of *Kiddush Hahayyim*. [21] Otherwise the converse was true.

> ... The general principle of the Rabbis was to make martyrdom the last resort and to offer every possible alternative. For God gave His laws that 'man should live by them.' (Lev. 18:5) and not die. At times, e.g. during the persecutions following the Bar Cochba War, it was necessary to check the zeal of those burning to die in testimony of their faith. Therefore the verse in Leviticus was made the authority for limiting martyrdom to the three cardinal sins of murder, adultery, and idolatry. (TB Yoma 85b: San. 74a) ... The efforts of the Rabbis had to be directed to restrain rather than encourage martyrdom ... [22]

Kiddush Hahayyim is a constantly applied motif in the writings of Rabbinic Judaism. The works of Moses Maimonides (1135-1204), the acknowledged architect of Rabbinic tradition in the Middle Ages, are replete with examples of concern for dignified human survival.

> In this way did we learn to interpret this commandment. As He is called gracious, so shall you be called gracious. As He has been called merciful, so shall you be called merciful. As He is called holy, so shall you be called holy. In this fashion the prophets described God as slow to anger, abounding in loving kindness, righteous, true, pure, strong, etc. They did so to advise man of the good and proper ways to adhere to in order to imitate God with all of his powers and capabilities. [23]

Maimonides denies the validity of asceticism [24] and stresses the human rights of capital offenders. [25]

In subsequent Jewish history the theme of *Kiddush Hahayyim* may be traced through three major movements in Judaism: Musar, Hasidism, and Zionism.

Musar, a movement of moral reawakening through the study of traditional ethical literature and moral self-criticism, rests on a continuous search for meaning and fulfillment in human existence on earth. [26] The motive force of human existence, as understood by adherents of the Musar movement — which has survived in Talmudical academies in the United States, free Europe, and Israel — is to fashion one's life in such a manner as to reflect the attributes of God. Rather than abstain for the sake of abstinence, man is to hallow his everyday conduct because God Himself is the source of all life on earth. [27]

Hasidism emerged in Eastern Europe during the eighteenth century as a movement inspired by the need to affirm life and to create a meaningful pattern of existence in the face of realities almost too harsh to be borne; massacres by Bogdan Chmielnicki and his Cossack followers, slaughter by the Haidemack rebel bands, the mass disillusionment after the exposure of the pseudo-Messiah Sabbetai Zvi (1626-1676), and the resulting Sabbatian and Frankist heresies. Created by Israel Ben Eliezer, the Ba-al Shem Tov (1700-1760), and subsequently structured by his disciple Reb Dov Ber of Mezhirich (1710-1772), Hasidism views all of daily life as potentially sacred. For *Hasidism* every act, every relationship, every human experience is a way to reach out to God.

> "...We reach a fundamental point in Hasidic teaching, the sanctification of the Divine Name in daily life, and not only by practicing martyrdom when the circumstances demand it ..." [28]

Hasidism also rejects the concept of absolute evil; rather it views evil as a continuum that moves inexorably in the direction of the good. As the Ba-al Shem Tov said:

> ... In reality the interpretation is not as generally held: that is to say there is absolute 'evil', really evil is also good, only a lower degree of absolute good ... thus when one does good, evil also becomes good ... In other words the reality of evil does not exist in man, only many levels of the good exist. The lowest levels being the human passions and desires that arouse man's will. If man directs these towards the good, they are included within the good. However, if they are directed towards the evil, they become evil. Thus one may conclude that the Creator did not create absolute evil, only many levels of the good, and only man can actualize 'evil' ... [29]

On another level, *Hasidism* holds with the Talmudic doctrine which explicates that the way to reach out to God is through joy. The Talmud equates piety with joyfulness and rejoicing as it teaches:

"... We must learn that the *Shechinah* (the Divine presence) rests upon man neither through gloom, nor through sloth, nor through frivolity, nor through levity, nor through idle talk save through joy in connection with a mitzvah as it is written, 'and now bring me a minstrel, and when he played the hand of the Lord came upon me.' " (2 Kings 3:15). [30]

Hasidism proposes that it is a *mitzvah* to rejoice. As a result *Hasidism* rejected abstinence and asceticism as valid expressions of religious faith and piety.

Rabbi Baruch, the Ba-al Shem Tov's grandson, related: "They asked my grandfather, the holy Ba-al Shem Tov, '... Indeed we know that in former times pious people would fast from Sabbath to Sabbath, but you our revered one nullified self-denial, saying that he who denies himself is a sinner worthy of divine judgement. Therefore tell us what does this imply?'

The Ba-al Shem Tov responded: 'I came into the world to teach a different way through which man can acquire three things: the love of God, the love of Israel, and the love of Torah — and there is no need for self-denial'. . ." [31]

It is possible to conclude as one views *Hasidism* that it sought to help the individual Jew cope with his daily life out of his religious tradition. It provided the individual with a response based on hope with which to meet the reality of poverty and suffering. *Hasidism* provided the masses with an intimation of Divine joy which helped brighten for them the dreariness of life under quasi-feudal social and economic restrictions. Hasidic leaders were able to communicate that feeling to their fellow inmates even in the ghettos and concentration camps of the Holocaust. Survivors of the Holocaust have told countless stories of Hasidic rebbes leading their flocks to gas chambers and execution sites amidst fervent singing and dancing.

The beginnings of modern Zionism as a political movement that orchestrated the actual return of Jews to Palestine to restore their people in their ancient homeland, are linked in part with the new wave of government sponsored persecution that overwhelmed Russian Jewry following the assassination of Tsar Alexander II in 1881. For the Jews of the Tsarist empire, the two decades that ensued were years of terror culminating in the Kishinev pogrom of April 11, 1903. This violent attack left almost 50 Jews killed, 92 severely wounded, 500 with lesser injuries, 700 Jewish homes burned to the ground, 600 shops looted, and 2,000 Jewish families homeless and destitute. [32] In the light of contemporary events these numbers seem to be insignificant, yet they had important historical implications.

This period, 1881-1903, and the accelerated oppression and persecution that it brought traumatized the Jewish community of Tsarist Russia. It caused thinking Jews, traditionalists and non-traditionalists alike, to reappraise basic Jewish values. It raised critical questions concerning Jewish survival in both physical and spiritual terms. In the process they moved in two directions; a reexamination of the Jewish views on martyrdom as well as the struggle for the restoration of Jewish peoplehood and nationhood through political Zionism. These in turn focused on meaningful Jewish living in the restored homeland in the context of the Jewish past, its present condition, and future perspectives. Thus in fact, they responded to the age-old call of *Kiddush Hahayyim*.

For many, the suffering that this period brought on could not be considered to be martyrdom in the classical sense of *Kiddush Hashem*. This attitude can be detected, for example, in the poetry of Chaim Nachman Bialik, later to be considered the poet laureate of Jewish nationhood. He visited Kishenev shortly after the pogrom as head of the Jewish Investigation Committee. For him, as for others, Kishinev did not represent *Kiddush Hashem*. He came away distressed, not by the physical damage he saw but by the attitude of the survivors. He saw a group of timid, cringing people who confronted their tormentors with helpless acquiescence. In his poem *B'ir Haharega* (In The City of Slaughter), written after his return from Kishinev, Bialik pitilessly castigates the people for their failure of nerve, cringing before their tormentors, and failing to stand fast and fight. No longer were they scions of the Maccabees he lamented:

> It was like mice that they fled,
> Like roaches they scurried and hid,
> Trapped, like dogs they died. [33]

In an agonized cry he calls out that both their lives and their death were meaningless.

> I grieve for you, my children. My heart is sad for you.
> Your dead were vainly dead; and neither I nor you
> Know why you died or wherefore, for whom, nor for what laws
> Your deaths are without reason, your lives without purpose. [34]

For Bialik they became wanderers bereft of pride and dignity. Beggars among the nations, not martyrs, but ne'er-do-wells peddling their miseries from door to door, abandoned by all, even their God.

> On their brows, the mark of death,
> their hearts battered desolate.
> Their spirits dead, their vigor fled;
> their God has utterly forsaken them. [35]

Neither their suffering nor their response fit into the classical Jewish understanding of martyrdom and *Kiddush Hashem*. These did not reflect the willingness to sanctify God's name through death when it was impossible to do so through life.

This whole period beginning with the events of 1881 and climaxing with the Kishinev pogrom represented a turning point in Jewish history as well as in Jewish attitudes. These events demonstrated that even in an age of enlightenment, it was still possible for mobs to treat Jews like animals with the full approval and support of lawful governmental authorities. We note tangentially that in this respect it is a precursor of Nazi persecution. One of the more immediate effects of Kishinev was the realization that passivity was deadly. Jews realized that they had no one but themselves to depend on for their survival. A direct result was the emergence of a Jewish self-defense organization willing to resist and fight to protect Jewish life, honor and dignity.

A second result was the emergence of Zionism no longer just as an eschatological vision for the future but as a political reality. The protagonists of modern political Zionism understood that under such conditions, the most effective way of restoring the dignity and viability of the Jewish people was to emphasize Jewish nationalism as the way of Jewish survival perpetuating the sanctity of Jewish life. It reflected the Jewish will to survive as a distinct cohesive and identifiable people. Its goal was not the maintenance of the *status quo* but the creation of new conditions which would be conducive to physical and spiritual normalization of Jewish life. Its objectives were stated not only in religious terms, but also in such secular terms as culture and nationhood. In the sense that its ideology was life-affirming, modern political Zionism, in its own way, expressed the sanctity of Jewish life.

The objective of political Zionism in both theory and practice was and is today the restoration of the dignity which the Jews had lost as a result of historical circumstances. The Odessa physician Leon Pinsker (1821-1891), among others articulated this theme in his classic (1882) essay *Auto-Emancipation*. [36] Through their own initiative and resources, the Jews were to create the conditions of their national rebirth. Another Zionist forerunner, the writer Peretz Smolenskin (1842-1885), noted in his essay "Am Olam":

> ... Israel never ceased and never will cease being a people. Even if we seek this with all our hearts, we will not succeed as long as we are a distinct faith. Even if freedom comes and as a result of pity we are granted citizen status, we will be citizens and yet not citizens ... [37]

Zionism not only rejected the passivity into which the Jews had lapsed through centuries of persecution and oppression; it also called for a spiritual renaissance. This theme is pivotal in the works of Ahad HaAm (Asher Zvi Ginsberg; 1856-1927), the great exponent of "cultural Zionism," who envisioned the restored Jewish homeland as a spiritual center even for those Jews who would remain in the Diaspora.

Zionism, in its various philosophical and organizational manifestations, is based on the concept of the existential integrity of the Jewish people, its right to live in dignity on its own soil. Instead of a philosophy of martyrdom, Zionist thought leads to a renewal of full Jewish life. As Smolenskin puts it:

> ... This hope revivified Israel's spirit during its wandering. Even now it unites the heart of the people in all the lands of its

dispersion . . . Thus hope of a future redemption was the source of consolation and salvation in times of oppression and in times of peace. Thus it is a contemporary and a future requirement . . . [38]

Political Zionism as the ultimate expression of *Kiddush Hahayyim* can be seen in the thought of Rabbi Abraham Isaac Kuk (1865-1935) who served as the chief rabbi of Palestine from 1921 until his death. A leading proponent of Orthodox Judaism he was closest to Mizrahi, the Orthodox Zionist Religious Party. He was one of the principal contemporary exponents of the relevance of the Zionist ideals to the concept of *Kedushah* in life.

Rabbi Kuk proposed that *Kedushah* (sanctity or holiness), is a pivotal concept of Judaism. For him all Jewish life, thought, and experience is centered around it. *Kedushah* subsumes all other values. He viewed *Kedushah* not as a theological abstraction, but rather as a dynamic and concrete part of life, allowing for its enhancement and elevation. He perceived of a continuum moving from the secular — the profane to the sacred — the holy. The profane serves as the material for the sacred and ultimately merges into the holy to become one all-pervasive entity.

> . . . An objective of the revelation of the secrets of Torah is to view the secular through the mirror of sanctity while acknowledging that the secular is not an absolute . . . Each approaches the other emphasizing unity. These values allow for the enhancement and elevation of humanity's spirit in contact with spirituality . . . It is necessary that sanctity be built on the foundation of the profane, for secularity is the material while sanctity is the mold . . . In the final analysis, sanctity will ingest, digest, and assimilate the profane. [39]

In Rabbi Kuk's view, the objective of Judaism is to maintain the process leading to the realization of *Kedushah* in everyday life. All human abilities and potentialities must be elevated, because life is an ongoing process leading both consciously and unconsciously to sanctity. It is applied to man the individual as well as man the social being. It is thus the end towards which both individuals and communities are organized. In political terms the nation provides the base for him.

> . . . The nation is built on the strength of its inner sanctity. It provides strength to the nation as well as to the world to elevate life and to illuminate the inner soul, the foundation of life-giving qualities . . . [40]

Rabbi Kuk viewed Zionism in this light. For him it represented the Jewish mechanism to bring *Kedushah* into life as it heralded and provided for the restored Jewish national existence. Thus he interpreted the physical labor of the *halutzim*, the pioneers who were rebuilding the Jewish homeland as manifestations of *Kedushah*. Though many of them were non-religious and in fact, denied the validity of Jewish theology and practices Rabbi Kuk counted their physical toil on behalf of their land and people as acts of *Kedushah*, sacred holy, sanctified acts.

> When we see people striving to achieve physical and secular goals as they are busy creating a nation, we must feel that they are moved not only by material but by sacred goals as well . . . We dare not despair in these acts nor close our eyes to the fact that the spiritual rests on the physical in all its aspects leading to a unified structure.[41]

To Rabbi Kuk *Kedushah* was dynamic, impacting on all human endeavor. There was nothing, either in man or in the universe, that was absolutely sacred or absolutely profane. All of life was potential *Kedushah.*

In Rabbi Kuk's view, the ideas of political Zionism were completely consistent with the basic tenets of traditional Judaism. He understood modern Zionism as one aspect of *Kedushah*. Hence, he respected it as a movement which, by restoring the Jews to free and dignified nationhood, would help make *Kedushah* a reality in Jewish life.

In conclusion, we have isolated and identified *Kiddush Hahayyim* as a core value in Jewish history, thought, literature, individual and communal life throughout the ages. What emerges is a concept basic to Judaism. Perhaps for some it is mystical in nature and inferred. Yet it is axiomatic to Judaism, constituting the soil out of which it was and is nurtured. As a value in Judaism, it has served to guide and support countless generations of Jews in their struggle for physical, material, and spiritual survival.

Its efficacy, enabling twentieth century European Jews to live with hope and if necessary to die with dignity under the most cruel tyranny that the Jewish world has ever known, cannot be measured in numerical terms. It can be evaluated only by its humanizing effect, allowing a life of Jewish dignity at least for some. It is this aspect which constitutes the subject of the present work

---

1. Solomon Buber, ed. *Pesikta diRabbi Kahannah* (Leik: n.p.. 1868) 102b.

2. Samuel Hugo Bergman, "Kiddush Hashem" ("The Sanctification of the Divine Name") *Machanayim, Journal of the Chief Rabbinate of the Israeli Defence Forces*, Hanukkah 5730, p. 18.

3. Ben-Zion Dinur, "Kiddush Hashem v'Chillul Hashem" ("The Sanctification and the Desecration of the Divine Name") *Machanayim, Journal of the Chief Rabbinate of the Israel Defence Forces.* Hanukkah 5720, p. 25.

4. Jacob Z. Lauterbach, ed., *Mekilta de-Rabbi Ishmael*, 3 vols., (Phila-

delphia: The Jewish Publication Society of America, 1933) Vol. 2, p. 25.

5. Leviticus Chapter 22 verses 31-33.

6. Dinur. *Op. Cit.*, p. 28.

7. See: The Ten Commandments (Exodus 20:2-15, Deuteronomy 5:6-18):
   The Holiness Code (Leviticus 19-20); Treatment of the poor (Deuteronomy 15:7-18); Justice in government (Deuteronomy 17:14-20).

8. Babylonian Talmud, Tractate Nezikim, Baba Metze-ah 62a.

9. Babylonian Talmud, Tractate Tohoroth, Oholot 7:1.

10. Babylonian Talmud, Tractate Nezikim, Baba Kama 91b.

11. Tosefta Terumot 7:20.

12. Midrah Rabah, B'reishit Rabbah 14:3.

13. *Ibid.* 9:7.

14. David Feldman, *Birth Control in Jewish Law*, (New York: New York
    University Press, 1968) p. 99. *Iggeret Hakodesh* as cited here appears
    in Al-Nakawa's *Menorat Hamaor*, edited by H. G. Enelow, published
    by Bloch Publishing Co., 1932. Vol. 4. pp. 87-113 *passim Perek Nsuay
    Ishah.*
    Know that sexual intercourse is holy and pure when carried out prop-
    erly, in the proper time, with proper intentions. No one should claim
    that it is ugly and unseemly. God forbid! for intercourse is called
    'knowing' (Gen. 4:1) and not in vain is it called thus . . . Understand
    that if marital intercourse did not partake of great holiness, it would not
    be called 'knowing' . . . we who have the Torah and believe that God
    created all in his wisdom (do not believe that He) created anything
    inherently ugly and unseemly. If we were to say that intercourse is
    repulsive then we blaspheme God Who made the genitals . . . hands,
    too, can perform evil deeds and they say they are ugly. So the genitals,
    whatever ugliness there is comes from how man uses them. All organs
    of the body are neutral; the use made of them determines whether they
    are holy or unholy . . . Therefore marital intercourse, under proper cir-
    cumstances, is an exalted matter . . . Now you can understand what our
    rabbis meant when they declared (Talmud Bavli Sotah 17a) that when
    a husband unites with his wife, the Divine presence abides with them.

15. Jerusalem Talmud, Tractate Nashim, Kiddushim 4:12.

16. Jerusalem Talmud, Nedarim 9:3.

17. Babylonian Talmud, Tractate Nezikim, Avodah Zarah 27b.

18. Babylonian Talmud, Tractate Moed, Yoma 85b.

19. Babylonian Talmud, Tractate Nezikim, Sanhedrin 74a.

20. Samuel Tanhum Rubinstein, *"Hatzalat Nefashot al Y'de Giluy Arayot B'Halakha"* (Halachah and Saving of a Life through Rape") *Torah She Ba-al Peh, Mosad Harav* Kuk (5732) 89.

21. See *Emek HaBakha*, a treatise published by the Italian Jewish physician Joseph HaKohen (1496-ca. 1578); accounts of the Chmielnitsky massacres in *Yeven Metzulah*, published in 1653 by Rabbi Nathan Hanover, and Jacob R. Marcus, *The Jew in the Medieval World: A Source Book, 315-1791*, New York, 1965, pp. 115, 131, 179 and 450.

22. Montefoire and H. Loewe, *A Rabbinic Anthology*, (Philadelphia: Jewish Publication Society, 1960) p. 495. Addendum to extract 1401.

23. Rabbenu Moshe ben Miamon, *Mishne Torah Hayad Hahazakah*, 7 vols., (Jerusalem: Hotza-at El Hamekorot, 5714) Vol. 1, Hilchot Dayot 1:6, p. 23.

24. *Mishne Torah, Op. Cit.*, Vol. 1, Sefer Madah, p. 25, *Hilkhot Deyot* 3:1.

25. *Ibid.*, Vol. 7, Sefer Nezikin, Hilchot Rotzayach, pp. 118 - 1:4; p. 120 - 2:7; p. 127 - 7:1; p. 128 - 8:5-6. These passages deal with distinctions between manslaughter and premeditated murder, testimony in court, punishment, execution, and the biblical cities of refuge. Their tenor is to stress the human dignity of all men, including proven criminals.

26. Musar postdates Hasidism as a visible movement, for it was only systematized in 19th century Lithuania by Rabbi Israel Lipkin (1810-83), also known as Reb Israel Salanter. However, it is founded on much earlier works on Jewish ethics, including *Duties of the Heart* by Bahya ben Joseph ibn Pakuda (1050-1120), *The Gates of Repentance* by Rabbenu Yona ben Abraham of Gerona (d. 1263), *Paths of the Righteous* by Moses Hayim Luzzato (1707-74), and *The Ways of the Righteous*, published by an unknown author in 1581.

27. Bahya ben Joseph ibn Pakuda, *Duties of the Heart*, 2 vols., (Jerusalem: Hotza-at Kiryah Ne-emanah, 5725) Vol. 2., Abstinence, pp. 288-337 *passim*.

28. Bezalel Landau, *"Kiddush Hashem B'torat Hahasiduth"* ("The Sanctification of the Divine Name in Hasidic Teaching") *Machanayim, Journal of the Chief Rabbinate of the Israeli Defence Forces*, Hanakkuh 5720, p. 86.

29. Moshe Shelomo Kasher, ed., *Perakim B'machshevet Hahasiduth* ("Chapters in Hasidic Thought") (Jerusalem: Machon Torah Shelamah, 5732) pp. 45-47.

30. Babylonian Talmud, Tractate Moed, Sabbath 30b.

31. Martin Buber, Or *Ganuz, Sipurey Hasidim* ("The Hidden Light, Hasidic Tales") (Jerusalem: Hotza-at Schocken, 1969) p. 74.

32. *American Jewish Yearbook* 5564, 1903-1904 (Philadelphia: Jewish Publications Society of America, 1903) p. 20.
    See also:
    Herman Rosenthal, "Kishinef, *"The Jewish Encyclopedia*, 1st ed., VII, p. 512.

33. *The Writings of Hayyim Nachman Bialik* (Tel-Aviv: Hotza-at Dvir, 1939) p. 93.

34. *Ibid.*, p. 94.

35. *Ibid.*, p. 95.

36. Leon Pinsker, *The Road to Freedom: Writings and Addresses* (New York: Scopus Publishing Co., 1934) pp. 54-96, "Auto-Emancipation," *passim.*

37. Peretz ben Moshe Smolenskin, Essays, 4 Vols. (Jerusalem: Hotza-at Kerren Smolenskin, 5684) Vol 1. "Am Olam," p. 145.

38. *Ibid.*, p. 143.

39. Rabbi Avraham Yitzchak Hacohen Kuk, *Orot Hakodesh* ("Sacred Lights") (Jerusalem: Ha-agudah L'hoza-at Sifrei Harav Kuk, 5698) pp. 143-146, *passim.*

40. *Ibid.*, p. 146.

41. *Ibid.*, p. 323.

Part Two

The Ghetto as a Tool for Extermination

Chapter Two

The Ghetto:
A Tool For Extermination

On December 16, 1941, Hans Frank, Governor-General of German-occupied Poland, made the following announcement to his cabinet and his personal advisors:

> As far as Jews are concerned, I want to tell you quite frankly that they must be done away with in one way or another . . . As an old National Socialist I must say this: This war would be only a partial success if the whole of Jewry were to survive it, while we had shed our best blood in order to save Europe. My attitude toward the Jews will, therefore, be based only on the expectation that they will disappear . . .

> Gentlemen, I must ask you to rid yourselves of all feelings of pity. We must annihilate the Jews, wherever we find them and wherever it is possible . . .

> We cannot shoot or poison 3,500,000 Jews but we shall nevertheless be able to take measures which will lead, somehow, to their annihilation, and this will be done in connection with the gigantic measures to be determined in discussions with the Reich . . . [1]

The Nazi aim, as expressed by Frank, was to be accomplished through a systematic program of extermination which began in the ghetto and was completed in the death camps. The first phase in the step-by-step destruction of the Jews was a spate of restrictive laws designed to demoralize the Jewish community as a whole and to dehumanize the Jew as an individual. The anti-Jewish legislation drawn up by Frank's superiors in Berlin with exacting care called for the isolation, enslavement and starvation of the Jews to make them ripe, as it were, for mass liquidation.

In order to implement this program, it was necessary to segregate the Jews in specified geographic areas from which they would not be able to escape. Hence, the first Nazi move toward the goal of a *Judenrein* world free of both Jews and Judaism was to gather the Jews in their occupied territories and incarcerate and isolate them in ghettos. The establishment of ghettos represented a critical step in the process leading to "The Final Solution of the Jewish Problem," code name *Endlösung*. It was formulated as the official German governmental policy with reference to Jews at a conference convened by Heinrich Heydrich with the approval of Hermann Goering at *Am Grossen Wannsee* on January 20, 1942. The ghettos were designed to play a crucial role in the systematic elimination of the Jew from the body politic. It was a process that was to be completed in the concentration camps where mass murder would find its grimmest expression.

The ghettos established by the Nazis represent one of the most appalling chapters in the annals of human barbarity. But the response of the men, women, and children in these ghettos to the German attempt to convert them into non-persons gave the world a lesson in heroism of both body and spirit. Theirs was a shining example of how people can live meaningfully even under the most trying circumstances. The records of their endeavors inspires future generations.

Since Jews are human like other people, it must be admitted that within the ghettos there were those who were motivated by greed and selfishness, the dread of hunger, and the fear of death. With their sense of decency paralyzed they collaborated with the enemy. Yet at the same time there was hardly a ghetto in which men, women, and even children did not add their own acts of *Kiddush Hahayyim* to the composite image of Jewish pride and dignity that has evolved during the many difficult centuries of persecution and oppression.

The ghettos played crucial roles in the German structure geared to the systematic elimination of the Jew from the European society. The population configuration of any given ghetto was a cross section of the whole Jewish communal and social spectrum. In a sense, the ghettos became autonomous communities administered for the Germans by Councils which were variously named. These Councils were established as a result of specific directives sent by Heinrich Heydrich, the chief of the German security police. The first such directive, dated September 21, 1939, was followed by others. [2] These Councils of Jewish Elders came to be known as the *Judenrat*, (literally "Jew Council"). Generally, they were placed under the direction of the *Altester der Juden* (literally "Jew Elder"). Various departments of the *Judenrat* carried on the day-to-day activities authorized by the Germans.

The *Judenrat* and *Altester der Juden* were the official links between the Nazis and the ghetto population. They were the instrumentalities used to accelerate the *Final Solution* which required the concentration of Jews in well-defined areas. To this end ghettos were established in cities with pre-existent Jewish communities to which Jews from the surrounding areas were shipped. As already noted, Kovno, Lodz, Vilna, and Warsaw were historically such focal points of Jewish life and culture. In each the Nazis established a ghetto. In each, the *Judenrat* and the *Altester der Juden* were authorized by the Germans to carry on those specific activities that were assigned to them. Through them, the German authorities controlled the life of the Jewish population within the ghettos. Thus these bodies were pivotal. They were the focus of everything that occurred in the ghettos.

KOVNO

Jews had been living in Kovno on and off since the 17th Century. Beginning with the second half of the 19th century, Kovno, like Vilna, became known as a center of Jewish cultural activity. Kovno was the home community of the Talmudic scholar, Isaac Elhanan Spektor. It was famous for its Talmudical academies. The Yeshiva of Slobodka (Vilijampole), a Kovno suburb, became world famous in Rabbinic circles. The Yeshiva *Or Hayim* was a center of *Musar*, a movement devoted to Jewish ethical renewal. Kovno was a pivotal traditional Jewish community, yet it contributed such great names as Abraham Mapu, the novelist, to the modern Hebrew literary renaissance of the 19th century.

Kovno had been part of Tsarist Russia and was occupied by German forces during World War I. Between 1920 and 1939 Kovno (Kaunas) was the capital of Lithuania. Like Vilna, Kovno was occupied in July 1940 by Soviet troops who held the city until war broke out between Germany and the Soviet Union. On June 24, 1941 Kovno was captured by the Germans. The ghetto was established less than two months later, on August 15, 1941. [3] Immediately upon the arrival of the Germans, the city's 35,000 Jews were terrorized not only by the Germans, but also by the Lithuanian Fascists who had welcomed the Nazis as liberators. It is estimated that about 7,000 Jews were killed in Kovno during the first three weeks of German rule.

When the Kovno ghetto was first established, it contained approximately 29,760 Jews in an area which previously had accommodated no more than 7,000. Eventually, these ghetto inmates were to be joined by thousands of Jewish deportees from Germany proper, from Austria, and from the part of France that had been officially occupied by Germany. The ghetto was ringed by a barbed-wire fence; its gates were guarded jointly by German police and by members of the Jewish ghetto police force organized by the Germans to keep order within the ghetto. In years to come, there were historians who condemned the members of the Jewish ghetto police as traitors who collaborated with the Germans in hopes of obtaining extra food rations and other privileges. It should be noted, however, that many of those who joined the ghetto police were motivated not by personal greed, but by the hope that by helping preserve law and order in the ghetto, they might be able to save their fellow Jews from arrest, deportation, and death. [4]

The administration of the Kovno ghetto, like that of the other ghettos in Nazi-held Eastern Europe, was entrusted by the Germans to a *Judenrat* which was directly responsible to the German City Commissioner. (In Kovno, the *Judenrat* was also known as *Aeltestenrat* or "Council of Elders"). Dr. Elhanan Elkes, a well-known physician and Zionist leader who met his death in Dachau, was chairman of the Kovno *Aeltestenrat* throughout the period of the ghetto's existence. In Kovno, as in other ghettos, the *Judenrat* was the mechanism employed by the Germans to provide a labor pool for diversified forced labor. This involved sorting out the population into productive and non-productive categories, the distribution of work certificates, and the transfer of the population from one section of the ghetto to another. The *Judenrat* was also responsible for the accumulation of Jewish property for German expropriation.

The first step in the annihilation of the Kovno ghetto was the massacres perpetrated at the Ninth Fort outside the city beginning on October 29, 1941. When the Soviet forces launched their attack on Kovno in July 1944, the Nazis liquidated the ghetto, using grenades and other explosives to kill Jews hiding in underground bunkers. The Jews who still survived were deported to German proper: the men to Dachau and the women to Stutthof.

LODZ

Located in central Poland, Lodz possessed the second largest Jewish community in that country between the two World Wars. It is estimated that in 1931, Jews constituted over 30 percent of the city's total population.

Jews first settled in Lodz at the end of the 18th century, drawn in part by the city's flourishing textile industry. Despite the anti-Jewish policies of Poland's minister of finance during the 1920s, Lodz's garment industry was almost entirely in Jewish hands; Jews were also engaged in such building and related trades as paving and carpentry. Between the wars, the Jewish community of Lodz enjoyed an active cultural and organizational life, including a number of Hebrew authors and poets, Jewish musicians, and many Zionist groups.

On September 8, 1939 the Germans entered Lodz and promptly renamed it Litzmannstadt. In October the German authorities disbanded the official Jewish community board and replaced it with a *Judenrat*. The *Judenaelteste*, chairman of the *Judenrat*, was Chaim Mordecai Rumkovski, whom many Jews regarded as a pawn of the Germans, but who eventually went to Auschwitz to share the lot of his fellow Jews.

In December 1939, Jews living in the elegant downtown streets of the city were evicted from their apartments; their former homes were turned over to *Volksdeutsche* (ethnic Germans). In January 1940, the Jews were segregated into the Old City and the Baluty area. It was in this enclave that the ghetto was formally established on February 8, 1940. On March 1 the Germans organized a pogrom to drive the last remaining "free" Jews into the ghetto and it was sealed off from the rest of the city on April 30. Between September 1939 and May 1, 1940, some 70,000 Jews, including many of the community's cultural and intellectual elite, the wealthy and the young, had fled the city, some of them to Warsaw and other parts of Nazi-held Poland, still others eastward into the Russian occupation zone.

Left in the ghetto were 164,000 Jews crammed into an area covering less than two square miles. [5] The ghetto was divided into three areas, each surrounded by barbed wire and a chain of *Schutzpolizei* (security police) posts but connected with one another by bridges and gates. Chaim Rumkovski managed the ghetto's affairs under the direction of Hans Biebow, head of the German ghetto administration.

The Germans orchestrated the sequence of events in the Lodz ghetto in a manner designed both to keep the Jews under constant tension and to decimate the ghetto's population. Periods of relative calm alternated with pogroms, starvation, forced labor, confiscation of whatever property the Jews still possessed, and mass deportations to the "extermination center" at Chelmno. Between January and April 1942, 44,000 Jews were deported from the Lodz ghetto. By September 1942, the ghetto's population had dropped to 89,446. The final liquidation of the ghetto began less than two years later, in June 1944. By September 1, 1944, 145,680 Jews had been sent from Lodz to their death in Auschwitz and Chelmno.

VILNA

Jews had been living in Vilna since the 16th century. A center of Jewish scholarship since the 17th century, one of its Talmudic luminaries was Elijah ben Solomon Zalman, more popularly known as the "Gaon of Vilna". Because it was a great Talmudic center, Vilva came to be known as "Jerusalem of Lithuania."

Originally a part of Tsarist Russia, Vilna was first occupied by German forces during World War I. Germany's defeat in 1918 was followed by a struggle between the succession states of Poland and Lithuania for the possession of Vilna. From 1922 until the outbreak of World War II, Vilna belonged to Poland. During this interwar period, Vilna continued to be a center of Jewish learning. It was renowned not only as a center of Talmudic and religious learning, but also as a community where *Haskalah*, modern Jewish culture, flourished. Vilna was, for example, the birthplace and home community of the Jewish Ethnographical Society's museum and archives, and of YIVO, the Yiddish Scientific Institute, both of which attracted scholars from all over the Jewish world. It was also a center of Zionism. The period between the two World Wars witnessed the establishment of a network of elementary and secondary schools in Vilna where Hebrew was either the principal language taught or, in fact, the sole language of instruction.

In September 1939, when Russia and Germany split Poland between themselves, Vilna was occupied by Soviet troops, but a month later, Russia ceded the city to the republic of Lithuania, a neutral state. As a result, Vilna soon became an island of safety for thousands of Jewish refugees fleeing German-occupied Poland.

When Lithuania lost her freedom in July 1940, Vilna reverted to Russian rule. The Soviet authorities closed down all "official" Hebrew cultural institutions and Zionist organizations, deporting many leading members of the Jewish community into the interior of the Soviet Union.

Less than a year later, in June 1941, war broke out between the Soviet Union and Nazi Germany. When the Germans marched into Vilna on June 6, 1941, they were welcomed by the populace with flowers and cheers as liberators from Communist rule.

Between that date and September 6, 1941, when the German occupation authorities established the Vilna ghetto, some 20,000 of Vilna's 60,000 Jews were murdered at Ponary, a wooded resort area about 10 kilometers outside the city, which had been reserved by the Germans to serve as an "extermination center" for Jews.

Hingst, the German district commissar, divided the Vilna ghetto into two separate sections. The larger of the two housed able-bodied Jews who could be employed to good advantage by German industries. The smaller, the "Little Ghetto", served as a death pen for the very young and the very old whom the Germans considered of no use to their war effort. On October 29, 1941, about seven weeks after the establishment of the two ghettos, the "Little Ghetto" was liquidated and its entire population sent to its death. [9]

The Germans appointed Jacob Gens as Vilna's *Judenaelteste*. Gens, who had been an officer in the Lithuanian army and subsequently an official at the Kovno city jail, was to be shot by the Gestapo on September 14, 1943, when the ghetto was liquidated. In his capacity of ghetto leader and chairman of the *Judenrat*, Gens was responsible to the German authorities for the preservation of law and order in the ghetto. Under his chairmanship, the Vilna ghetto *Judenrat* functioned through a system of departments, following the procedure in other ghettos. Its labor department was under orders to harness a pool of Jewish labor for German and Lithuanian factories. Other departments were industry, supply and distribution, health and child care, and housing and social welfare.

Side by side with, but clearly distinct from, the German-sanctioned ghetto leadership, there existed in the Vilna ghetto various Jewish underground political organizations, successors to the groups that had existed in Vilna prior to the war. Early in 1942, these organizations joined to create a united fighting force (*Fareinigte Partizaner Organizatie*) under the command of Yitzhak Wittenberg, Joseph Glazman, and Abba Kovner. The Jewish partisan fighters were active not only within Vilna itself, but also in the woods outside the city, smuggling ammunition into the ghetto, issuing underground news bulletins, forging documents, and sabotaging German military installations. Many of the Jews who escaped from the ghetto and joined the partisans in the woods survived the war. Wittenberg and Glazman were to meet their end at the hands of the Gestapo; Kovner lived to fight in Israel's War of Independence and to continue his literary activity in Israel.

The Germans used the Vilna ghetto as a staging area for a carefully spaced program of *Aktionen* (mass killing operations). During a single *Aktionen* in the spring of 1943, 26,000 Jews from Vilna were murdered in Ponary. [10] The victims were moved from Vilna to the resort area under the pretext that life for them would be easier there, and food more plentiful. Many Jews, believing the Nazi canard, volunteered to go of their own accord.

In August 1943, those Jews still surviving in the Vilna ghetto were deported;

the men were sent to Estonia, the young women to Latvia, and the children, the old, and the infirm to the death camp of Maidanek. By the end of September 1943, only 3,000 able-bodied Jews were left in Vilna. They were employed at the Keilis fur manufacturing plant and at HKP, the "Military Vehicles Park" where German army vehicles were stored and serviced. On July 2 and 3, 1944, these survivors, too, were taken to Ponary and murdered. This was the end of the Vilna ghetto.

Before they were physically annihilated, the inmates of the Vilna ghetto were subjected by the Nazis to systematic attempts at dehumanization. Living conditions in the Vilna ghetto were identical with those in the other East European ghettos established by the Nazis. In the light of the atrocities committed by the Germans, the positive activities conducted by the inmates of the Vilna ghetto, which will be studied in subsequent chapters, become all the more meaningful and significant. These activities represent attempts to live meaningfully as long as possible.

Typically, the Nazis restricted the movements of Jews outside the ghetto, even before the ghettos were sealed off from the "Aryan" sectors. Jews were not permitted to use public transportation or to pass through certain streets. They could do their marketing only at specified hours — at times when, as a rule, most of the desirable merchandise had already been bought up by the non-Jews. Jews were not permitted to sell their property or possessions to non-Jews. Books owned by Jews had to be surrendered to the authorities. Jews were forbidden to buy newspapers or magazines outside the ghetto area.

The Jews in Vilna were ordered to sew distinctive identification badges on their clothing. Hardly had one type of badge been specified when a new official order was issued replacing it with another. Thus, on July 4, 1941, the Jews were ordered to wear a piece of cloth, ten centimeters square, marked with a yellow "J" (for "Jude") on the back and on the chest. A few days later a new directive was announced, ordering Jews to detach the square badge from their clothes and to exchange it for a blue armband with a white Star of David, to be worn on the left arm. On August 3, the armband was ordered replaced by a yellow badge with a Star of David, to be worn on the back and chest. These constantly changing directives were intended as an added harassment to keep the Jews in a perpetual state of confusion, tension, and anxiety. [11]

As far as the Germans were concerned, the primary function of the ghetto population was to provide the German war effort with a steady labor pool. There was more than one way in which to recruit this Jewish labor force. Sometimes, Jews were simply picked up in the ghetto streets and shipped off to a labor project site. Another technique was to impress upon the Jews that only those who were willing and able to work would be permitted to survive a little longer:

> The basis for our survival in the ghetto is work, discipline and order. Every able-bodied ghetto inmate is a pillar upon which our survival depends.
> There must not be any among us who despise work. [12]

The most precious possession of the ghetto inmate was the *Ausweis*, the employment certificate which stated that the bearer was able to work. The *Ausweis* enabled the bearer, and at times also the members of his immediate family, to survive in the ghetto. Without an *Ausweis*, a Jew in the ghetto had no way of "legitimizing" himself. The Nazis used the *Ausweis* as yet another instrument of persecution to demoralize the ghetto Jews and to set one against the other. From time to time orders were issued changing the color of the *Ausweis* from white to yellow and then to red. At one point, each *Ausweis* was required to show a photograph of the bearer; at another point, no photograph was permitted. All this, of course, meant that ghetto inmates had to keep applying to the authorites for new *Ausweis*. At the same time, there was always the threat that some of the applicants would not be given a new *Ausweis* in exchange for the old. For instance, on September 12, 1941, Field Marshal Wilhelm Keitel forbade the German army to issue further *Ausweis* to Vilna Jews who were then working for the Transport Command and the Armaments Office.[13] Such announcements spread terror among the Jews in the ghetto, for without an *Ausweis* one was in constant danger of being picked up for deportation and death, usually at the extermination center of Ponary.

The very name of Ponary struck fear in the hearts of the ghetto Jews. Before the war, Ponary had been a popular country resort. When the Russians occupied Vilna, Ponary became the site of an oil depot, complete with storage pits. During the period of Nazi occupation, however, Ponary was the primary execution site for those of Vilna's Jews who were deemed of no further use to the German war machine and were consequently marked for annihilation. It was at Ponary that most of the Jews who did not succeed in escaping from the Vilna ghetto met their death.[14]

WARSAW

Warsaw, the ancient capital of Poland, apparently received its first Jews at the end of the 14th century. During the 19th century, Jews played an important role in the city's finance, commerce, and industry. Between the two World Wars, Warsaw, as the capital of the Polish republic, served as headquarters for all Jewish movements and political parties in Poland. These movements included the ultra-Orthodox Agudath Israel, the Mizrachi (Religious Zionist) movement, the various other Zionist groupings ranging from the right-wing Herut to the leftist labor parties, and the anti-Zionist Socialist Bund. Each movement had its own school system, using Polish, Hebrew, or Yiddish as its language of instruction.

The Germans entered Warsaw on September 29, 1939. By December, the city's 400,000 Jews had been subjected to harsh restrictions.[15] All Jews, including those who had converted to Christianity (assimilation and conversion were frequent phenomena among Warsaw's Jews), were required to wear a distinctive armband, and Jewish-owned businesses were required to be marked conspicuously with a Star of David. Jewish-owned loan and mortgage establishments were placed under the management of non-Jewish commissars. Jews were forbidden to use public transportation and to enter the city's main post office on Warecki Street. None of the Jewish schools were permitted to reopen for the fall session.

By the end of the first year of German occupation, Jews were no longer permitted to enter Warsaw's public parks or to use its municipal promenades, [16] and Jews were required to step off the sidewalk to make way for approaching German soldiers or civil servants. Non-Jewish bookstores were forbidden to sell German books to Jews.

The first German plans to segregate the Jews of Warsaw in a ghetto had been announced as early as November 4, 1939. The Germans made no move to implement this proposal until October 3 of the following year, but once the decision had been formally made and approved, the Nazi overlords acted with dispatch.

On November 15, 1940, the area set aside for the ghetto was sealed off from the rest of the city. A district covering some 840 acres, or 2.4 per cent of the city's total area, had been set aside to house almost 400,000 Jews, or fully one-third of Warsaw's total population. [17] The ghetto was surrounded by a wall built and paid for by the Jews themselves under the orders of the Nazis. In the fall of 1941 the area of the ghetto was still further reduced, though the ghetto's population at its peak was 500,000. The periodic population decrease caused by deportation was more than offset by the constant influx of new arrivals who had fled or had been brought in by the Germans from other parts of Poland.

One of the fortunate few who managed to escape from the Warsaw ghetto before its destruction recorded his personal recollections of the mass movement of nearly half a million Jews into the ghetto area.

> Try to picture one-third of a large city's population moving through the streets in an endless stream, pushing, wheeling, dragging all their belongings from every part of the city into one small section, crowding one another more and more as they converged ... Pushcarts were about the only method of conveyance we had, and these were piled high with household goods, furnishing much amusement to the German onlookers who delighted in overturning the carts and seeing us scrambling for our effects ... In the ghetto ... thousands of people were rushing around at the last minute trying to find a place to stay. Everything was already filled up but still they kept coming ... The narrow crooked streets of the most dilapidated section of Warsaw were crowded with pushcarts, their owners going from house to house asking the inevitable question: Have you room? The sidewalks were covered with their belongings. Children wandered, lost and crying, parents ran hither and yon seeking them, their cries drowned in the tremendous hubbub of half a million people. [18]

Thousands of Jews in the Warwaw ghetto remained homeless; some slept in courtyards. Fully 60 per cent of the ghetto population had few or no visible means of support. Those fortunate enough to find work labored about 12 hours for average daily wages of 20-30 zloty,[19] or $4.00-$7.00; (during the early phase of World War II, five zlotys were the equivalent of $1.00). The small official food rations which were irregularly brought into the ghetto by the Nazis for sale were of the most inferior quality; nonetheless, they promoted smuggling, black marketeering, and begging, even by children. Starvation was rampant. Mary Berg, a young American girl who had accompanied her parents on a visit to relatives in Poland and had been stranded there during the war, recorded her experiences in the diary she kept in the Warsaw ghetto:

> The prices of foodstuffs are going up. A pound of black bread now costs four zlotys, of white bread six zlotys. Butter is forty zlotys a pound; sugar, from seven to eight a pound.
>
> ... When a hungry person sees someone with a parcel that looks like food, he follows and, at an opportune moment, snatches it away, opens it quickly and proceeds to satisfy his hunger ... No, these are not thieves; they are just people crazed by hunger.[20]

Due to the perpetual famine, the ghetto was constantly plagued by epidemics, particularly typhus. By the summer of 1942, a total of 100,000 inmates of the Warsaw ghetto had died of "natural" causes.[21]

As in the other ghettos, the Germans divided the population of the Warsaw ghetto into two categories: productive and non-productive. To be classed as non-productive was, in fact, to be condemned to death, for the "non-productives" were systematically rounded up for what was euphemistically referred to as "resettlement" — deportation to the extermination camps. The "productives" were either allowed to remain in the ghetto or were relocated to projects where their labor was needed. However, this was only a temporary reprieve, for once their usefulness to the German war effort was considered to be at an end, the "productives" too, were sent to their death. The Germans required the *Judenrat* to supply them with a specific quota of Jews to be deported. The program of mass deportations of Jews from the Warsaw ghetto began on July 22, 1942, with the demand that the *Judenrat* provide a daily contingent of 5,000 – 7,000 individuals for deportation as "unfit for work."[22] When the *Judenrat* failed to meet this quota, flying squads of Germans, assisted by members of the Jewish ghetto police, invaded the ghetto, cordoned off specified streets and buildings, and "selected" individuals to be dispatched to the *Umschlagplatz* (transfer point) for transportation to the death camps. Between July 22 and September 9, 1942, some 310,322 Jews were shipped out of the Warsaw ghetto, leaving behind 40,000 "legal" residents and 30,000 "illegals."[23]

"Jewish Warsaw is in its death throes," Chaim Kaplan, who had been a respected member of Warsaw's Jewish community for 40 years before the war, wrote in his diary on August 2, 1942:

> Jewish Warsaw is dying. An entire community is going to its death! The appalling events follow one another in such abundance

that it is beyond the power of a writer of impressions to collect, arrange and classify them, particularly when he himself is caught in their vise — fearful for his own fate for the next hour, scheduled for deportation, tormented by hunger, his whole being filled with the fear and dread which accompanies the expulsion . . .

. . . A blockade was made on Leszno Street . . . and within two hours about 2,000 people were brought to the transfer point. All of them went forth empty-handed, naked or half dressed. Woe to that family which must be routed out by the Nazis or their minions, the "alert" Ukrainians and Lithuanians. The victims emerge beaten and sore, naked as the day they were born . . .[24]

This was the last but one entry in Kaplan's diary. He did not survive the war. (Two decades later, the diary was found intact in a kerosene can on a farm outside Warsaw).

The second phase of the mass annihilation process in Warsaw began on January 1, 1943, with the liquidation of the ghetto's hospitals and the murder of their patients. Every aspect of life in the Warsaw ghetto was paralyzed. This total breakdown triggered the first organized armed resistance within the ghetto. That struggle was to assume historic dimensions with the final Warsaw ghetto revolt, which began on April 19, 1943 and grew into a full-fledged battle between the ghetto fighters and a special German combat group with attached artillery units and a German general in command. The Germans attacked the ghetto with automatic rifles, machine guns, flame throwers, mortars, and tanks. The Jews, armed with rifles, a few machine guns, hand grenades and homemade Molotov cocktails brought the invading Germans to a halt. The fighting ended only on May 16, after disease, starvation, and mounting casualties from the German shelling of the ghetto finally brought about the collapse of the defenders.

Concerning Resistance

The heroism of armed Jewish resistance was matched by another, quieter struggle — spiritual in nature — not only within the Warsaw ghetto but also in the other ghettos of Eastern Europe: the determination of a goodly number of ghetto Jews not merely to vegetate until Hitler was defeated or until they were killed, whichever would come first. They resolved to conduct their lives not as hunted victims but as human beings who hoped to see a better future, or if they could not survive the war, then at least make the Germans understand that though they might succeed in killing the Jews, they would not succeed in divesting the Jews of their human dignity. These Jews knew that their end might be *Kiddush Hashem*, the sanctity of martyrdom, but while they lived they would implement in their daily activities the age-old principle of *Kiddush Hahayyim*, as they lived meaningful lives, Jewishly and otherwise. They would strive to educate their children, to continue their Jewish studies, to observe their religion, and even to carry on the Zionist struggle for the Jewish

Homeland as if the ghetto were just a transient episode. Scholars of Jewish law would continue to study and teach; poets, composers, and writers would not permit ghetto life to throttle their creativity, and artists would record the ghetto experience on paper and canvas for future generations.

In these respects, the four ghettos described here — Kovno, Lodz, Vilna, and Warsaw — do not present a unique phenomenon; rather, they illustrate experiences and responses that occurred in ghetto communities throughout Nazi-occupied Eastern Europe, where despair and resignation were matched by the will to live and faith in the future.

We characterize this phenomenon of creative acts as spiritual resistance against the Nazi oppressors in the form of activities carried on in the face of dire suffering. We note that in the ghettos these activities may be classed in two distinct categories: "permitted" and "clandestine."

The "permitted" activities were those sanctioned by the German authorities and openly conducted under the auspices of the ghetto's *Judenrat*. They were, of course, defined and limited in terms of the German objectives: the liquidation of the Jews and the reduction of all occupied areas to the status of a colonial hinterland in the service of the Greater German Reich. [25] Accordingly, the Germans permitted and even encouraged such activities as they felt were consistent with their war aim, not only among the general population but also among the Jews in the ghettos. They would not allow academic studies for an "inferior" race, but at one juncture it was not too difficult for the Jews in the ghetto of Lodz to obtain permission for organizing vocational training courses, since the Germans viewed such courses as a source of future cadres for the Jewish slave labor force. These courses proliferated in many ghettos. [26]

But the Jewish communities were not satisfied with the bare minimum of activity permitted or supported by the authorities. They made many attempts — some official, others "unofficial" — to extend the scope of their endeavors. The "permitted" vocational training courses, for instance, were frequently used for the "clandestine" purpose of giving the students an academic education as well. Under the camouflage of vocational training it was possible to teach subjects which the authorities could not control. The story of the vocational school in the Kovno ghetto is a good illustration. With the support of the *Judenrat*, a group of devoted ORT teachers (ORT is a worldwide Jewish vocational training agency which had its beginnings in Eastern Europe in 1880) started a vocational school for 40 students. Because the people in the ghetto were anxious to help ensure their children's survival by making them "productive," the number of students grew steadily and by February 1944 had an enrollment of 480. This vocational school became the center of cultural activites not only for the young, but also for all the other inmates of the Kovno ghetto. [27]

In addition to the "permitted" activities, there was a whole spectrum of others that were carried on secretly. Since they were "illegal," they involved the risk of severe penalties. But in fact it is this second "clandestine" category of ghetto activities which reflects the true response of the Jewish victims to the

Nazi attempt to enslave not only their bodies but also their minds and souls. These activites were educational, cultural, journalistic, creative, religious, multiform in nature but all sharing two common goals: They were directed to the elevation of life under the most difficult of circumstances and they reflected the life-affirming quality of Judaism.

1. The Trial of the German War Criminals. *Proceedings of the International Military Tribunal* (Nuremberg, Germany: Part II 3rd December to 11th December, 1945, from official transcripts published under authority of H. M. Attorney-General by His Majesty; Stationery Office, London, 1946. Document 2233 D-PS Exhibit USA 281, Identified CV 1941, October-December p. 76, line 10; p. 77 line 33.

2. Isaiah Trunk, *Judenrat* (New York: MacMillan Co., 1972) pp. 2-5; 10-13 *passim*.

3. See Appendix I for map of Kovno ghetto.

4. Trunk, *Op. Cit.*, pp. 515-524 *passim*.

5. See Appendix II for map of Lodz ghetto.

6. Isaiah Trunk, *Lodzer Geto* (New York: Yivo Institute for Jewish Research and Yad Vashem, 1962) p. 304.

7. See Appendix III for map of Vilna ghetto.

8. Lucy S. Dawidowicz, *The War Against the Jews* (New York: Holt, Rinehart and Winston, 1975) pp. 201, 285.

9. Mark Dworzetsky, *Yerushalayim de-Lita in Kampf un Umkum* ("Jerusalem of Lita, in Struggle and in Death") (Paris: Yiddishen Nationaler Farband in America and Yiddishen Folksfarband in Frankriech, 1948) p. 136.

10. *Ibid.*, pp. 422-428.

11. Herman Kruk, *Tagbukh fun Vilner Ghetto* (New York: Yivo Institute for Jewish Research, 1961) p. 470.

12. Dworzetsky, *Op. Cit.*, p. 142. From a poster which appeared in the Vilna ghetto on July 5, 1942.

13. Nora Levin, *The Holocaust* (New York: Thomas E. Crowell Co., 1968) p. 248.

14. Kruk, *Op. Cit.*, pp. 24, 51, 191-193, 229-232, 317-319, 512-517. See also: Dworzetsky, *Op. Cit.*, pp. 53-56, 423-428.

15. Chaim A. Kaplan, *The Scroll of Agony* (New York: The MacMillan Co. 1965) p. 85.

16. *Ibid.*, pp. 282, 318, 349, 359.

17. See Appendix IV for a map of the Warsaw ghetto.

18. Tosha Bialer, "Behind the Walls," *Collier's Magazine*, February 20, 1943, p. 17.

19. Raul Hilberg, *The Destruction of the Jews of Europe*, (New York: Quadrangle Books, 1961) p. 172.

20. Mary Berg, *Warsaw Ghetto Diary* (New York: L. B. Fischer Co., 1945) p. 116.

21. Hilberg, *Op. Cit.*, p. 171.

22. *Ibid.*, p. 313-318.

23. *Ibid.*, p. 320.

24. Kaplan, Chaim, *Megilat Yesurim* (Tel Aviv: Hotza-at Am Oved and Yad Vashem, 1966), p. 559.

25. Trunk, *Judenrat, Op. Cit.,* p. 196.

26. *Ibid.,* p. 205.

27. *Ibid.,* p. 206-207.

Part Three

Kiddush Hahayyim
and
The Ghetto Community

Introduction

Towards a Definition
of the Jewish Community

The term Jewish Community is difficult to define. At one and the same time it refers to the total group of people who consider themselves to be Jews or who are considered by others to be Jews as well as to the structure organized to serve their needs. Without the former, obviously the latter could not exist. Historically, at times, the Jewish Community formalized its own structure; at other times it was imposed upon it. The community functioned through its leadership as well as through a table of organization, often quite elaborate. Within the communal structure there were also subgoups representing different political, educational, cultural, religious, social and other viewpoints. These, too, functioned to meet communal needs, but usually they were independent of the central Jewish communal authority though often cooperating with them.

The Jewish Community as it was organized served to meet unmet Jewish needs of the Jews as individuals, as members of the Jewish group, and as a corporate entity. The organized Jewish Community responded to many and diverse needs. Among them we can list education, culture, religion, social service, health, and politics.

We have noted the structure imposed upon the Eastern European Jewish Communities trapped in the ghettos by the Nazis. Side by side with that structure a clandestine Jewish communal mechanism evolved. Here we will investigate how this latter mechanism operated in the various areas to enhance the efforts of the Holocaust victims to withstand the Nazi efforts to dehumanize them.

Chapter Three

Educational Activities

Nachman Blumenthal, a literary critic who survived the Holocaust has written a monograph dealing with educational problems arising during the Holocaust. In this work he discusses the goals of the educational structure that was developed in the ghettos. In his view, even in the ghettos, the educational process, by its very nature, fulfilled a positive function, building toward the future despite a seemingly hopeless present. [1] Education in the ghetto was an act of affirmation which served as a focal point in the whole structure of Jewish life during the Holocaust period.

> The same ideal, this faith in the future, was also the goal of the Jews who lived during the Holocaust . . . in the most difficult of circumstances. The question that most disturbed them was, "What will be the fate of the younger generation?" They did everything possible to enable this generation to study, while the young people themselves showed a strong inclination to study . . . More than in normal times, the young aspired to become educated, out of their faith that the ghetto situation was only a transient phase and that eventually things would revert to their former state . . . [2]

On October 8, 1939, the High Command of the German occupation forces in Poland permitted all the schools that had operated previously to reopen. On the strength of this order, some Jewish schools also reopened; this was before the Nazis set up ghettos for the Jews. By the end of November, the German civil authorities, who, in the meantime, had replaced the military command, ordered the Jewish schools closed again, under the pretext that Jewish schools would help spread epidemics. In Warsaw, the last Jewish school was closed on December 4, 1939. (Non-Jewish elementary schools were permitted to remain open, under the condition that they would dismiss any Jewish teachers and refuse to admit any Jewish students.) The Jewish teachers who lost their jobs as a result of the closing of the Jewish schools and their exclusion from the non-Jewish schools appealed to the Warsaw *Judenrat*, to CENTOS (the Federation of Associations for the care of Jewish Orphans in Poland), and to other Jewish organizations, petitioning them to open a camouflaged school program under the guise of "child protection." In a memorandum submitted to the *Judenrat*, the teachers stated that in Warsaw there were 50,000-60,000 Jewish children between the ages of five and twelve, including thousands who had been left without adult supervision. Eventually, on the initiative of CENTOS and workers from other Jewish educational organizations, children's soup kitchens in Warsaw were utilized to conduct an "unofficial" educational program a few hours daily, thus keeping thousands of young children properly supervised and occupied.

On September 11, 1940, at the end of the first year of German occupation, Governor General Hans Frank authorized the local *Judenrat* to reopen elementary and vocational training schools and to train teaching personnel. These schools were supervised by the German authorities. The *Judenrat* had to apply to them for permission every time it wanted to open a new school.

The Warsaw *Judenrat* now appointed a school board consisting of representatives of defunct Jewish educational organizations. This board petitioned the appropriate German authorities for permission to open Jewish elementary schools in the Warsaw ghetto. Just then the German department of sanitation suddenly announced that the opening of Jewish schools in the ghetto would aggravate the typhus epidemic that had broken out earlier. Actually, the epidemic had abated by that time. It was clear that the health situation was merely a Nazi pretext to sabotage the endeavors of the Jewish community to establish their own educational system in the ghetto.

In January 1941 the school board renewed its efforts to obtain permission for setting up schools, but once again without success. Finally, in April, permission was granted to open several elementary schools accommodating a total of 5,000 children. [3] Eventually, by December 1941, a total of sixteen elementary schools with a total enrollment of 10,000 children or twenty percent of all children of elementary school age in the Warsaw ghetto had been opened. Of the unenrolled eighty percent, some 35,600 children attended the "unofficial" classes run by CENTOS in the soup kitchen. Others were in the *komplety* (private underground classes conducted by individual teachers on their own) but still others did not attend school at all. Many were too preoccupied with the task of helping keep their families alive by smuggling food into the ghetto.

The newly opened elementary schools were based on a three-year curriculum, but some of the schools added fourth and fifth years. They were patterned on the school system that operated in the Warsaw Jewish community before the war, when each of the major Jewish religious and cultural organizations had its own schools to disseminate its ideals. Of the sixteen elementary schools opened in the Warsaw ghetto, three were affiliated with the Yiddishist secular CYSHO, three with the Zionist Tarbut movement, one with the Yiddush-Hebrew Shulkult, and five with the Orthodox religious movements. The remaining four schools were non-aligned and, unlike the others, used Polish as the language of instruction.

Several secondary schools were also permitted in the Warsaw ghetto, but these were expressly limited to vocational, agricultural, and teachers' training curricula. The Germans did not want the Jews in the ghetto to train academicians and professional people.

Both the elementary and the secondary schools operated under the ever-present threat of forced closure without prior notice under the pretext that they had done or taught something that displeased the German authorities.

The ghetto schools operated under the most primitive physical conditions. In Vilna, for instance, where the total ghetto school population as of March 1943 numbered 1,700,[4] teachers and students rebuilt the bombed-out school buildings together. They salvaged whatever broken school furniture they could find or else built their own furniture from the debris they had gathered, improvising desks and benches from smashed doors and pieces of lumber. Sometimes students stood alongside the classroom walls, supporting their notebooks on the backs of those standing in front of them. They chopped wood, found in the debris of bombed-out buildings, to heat their schools. The teachers improvised educational materials by mimeographing textbooks. Teachers and students alike were able to function despite the high absenteeism due to cold weather, lack of clothing and shoes, the privation and even the epidemics that were part of ghetto life.[5]

In the Lodz ghetto the schools also struggled against technical obstacles imposed by the Germans. In the winter, classrooms went unheated because the ghetto's coal rations were sufficient only for heating factories and workshops. Many of the teachers who had taught at Lodz's Jewish schools before the war, especially those who had been active in Jewish communal life, fled east to the Russian-occupied sector. Those who remained behind were ill-prepared to teach in Yiddish or Hebrew. Then, too, there was a lack of textbooks, particularly in Yiddish, because the bookstores had been destroyed in the war or their stock had been confiscated. As in the Warsaw ghetto, the teachers in Lodz mimeographed their own textbooks and composed some of the textbooks themselves. The school system in the Lodz ghetto came to an abrupt end in October 1941, when school premises had to be evacuated and converted into shelters for almost 20,000 newly arrived Jewish deportees from Central Europe.[6]

The ghetto communities used every possible means — legal, quasi-legal, and illegal — to strengthen their educational systems. The means were conceived and implemented by Jewish activists in the ghettos, sometimes with the approval of the "official" Jewish authorities — that is, the *Judenrat* — but in most instances, they did not ask for such approval. Quasi-legal activities in the ghetto generally involved grafting upon the structure of an officially approved institution — a vocational school, for example — various educational functions not initially intended for that particular institution. As we have already seen, the soup kitchens and dining halls operated by CENTOS became more than merely places where free meals were served. They became centers for informal clandestine classes conducted by teachers who posed as soup kitchen or child care workers.[7] A good illustration of this sort of activity is the statement of aims for the clandestine educational program and activities that were actually conducted at three children's soup kitchens in the Warsaw ghetto, (Karmiltzka 29, Novolifka 39, and Krochmala 96):

1. We proposed to convert the public soup kitchens into educational centers to educate and influence our children.

2. Above all, through our concern for the health of the children, we hope to develop in them a sense for hygiene and beauty.

3. Notwithstanding the perilous times in which we are living, we hope to strengthen the spiritual lives of the children.

4. ... We hope to prepare the groundwork for converting the food centers into children's collectives ...

5. We shall try to provide children with opportunities to experience normal emotions, particularly joy, as often as possible.

6. We shall see to the social and moral education of the children by developing in them appreciation for friendship, sociability and a sense of responsibility with special emphasis on punctuality.

7. We aim to develop the mental capacities of the children in every way possible.

8. We will seek to instill in the hearts of the children a love of the Hebrew language and for Jewish culture. [8]

Clearly, then, these and the soup kitchens of other ghettos served their patrons something more than food. They were concerned as much with the spiritual well-being of the children as they were with their physical well-being.

In the Vilna ghetto, underground educators stressed their own teaching program, making Jewish religious, cultural, and moral survival the focal point of their clandestine activities:

Our Principles of Education
- A sense of national Jewish dignity.
- Love of the history of our people, with particular attention paid to the period of our national independence and the fighters for the freedom of our people: the Hasmoneans, Bar Kokhba and the heroes of Masada.
- Knowledge of the Present State of our people: Jewish life in all the Jewish communities.
- Faith in the future of our people ...
- Love of work and freedom.
- Love of mankind, and for the fight against oppression, the

partnership of all the nations in the fight for a better and just world.

- Knowledge of the Land of Israel (Palestinography) to be taught as a subject in its own right.
- Religion taught as a non-obligatory subject for students who wish to become acquainted with the principles of our religion. [9]

Vocational training was not only permitted but actually encouraged by the German authorities, in order to convert what they considered parasites into useful tools of the labor force under Hitler's new order. But the ghetto leadership converted the Jewish vocational schools into institutions offering an education never envisioned by the Nazi overlords.

One of the noteworthy institutions of this kind was the ORT Trade School in Kovno, which was opened in the early spring of 1942 with forty students who had enrolled for a locksmith course. This school had been set up on the initiative of ORT teachers with the aid of the Kovno *Judenrat*. Eventually it added courses for training tinsmiths and carpenters. Later there was a course in horticulture, and there were classes for girls in tailoring and embroidery. Much of the teaching equipment had to be smuggled into the ghetto from the outside, a completely illegal operation performed by the teachers at the risk of their lives. At the same time, the teachers blended into the school's vocational training program clandestine, strictly forbidden courses in art history, color theory, painting, and drawing. The school sponsored a choral society with 100 members, a library, and a series of evening lectures held in the utmost secrecy. At the peak of its development in February 1944, six months before Kovno was liberated by Russian troops, the ORT school had a student body of 440 young people.

Officially approved vocational courses for adults became a cover for other courses — chemistry, pharmacy, nursing, mechanics, electronics, art, accountancy — which were, in fact, of university rather than secondary school caliber.

University level courses were strictly forbidden in the ghetto, but there were teachers who risked their lives to organize such classes and students sufficiently motivated to attend them. Thus, in May 1941, when the German authorities approved a health program in the Warsaw ghetto to combat the spread of disease, a Dr. Zweibon, who had taught at the University of Warsaw before the war, used it as a guise to develop a program offering a full complement of medical courses to 500 students. Dr. Zweibon's course of study was on the level of accredited medical schools. [10] Comparable professional training programs were also developed in other ghettos in other fields of study. In the Lodz ghetto an academic high school was opened in the early fall of 1941 and soon had an enrollment of 125 regular students. The courses included mathematics, physics, biology, chemistry, psychology, philosophy, pedagogy, philology, engineering, statistics, and — last but by no means least important — Judaic studies. The lectures, opened not only to students but to the general adult ghetto public, were well-attended, sometimes drawing as many as 400 listeners but never less than 100. Frequently, the halls in which the lectures were given were filled to overflowing with standing room only outside the hall. [11]

Informal lectures in Jewish studies were organized for adults to imbue the listeners with hope for the future and pride in their Jewish identity. In the Vilna ghetto during the summer of 1942, one Eliezer Goldberg gave a complete course on Jewish history; his lectures dealt with such subjects as the Sadducees, Judaism and Hellenism, the Diaspora, and the period of Ezra and Nehemiah following the Babylonian exile. The lecture series was announced by means of circulars hand-lettered in ink and crayon on lined ledger sheets. [12] In his lectures, delivered in Yiddish, Goldberg stressed the positive aspects of Jewish history, with particular emphasis on events that had implications for the contemporary situation. He sought to impart to his audiences the conviction that the Jewish people would emerge triumphant from this ordeal, too. Each lecture was painstakingly prepared and presented from meticulously handwritten notes. [13]

It was through such means that the people in the ghetto sought to defy the Nazis by affirming their right to exist and demonstrating their resistance against the dehumanization that was an integral part of the German war on the Jews.

When such quasi-legal devices as academic courses under the guise of permitted vocational training proved inadequate, they turned to other underground educational activities which were unequivocally forbidden by the German authorities and usually with the disapproval of the *Judenrat*. Among such activities were underground classes, held in locations scattered through the ghetto, popularly known as *komplety* ("groups"). Found in many ghettos, the *komplety* were not structured, formal educational groups but private, clandestine units clustered around individual teachers. Usually comprised of from three to six students of all ages, these units were organized either at the initiative of the teachers or very often by the students themselves who would constitute themselves into a group and then approach a teacher of their choice. The subject matter taught in the *komplety* depended on the competence of the individual teacher and on the interests of the students. The courses would be held at private apartments, with the meeting place changed frequently to avoid arousing the suspicions of the police. Students would volunteer to act as "watchmen" posted at appropriate places outside. When they spotted Nazis or other suspicious-looking individuals approaching the house, they would warn the teacher; then the class would "shift gears" to create the impression of an "innocent" club or play, song, or story-telling group.

Youth movements played a prominent role in "illegal" educational activities. In the Warsaw ghetto the underground leadership established two academic high schools: the *Dror Gymnasia* and the Hebrew *Gymnasia*. Dror, (the word means freedom) was a Zionist youth movement expressing the ideology of Labor Zionism. The Hebrew *Gymnasia* drew students from the

Tarbut movement for the dissemination of the Hebrew language and literature, which before the war had a network of educational institutions in
Poland. A detailed description of the *Dror Gymnasia* is provided in its Hebrew
language underground publication entitled *Korespondentziah P'nimit* (Internal Correspondence). An entry dated July 7, 1942 details the growth of the
D'ror Gymnasia from the time of its inception in the summer of 1940 with three
students. By the time of the *Korespondentziah* report, the school boasted a student body of 120 and a staff of thirteen. The courses included languages —
Hebrew, Yiddish, Polish, German, French or English, and Latin — general
and Jewish history, Jewish sociology, Bible, and sciences such as physics
and mathematics.

> Most of the students have no means of support. Many of them
> study without paying tuition . . . The school derives its income
> from three sources: (1) Tuition; (2) Contributions from several
> communal organizations and (3) direct assistance from the
> movement itself.

> During the most recent period the financial situation has
> deteriorated. The students assume their share to the best of their
> ability. The second source of income has ended; even the re-
> sources of the movement have dwindled. Only thanks to the
> dedication of the teaching staff will we be able to complete this
> academic year.

> The gymnasium is administered by a committee of three: a
> teacher, the secretary of the gymnasium, and a member of Dror's
> Central Committee. There is a pedagogical committee to decide
> on pedagogical matters. Basic policy is determined by the Central
> Committee of Dror. [14]

Almost all the students were members of a student organization, *Ba
Ma'aleh*, which was described in the *Korespondentziah* report as a sort of
"student's republic." The activities of the organization included mutual aid,
provision of textbooks, the planning of Jewish holiday celebrations and also
of activities on behalf of other young people in the Warsaw ghetto.

In addition to the gymnasium, Dror in the Warsaw ghetto developed com-
plementary undertakings such as teacher training and the creation of text
materials. Its leaders organized a series of clandestine teachers' seminars
which were conducted behind locked doors. Concerning the first such
seminar, it was noted:

> All day long, guards were posted to protect us against any unan-
> ticipated intrusion.

> Outside, there was fear and desperation, while inside they
> dreamed their dreams of how to destroy the reign of evil . . . They
> also took counsel on how to maintain the human dignity of the
> Jew despite the despair of the ghetto life.

... This was the first teachers' seminar of the Jewish underground. When it became known in the broader community there was a furor. I remember delegations from various groups warning us of the dire consequences we would cause for all Jews in the ghetto.

... Gradually, however, their attitude changed, and the work of the seminar continued and ended peacefully ... One of the delegates (even) compared us to the Marranos of Spain. People became enthusiastic at the sight of young people ready and willing to sacrifice themselves in this manner ... [15]

The leaders of Dror felt that through these activities they were reinforcing the spirit of the young and thus counteracting the Nazi effort to rob Jewish youth of its sense of purpose and human dignity. This was why they were determined to bring all their resourcefulness to bear in order to carry on their educational program. Thus they were also actively involved in the preparation of textbooks and other educational materials. This activity was both arduous and dangerous.

When we started this extensive project, we realized that we had no textbook material for our teachers. No new books were published in the ghetto — nor any old ones, for that matter. So we had to create something out of nothing. We started an extensive publication program of our own.

The first new book to be published in the (Warsaw) ghetto was put out by Dror (in Yiddish): *Agony and Heroism in the History of Our People*. The book had 120 pages and was printed by means of a duplicating machine ... We sought to give to our youth accounts of heroism and self-defense from the history of our people. There were no typewriters in the ghetto, nor were there mimeographs. We had to labor long and hard until we succeeded in obtaining printing equipment from outside the ghetto. The greatest difficulty was the typing. This was dangerous work because our apartment was close to Pawiak (the big prison) where the Germans were around all the time. Sometimes we could not even type so much as one page in a whole day.

Sometimes the Germans would pass by and hear singing from our windows, and they didn't like it. How dared the Jews sing? They broke into our place, and it was only with difficulty that we managed to hide our typewriter from them. They went through all our rooms and said in amazement, "Such a lot of young Jews!" We replied, "They are refugees." Miraculously, they passed the printing room but did not enter it. That is how we were saved.

This, the first book to be published in the ghetto, was issued in an edition of 2,000 ... [16]

The educational and cultural work of Dror in the ghettos of Poland is only one example of similar endeavors by other organzations. Their commitment to the concept of Jewish survival in the face of Nazi persecution strengthened them in their resolve to promote Jewish educational, cultural, and spiritual values among the young no matter what the circumstances or the risks entailed.

In the Vilna ghetto, the *B'rit Ivrit* (Hebrew-speaking Federation) popularized the study of the Hebrew language and culture. Dr. Mark Dworzetsky, the historian of the Vilna ghetto, wrote:

> There were times when heavy clouds hung over the ghetto and no one had the heart to organize *B'rit Ivrit* classes, or else many of the leaders were preoccupied with other important tasks. But at such moments Israel Diminstein (one of the leaders) would say to our comrades: 'Hebrew must be heard until the last day of this ghetto. Our house is on fire, and time does not stand still.' So we continued the activities of *B'rit Ivrit* until the last days of the ghetto. [17]

Among other activities, the *B'rit Ivrit* launched the *Hevrah Mada'it Ivrit* (Hebrew Society for Scientific Research) which was devoted to the study of Hebrew and Jewish literature. Under its aegis two scholars, Drs. Zemach Feldstein and Z. Kalmanovitz, presented a series of scientific studies on the writings of the Hebrew essayist Ahad Ha-am, the letters of Theodore Herzl, and other Jewish historical documents. Moshe Ilitzky delivered a major treatise in Hebrew, entitled "Jewish Humor Under All Conditions." *B'rit Ivrit* also set up a Hebrew writers' group which embarked on the project of collecting in written form all the important Hebrew lectures delivered under the auspices of *B'rit Ivrit* and the *Hevrah Mada'it Ivrit*.

From this overview, it is logical to conclude that educational activities as they were created and orchestrated in the ghettos were effective in building inner Jewish defenses for at least a segment of the trapped populace. In the final analysis, perhaps these activities saved few lives, yet without doubt they added a period of meaningful living to the years they lived. In the aggregate they assured the survival of the Jewish spirit, contributing to the victory of that spirit over Nazism.

Chapter Four

Cultural Activities

In addition to formal and informal classes and lectures, the ghetto inmates initiated a wide range of cultural activities in such areas as drama, music and art. Libraries were organized, programs commemorating Jewish holidays and important events in Jewish history were held.

Though the frequency, variety, and nature of these activities depended on prevailing conditions and hence varied from ghetto to ghetto, they all shared a high level of sophistication and structure. As with educational activities in the ghetto, so, too, certain cultural activities were authorized and were encouraged by the Germans while others were considered illegal and had to be conducted clandestinely. Although it became increasingly difficult for the Jews to continue their culture programs as the Nazis moved closer to the "final solution," they steadfastly refused to abandon them. For ghetto activists these activities were in fact manifestations of spiritual resistance and vehicles to express and define their humanity.

Thus, besides being a symbol of spiritual resistance, cultural activities in the ghetto served as an antidote to the corrosive realities of day-to-day ghetto life, developed to enhance individual self-respect and reinforce the sanctity of the human image through a sense of personal worth. The key word was *oishalten*, a Yiddish term best translated as "to withstand" or "to endure." Cultural activities in the ghetto were not looked upon as luxuries but as necessary means of survival in the face of Nazi pressures.

Cultural activities strengthened the hope of the ghetto inmates that a better future still lay ahead for them and the conviction that, even in the most difficult of circumstances, they must avail themselves of every possible means to prepare for that future. It was through these means that they reinforced their sense of human dignity.

In this connection, it is significant to note a study conducted by the Warsaw ghetto's historian Emanuel Ringelblum (who was to die at the hands of the Nazis in March 1944) as part of his secret archival project known by the code name of *Oneg Shabbat* (Sabbath Delight). Entitled "Two and A Half Years of War," this study was conducted during the winter of 1941-42 and intended to include a series of fifty interviews with leading cultural figures in the ghetto.

Fragmentary materials discovered after the war, hidden in milk cans in the rubble of the ghetto, (what is left of this collection of historical material is now known as the Ringelblum Archives) indicate the scope of this study, which included such areas as education, economics, religion, Zionism, and cultural activities. Its objective was not simply to evaluate the contemporary situation but to consider prospects for the future, when the war would be over. In fact, the subtitle of the Ringelblum study is "Reflections, Evaluations and Perspectives for the Future." One of those interviewed, the writer Aaron Einhorn, described in the following terms the one positive moment in ghetto life:

> The only bright spot is the fact that the Jews are clinging so tenaciously to life ... This give us a glimmer of hope that the Jewish masses in the ghetto will persevere; that they will survive this hell and live to see better times. [18]

Institutional structures were devised to organize and conduct the cultural activities that developed in the ghetto. Although they varied from place to place, there usually were parallel structures; that is, those approved by the authorities, which operated legally, and those that were only quasi-legal or altogether illegal. Some of the activities were carried on under the aegis of a structure with the widest possible representation from the entire spectrum of a particular ghetto community. In other instances the structure was provided by one particular already existing Jewish organization, or else it was the work of interested individuals.

From 19 loose papers, part of the journal of an unknown chronicler, it is possible to reconstruct the development of the cultural structure in the Lodz ghetto. It moved through several phases. The key was the establishment of the *Yiddishe Kultur Geselshaft Litzmannstadt Ghetto* (Jewish Culture Society of the Litzmannstadt Ghetto) in November 1940. Though the Society was founded on the initiative of the Yiddishist, secularist *Bund*, its intent was to cut across political and religious lines and to spread Jewish culture as broadly as possible among the ghetto masses. To this end the Bund called upon both YIVO (the Yiddish Scientific Institute) and ORT (the worldwide Jewish vocational training agency) to cooperate with all of the other interested parties. The only requirement set by the Bund was that all participants in the Society should display a positive attitude toward the Yiddish language. The Society planned a multidimensional program including a library, a people's university, Yiddish study circles, a dramatic group, concerts, lectures and athletic events.

Several months before, in July 1940, a program of musical activities was inaugurated in the Lodz ghetto in the form of an instrumental group sponsored by Slonce, an agricultural organization.

Mordecai Rumkovski, chairman of the Lodz *Judenrat*, felt it necessary to bring the entire cultural structure of his ghetto under his control. Having noted the success of the quasi-legal Culture Society, he absorbed this whole structure into his administration in the form of a *Kultur-Haus* (Culture House). This institution became the focal point of all "legal" cultural activities in the Lodz ghetto. The Vilna ghetto, too, had a *Kultur-Haus* (directed by the Yiddish philologist and translator Zelig Kalmanovitch) and a *Ghetto Vissenshafts Institut* (Ghetto Scientific Institute), whose work was coordinated by Herman Kruk, the diarist of the Vilna ghetto.

The Warsaw ghetto developed an underground umbrella organization, YIKOR (Yidishe Kultur-Organisatie) Jewish Culture Organization, under whose auspices Jewish cultural activities were planned and conducted. Among the founders of this organization was Emanuel Ringelblum. YIKOR's particular concern was to stem the tide of assimilation and Polonization in the ghetto. The first task YIKOR set for itself was to make Yiddish, rather than Polish, the language of the Warsaw ghetto. Then it moved on to become the fountainhead of the ghetto's cultural life, sponsoring a broad array of cultural activities and stimulating the formation of cultural "house committees" in the warren-like tenements occupied by the ghetto inmates. Then it either acted directly to organize various evening events, such as lectures, musical recitals, and literary evenings, or it supplied the talent requested by the "house committees." YIKOR even sponsored literary contests complete with judges and prizes.

Concerted efforts were made to bring culture to the masses wherever they congregrated – in public soup kitchens or in ghetto factories and workshops. It was frequently possible to organize "illegal" cultural activities in these places under the guise of "permitted" recreation and entertainment. In Lodz, during the first half of 1943, revues were staged in ghetto workshops with casts consisting of individuals who either worked in those shops or had been borrowed from other places of work.

> The songs from these revues were popular throughout the ghetto. Yanowski's humor and satire brought cheer into the depressed ghetto life. Moshe Pullover, the actor who organized the *Avante Garde* Ghetto Theater, wrote in his memoirs:

> No matter how much hunger stalked the ghetto with giant steps, you could hear singing in the ghetto workshops. When you sang while you worked, you could forget everything, even that we were in the ghetto. People would say, 'Today we'll go to the theater in the attic; tomorrow we'll go see a play in the basement.' We joked with one another. We did not realize how serious our situation in the ghetto really was.[19]

Workshops also served as a cover for cultural activities of a more serious nature. In Vilna, "courses" in Yiddish and literary lectures on such figures as Sholem Aleichem and I. L. Peretz were held in an overcoat factory. This particular workshop even housed a secret library of several hundred books in Polish and Yiddish, covering such diverse areas as history and poetry.

In Warsaw cultural and musical programs proliferated. In order to encourage these artistic expressions and at the same time to prevent chaos, a coordinating agency known as *Vaadah Markazit Le Hatzagot* (Central Council for Cultural Performances) emerged in September 1940.

There was a comparable development in Vilna. On February 17, 1942, an Organization of Artists and Writers held its first meeting under the chairmanship of Zelig Kalmanovitch. Some 100 writers, musicians, artists and actors attended. The group set as its goals:

1. To activate, even if only for a brief period, the creative spirit in the ghetto, freeing them from the pervasive atmosphere of despair; also, to arouse in them a spirit of hope for the future linked with the Jewish past.

2. To attempt to give material assistance to its members by providing them with suitable work as well as dignified communal support in both financial and material terms.[20]

Membership in the Vilna organization was open to anyone involved in cultural endeavors. In addition to sponsoring all kinds of events, the group encouraged its members to be creative in their fields and established a publishing office, *Hotzaat Ha-Ghetto*, (Ghetto Publishing House). It acquired a variety of literary manuscripts and musical scores created in the ghetto with the intention of publishing them after the war.

The various Zionist organizations that functioned in the ghettos fulfilled similar roles in line with their aim to work for the Jewish national renaissance through Jewish cultural activity.

The cultural activities conducted in the various ghettos were imbued with a clearly articulated purpose: the enrichment and elevation of life in the ghetto. This spirit is reflected by a report smuggled out of Warsaw and addressed to YIVO, the Yiddish Pen Club, and to the literary figures Sholem Asch, J. Leivick, Joseph Opatoshu, and Raphael Mahler, all of whom had settled in the United States. Dated March 1, 1944 and signed by Emanuel Ringelblum and the veteran left-wing Labor Zionist Dr. Adolf Berman on behalf of the Warsaw ghetto's cultural committee, it is the final report of the cultural work that was carried on in Warsaw as it became clear that the ghetto was about to be liquidated. Tangentially, it is sad to note that this report was penned six days before Ringelblum's death. Ringelblum was among a group of 38 which included his wife and son who escaped to the Aryan side after the destruction of the ghetto and were sheltered by a Polish worker, Mierlzyslaw Wolski. On March 6, 1944 a Polish informer led the Gestapo to their hiding place and all, including Wolski, were executed.

Berman and Ringelbaum summarized the intent and nature of their activities in the following words:

. . . These organizations have carried on their selfless endeavors until the last moment, as long as the faintest spark of life still remained in the Jewish community . . .

The slogan of Jewish communal activity in the Warsaw ghetto was "Live in dignity and die in dignity!"[21]

Music and Theater

Musical and dramatic arts in the ghettos provided a moral boost through opportunities for creative self-expression. Through music and the theater, the ghetto residents proved to themselves and to others that they were still human beings, with normal creative impulses.

A number of significant musical activities took place in the Vilna ghetto. Abraham Sutzkever, a Vilna Yiddish poet who survived the Holocaust and eventually settled in Israel, tells of the formation of a symphony orchestra in the ghetto under the baton of the conductor Wolf Dormashkin. This orchestra boasted of a piano which had been secretly smuggled into the ghetto piece by piece and reassembled there. Sutzkever reports that during the period of searches preceding the establishment of the Vilna ghetto, many Jewish musicians had buried their instruments to keep them from falling into the hands of the Nazis. After they had moved into the ghetto, their instruments were unearthed and transported to them through tunnels that passed beneath its walls; some musicians had their instruments smuggled into the ghetto by Jews who had been assigned to work in the "Aryan" sector of the city. [22] The Vilna ghetto orchestra eventually numbered forty members. It presented about thirty-five concerts with a repertoire of works by Tchaikovsky, Dvorak, Mozart, Chopin, and Beethoven. Sutzkever also recalls the existence of chamber ensembles.

Yediot Ha Ghetto, the official news gazette of the Vilna ghetto, reviewed the opening concert in glowing terms, commenting on the technical skill and musical talent of both the members of the orchestra and the soloists. It also noted the response of the audience and explained the difficulties under which the orchestra had been formed and developed, concluding with the following accolade addressed to both the orchestra and the ghetto community which attended the concert:

> The recent concert represented a giant step forward in the development of the symphony orchestra, as described by one of its own members, Dr. Kanovsky. He stressed particularly the great accomplishments of W. Dormashkin, as well as the devotion of the musicians, most of whom were working during the day for government operated enterprises, so that they had to rehearse until late in the night . . . [23]

The Vilna ghetto also boasted of several Hebrew choral societies. One such group was organized by the *B'rit Ivrit* under Dormashkin's direction. It specialized in *halutz* (Palestine Jewish pioneer) tunes, Yemenite and Hassidic melodies, and folk songs, including Biblical passages set to music. One of its major feats was a rendition of Zemach Feldstein's Hebrew translation of the opera *Aida*. Another choral society, the *Makhelah Ivrit Ketanah*, (The Little Hebrew Choral Society) ultimately numbered fifty members; its most popular numbers were Zionist songs such as "Yerushalayim," "Omrim Yeshnah Eretz", and "Alee Lehavah." In addition, there was a conservatory which offered classes in piano, violin, and voice to almost 100 students.

Young musicians were encouraged to compose music; in the Vilna ghetto, competitions were held for this purpose with cash prizes awarded to the winners. [23a]

· In Lodz, prior to the establishment of Rumkovski's *Kultur-Haus*, there had been some highly successful musical groups, including a symphonic ensemble consisting of thirty-five musicians, which by the end of 1940 had offered seven performances. [24] A chamber ensemble gave concerts for professional people at the public soup kitchens. In October 1940, choral societies were organized. The *Ha-Zamir* choral society, which existed before the war, resumed its activities and amalgamated with the *Shir* Choral Group and a symphonic ensemble. This newly augmented group presented its first concert on October 30, 1940, with works by Haydn, Mozart, Gluck, and Weber. Subsequent concerts were devoted to works by Tchaikovsky, Schubert, and Rubinstein; during 1942, concerts were given every Wednesday evening. [24a] These performances and recitals continued until January of 1944, when the Nazi authorities confiscated all instruments in the Lodz ghetto. Despite Nazi restrictions, there even was a School of Music. [25]

As for the theatre, the most popular form of dramatic presentation in the ghettos were musical reviews. Usually the themes were taken from ghetto life, with sarcastic overtones. In the Lodz ghetto, these performances were directed primarily by Moshe Pullover, director of the *Avant Garde* studio theatre, which performed twice each week. It is estimated that during 1941 some 70,000 individuals viewed these performances either at the *Kultur-Haus* or at ghetto factories. [26] A choreographic studio was developed to provide dancers for the plays, and for a short time in 1941 there was a marionette theater for children.

The theatre was also active in the Vilna ghetto. One dramatic group staged revues and potpourris of drama and song along with legitimate stage plays. The inaugural program of this group on January 16, 1942 included a choral reading from the works of the Hebrew poet laureate Chaim Nachman Bialik, selections from the well-known Yiddish play *Mirele Efros* and from the works of the cantor-musicologist Abraham Idelsohn. Yiddish language musical revues included such titles as "You Never Know," "Pesha and Resha," and "Moishe Stands Firm." [27]

Legitimate theater, too, flourished in Vilna. Beginning on July 20, 1942, a number of Yiddish plays were presented in the ghetto, among them such works as Peretz Hirschbein's "Green Fields," Otto Indik's "The Man Under the Bridge," Berger's "The Deluge" and Sholem Aleichem's "Tevye the Milkman." During 1942, some 120 performances were presented in the Vilna ghetto to an estimated audience of 38,000. [28]

In addition to the Yiddish theatre, the ghetto of Vilna had a Hebrew theater troupe, whose most significant performance was a Hebrew version of Pinski's Yiddish classic, "The Eternal Jew." [29] The prime movers in the establishment of this Hebrew players' company were ghetto young people. The very fact that

Hebrew was used in these stage presentations had a salutary effect on ghetto morale. The play highlighted struggle and revolt and emphasized hope in the future of Jewish peoplehood.

In Warsaw, there were five Jewish theatres, three of which performed in Polish and two in Yiddish. Plays were presented in the Eldorado, Pamina, Azazel Hahadash and Teatron Cameri Theaters and in other halls equipped with a stage. The content and quality of the performances varied; they included such productions as "Mirele Efros," Moliere's "The Miser," and an operetta created in the ghetto dealing with local themes. [30] In addition, there was a Hebrew theatrical company; later, there were children's theaters and even a marionette theatre to entertain the young.

The musical and dramatic activities in the Warsaw ghetto first began in response to the 7 p.m.-5 a.m. curfew imposed by the Germans. Initially, many of the ghetto inmates spent the curfew hours in political discussions; others wiled away the time with card playing. One day, on November 8, 1939, someone had the bright idea of breaking up a long evening of card playing with a program of entertainment starring Simcha Fustel, one of the most popular Polish/Jewish actors who before the war traveled widely and at one time co-starred with Molly Picon. (He was to die in the Maidanek extermination camp.) Fustel's performance was a success. As a consequence, others followed the same pattern and invited Fustel or other well-known artists such as the folk singer Ida Arvest, the operatic singer Regina Zukor, and the husband-and-wife team of David Zaiderman and Chana Lerner to perform. In September 1940, the *Vaadah Merkazit L'Hatzagot* (The Central Coordinating Committee) emerged in the Warsaw ghetto to match artists and audiences, establish fees, and protect the artists.

Early in 1940, the German authorities permitted musical revues at a Jewish cafe, the Cafe Gartner. The Melody Dance Hall, too, introduced a musical revue program. The first shows presented at the Melody were in Polish and featured Jewish artists who had formerly acted on the Polish stage but had been excluded from Polish theater by the Germans. Later, the Melody Dance Hall turned to Yiddish shows.

As in other ghettos, lovers of music and drama in the Warsaw ghetto not only concerned themselves with creating immediate opportunities for artists to use their talents, but also made an effort to induce musicians and actors to think in terms of continued professional growth in a hoped-for future of freedom — in Poland or elsewhere. On April 20, 1941, Mary Berg noted in her diary the results of one such contest in Warsaw:

> The cafe contest was a tremendous success and during the three days it lasted, the place was packed to the rafters. There were prizes for singing, dancing, recitation, and performance on instruments.
>
> Stanislawa Rapel, a pupil of Janina Pruszycka, won the first prize for dancing. A six-year-old boy . . . received the first prize for

piano. This little boy is a real genius and an accomplished vir-
tuoso. [31]

Teen-aged Mary herself won first prize for singing "jazz songs in English".
The jury which distributed the awards consisted of Wladislaw Spielman, a
pianist; Helena Ostrowska, a vocalist; Stefan Pomper, a ghetto newspaper
editor; Bella Gelbard, the wife of an architect, and Tatiana Epstein, owner of
the cafe where the contest had been held. [32]

A similar contest was held in January 1942 for the purpose of discovering
budding talent. Contestants had to be below the age of 25; awards included ten
cash prizes totalling 1,500 zlotys (the equivalent of $300.00 at that time) and
opportunities for further training by musicians in the ghetto. [33]

Books and Libraries

Even in the ghetto, Jews maintained their self-image as the "people of the
book." They maintained libraries which made reading and study materials
available to the public. In addition, at great personal risk, there were those who
engaged in a systematic program of rescuing books and preserving them, carefully catalogued, in secret archives.

Before the war, each of Poland's major Jewish communities had well-
stocked libraries. In Vilna, the Strashun Library (founded in 1892) housed a
total of 40,000 volumes with an estimated clientele of 52,000 readers. Another
Vilna library, *Mefitze Haskalah* (Library for the Dissemination of Public
Enlightenment), had been the repository of 48,000 books and documents. In
Warsaw alone there were fifty Jewish libraries with a total of 265,336
books.

The Nazis set out systematically to destroy Jewish libraries and to confiscate
Jewish books. Soon after they occupied Warsaw, they ordered all Jewish book
stores and libraries closed. Early in 1940 the Germans permitted the opening
of private libraries under the condition that they stock only books in Yiddish
and Hebrew while they rid themselves of literature critical of Hitler or Nazism.
A few weeks later, in the spring, the Nazis once again declared all Jewish libraries illegal. Books with Jewish content were confiscated and shipped to
Germany for inclusion in a future museum of artifacts from the "extinct"
Jewish race. This see-saw policy toward Jewish libraries, much like the issuing
and countermanding of "Jew-badge" specifications mentioned earlier, was
designed to exacerbate the "war of nerves" against the Jewish population.

Nonetheless, certain Jewish libraries were maintained in the ghettos under
the aegis of the organized Jewish communities. Apparently the Germans, at
various times, were willing to tolerate a limited number of "official" Jewish libraries. In the fall of 1941, only days after the establishment of the Vilna ghetto,
the *Mefitze Haskalah* library was reopened — complete with a reading room
— and the *Judenrat* directed the library to take over all books left behind in the
homes of Jews who had been moved into the ghetto. By August of 1942, the library had amassed a total of almost 93,500 books and magazines, while it
registered almost 4,000 subscribers out of a total Jewish population of approx-

imately 17,000. In March 1943, Jacob Gans, the head of Vilna's *Judenrat* required that all books (except for prayer books and religious texts) still in private possession be handed over to the library. For a brief period in 1942 the Vilna library maintained a bookstore, which had an inventory of about 7,200 books; during August 1942 it sold a total of 198 volumes. The ghetto administration of Vilna even managed to introduce small collections of Jewish books to labor camps in the city's environs for use by Jews who had been sent there from the ghetto. [34]

In 1944 — the year of its liquidation — the Lodz ghetto had one private circulating library with 7,500 volumes and some 4,000 subscribers. [35]

Along with these "official" ghetto libraries there developed a network of "private" lending libraries operating without official sanction from the *Judenrat*. These were hidden in private homes or at locations camouflaged as children's play centers. The two rooms set aside in one such clandestine library in Warsaw were decorated with children's drawings and with shelves bearing dolls and stuffed animals. "Everything was arranged to give the location a less serious, more recreational appearance," Rachel Auerbach, a survivor of the Warsaw ghetto, later recorded in Tel Aviv. [36]

Another "illegal" library in Warsaw circulated books from suitcases until it found a secret home at the headquarters of CENTOS, the coordinating organization for the care of Jewish orphans at Leszno. Its operations were directed by Leib Shur, who had owned the Tamar Jewish publishing house in Vilna before the war, and Batya Berman, who, prior to the war, had been a librarian at Warsaw's Central Library. (Shur eventually collapsed under the double burden of ghetto life and his self-imposed underground labors and was found dead on August 5, 1942. He had hanged himself among his books.) In time, this library took in private collections and grew to more than 12,000 volumes. [37]

Frequently, individuals carried on "mobile library" operations, concealing books under their clothing as they carried them from one borrower to another.

Strenuous efforts were made by individuals and groups to rescue and preserve Jewish books and religious artifacts. During 1942-43, Inish Einhorn and the attorney, M. Naftalin, who were employed in the Lodz ghetto's bureau of research and statistics, systematically searched dwellings abandoned by Jewish deportees, gathering up books and religious articles which the deportees had left behind. In this manner, the two men were able to catalogue and save from the Germans, 30,000 books. Similar activities were conducted in the Kovno and Vilna ghettos. Herman Kruk, historian of the Vilna ghetto, reports that Alfred Rosenberg, Hitler's "expert" on racial theories and minister for the occupied East European territories, ordered a group of Jews in the Vilna ghetto to transfer the contents of the Strashun Library to the library of the University of Vilna, where a suite of rooms which had previously housed a "Marxist-Leninist Seminar" had been set aside for the Jewish books. Kruk recalls that the twelve Jews assigned to transfer the books managed to select a large number of these volumes and hide them in bunkers and warehouses so that the Nazi could not find them. [38]

On December 13, 1942, teen-aged Yitzchak Rudashevski, another Vilna ghetto diarist who did not survive the war, recorded his emotions as the ghetto celebrated the circulation of the 100,000th book in the ghetto library:

> Today the ghetto celebrated the circulation of the 100,000th book in the ghetto library. The festival was held in the auditorium of the theater. We came from our lessons. Various speeches were made and there was also an artistic program. The speakers analyzed the ghetto reader ... The reading of books ... is the greatest pleasure for me. The book unites us with the future, the book unites us with the world. The circulation of the hundred thousandth book is a great achievement for the ghetto, and the ghetto has a right to be proud of it. [39]

Commemorative Observances and Celebrations

As added boosters of morale, the leadership of the ghetto communities arranged public observances and celebrations that focused on the positive, creative aspects of the Jewish heritage. Most of these gatherings were strictly "illegal" and hence had to be held in secrecy, but they were well planned, executed, and popular.

Some observances honored significant anniversaries of prominent ghetto personalities, like Simcha Fustel's 25th anniversary on the Yiddish stage. Other events marked significant milestones in ghetto life, such as the first anniversary of the Yiddish theater in the Warsaw ghetto. Still other functions paid tribute to Jewish literary figures of the past, among them Mendele Mocher Sefarim (1835-1917) the renowned short story writer, Chaim Nachman Bialik (1873-1934) the poet laureate, I. L. Peretz (1881-1915) the Yiddish story teller, medieval Spanish-Jewish poet Judah HaLevi (1086-1140), and the beloved Yiddish literary figure Yehoash (1871-1927). The underground exhibition honoring Yehoash was held in Vilna in March 1943, six weeks before the ghetto was liquidated. It included samples of his Yiddish translation of the Bible and manuscripts of his other writings. There was even a bust of Yehoash by a ten-year-old boy named Walmark. Since it was strictly clandestine, the exhibit was open only at night. Among those active in arranging it was Abraham Sutzkever. In his personal reminiscences of life in the Vilna ghetto, Sutzkever wrote:

> ... the Literary Club arranged a Yehoash exhibit at the clubhouse of the Youth Club. For half a year I had been bringing into the ghetto from the libraries and museums of the city — outside the ghetto — all sorts of literature, paintings, letters and manuscripts relating to Yehoash, and also essays written about him by his contemporaries, including Peretz, Sholem Aleichem and Bialik ... [40]

Sutzkever smuggled the materials out of the German repositories at the risk of his life, because the Germans wanted them to remain in the museums as evidence of the "extinct" Jewish race. His report continues:

> This exhibition was clandestine and illegal. During the day the entrance was boarded up and concealed so that the Germans should not discover it. Then, at nightfall, we would open the exhibit to the ghetto public. [41]

In his diary, the high school student Yitzchak Rudashevski noted the acclaim with which the Vilna ghetto received the Yehoash exhibit:

> March 14, 1943
>
> The exhibition is exceptionally beautiful . . . The room is bright and clean. It is a delight to come into it . . . When you enter the exhibition, you see the youthful zeal (sic) and full of warmth. People entering here forget that this is the ghetto . . . The mood of the celebration was an exalted one. It was indeed a holiday, a demonstration on behalf of Yiddish literature and culture. [42]

The school children celebrated graduations and Jewish holidays with appropriate dramatic and musical performances. The programs stressed optimism and the certainty that a brighter world was awaiting the younger generation. In his history of the Vilna ghetto, Mark Dworzetsky notes one celebration held by the ghetto's school children in honor of *Tu b'Shevat*, the "New Year of the Trees." This holiday, which comes in late winter, marks the annual rebirth of plant life in the Holy Land. The celebration took the form of imaginary greetings from the children in the ghetto to the children of the Jewish Homeland (in what was then called Palestine). An address by one of the teachers ended on a note of high hopes:

> The hour will yet come when you, dear children, will be able to join with those children in the free Land of Israel in planting trees and singing songs. And your days in the ghetto will remain in your minds only as a distant dream . . . [43]

This same spirit of optimism permeated the festival arranged for the children and young people of the Vilna ghetto to commemorate the poet Chaim Nachman Bialik.

In his memoirs, Mark Dworzetsky discusses his feelings and those of the ghetto inmates at that time:

> And so Hayim Nachman Bialik came to the ghetto . . .
>
> No matter how great our sorrows and tears . . . we still are . . . not just a family but a community! Let us, therefore, even in the ghetto, spite the enemy and go on living and building like any other community or society. Death may come tomorrow — but today we will live and keep up our school and our lectures, our orchestra, our health institutions and our workshops. Perhaps if

we live to see better days, we will go forth from the ghetto with our school, with our institutions and with the skills they will have taught us. [44]

Through this overview it is possible to catch a glimpse of the complex structure of cultural activities created in the ghettos. A picture emerges of communities struggling against almost impossible odds to maintain a sense of humanity. In their striving they demonstrated that the human spirit cannot be repressed even if the human body is tortured and finally destroyed.

Chapter Five

Religious Activities

"Israel's faith is not just an abstract thing," an Israeli physician, public servant, and religious Zionist leader Yeshayahu Wolfsberg-Aviad, wrote less than a decade after the end of the Holocaust.

> The Torah and the observance of the *Mitzvot* give the Jewish people a hold on life ... The observance of the *Mitzvot* affords them an opportunity to demonstrate their faith anew each day ... Faith fulfills a unique function: it shields and it also saves ... all those who walk tall ... due to their faith ... [45]

Sara Nishmit, writing about survival values in ghetto life, recalls the words of Rabbi Aaronson:

> ...and there were those who, moved by their faith in God, did not permit themselves to hate; instead they chose another form of resistance. This form of resistance yielded spiritual strength as they fulfilled their religious responsibilities, even under the most dangerous circumstances; it also helped guard moral values and the Divine image of every Jew. As they struggled to maintain moral purity ... they continually battled for life-giving values ... [46]

Certainly the faithful observance of Jewish ritual during the Holocaust was an affirmation of faith, a manifestation, also, of the deep conviction that physical survival was not an end in and of itself. If Jewish survival was to have any meaning, the spirit, the Jewish religious tradition, had to be nurtured, strengthened, and kept alive as well.

When the Nazis occupied a country, they invariably imposed various restrictions on Jewish religious observance even if they did not consistently enforce these restrictions. Apparently much depended on the whims of local German Occupation authorities. In many ghettos the Nazis insisted that Jews on forced labor assignments report to work not only on the Sabbath, but also on the Jewish holidays, including, in some instances, Yom Kippur, the most solemn day of the Jewish year. In Lodz, in the fall of 1939, those businesses still operated by Jews were ordered to remain open on the High Holidays. Jews who failed to comply with the order were subject to severe penalties. Several months later, on January 26, 1940, the Nazis issued an official edict against Jewish public worship in Warsaw. However, this edict was rescinded, on March 4, 1941, and the *Judenrat* was permitted to conduct Jewish services in synagogues, prayer halls, and private homes, effective March 17 of that year. *Rosh Hashanah* and *Yom Kippur* were "officially recognized" as Jewish religious holidays, but this did not restrain the German authorities, who ordered the Jews to report even on those holidays for work which had been declared "essential."

The German authorities closed ritual baths, dissolved religious communal institutions, imposed severe restrictions on Jewish education, and prohibited the Kosher slaughter of meat. Rabbis were insulted and beaten in the streets.

Just as they did in the case of other German depredations, so, too, in the case of Nazi restrictions on religious observance the Jews in the ghetto devised various responses. They availed themselves of every "legal" option; at the same time they evolved clandestine underground facilities for the exercise of those religious activities which had been declared illegal. Among the very Orthodox, there were those who refused to compromise and insisted on the full observance of all the minutiae of Jewish law and custom no matter what befell them. Those who adhered to this view did so out of the sincere convic-'tion that by their rigorous attention to religious ritual they were strengthening their own will and ability to survive.

Moshe Prager, a deeply religious writer who survived the Warsaw ghetto and settled in Israel, recorded the slogan of the militantly Orthodox Jews in the Nazi camps and ghettos:

> You are a Jew! Do what you must!
>
> For us this was a life preserver, which saved us from drowning in a sea of despair even in the most terrible times when all hope was lost...
>
> It was at such moments of hopelessness that the slogan, "You are a Jew! Do what you must!" lit for us the path to follow in the darkness around us. [47]

Others made compromises of varying degrees in accordance with their own conscience, such as rationalizing one's religious conduct in the light of *Pikuah Nefesh*, that Jewish principle which gives first import to the preservation of human life.

Though at times Germans, as already noted, permitted Jewish public worship, they made efficient use of Jewish religious observances to harass the Jewish communities. Sometimes the Germans actively interfered with synagogue services. In Lodz, for instance, during the 1939 High Holiday season, SS men raided the great Synagogue during religious services and forced 400 worshippers into the street. They then ordered the Jews to put on their prayer shawls and conduct a mock service, complete with choral singing, which the Germans filmed for propaganda purposes. A large group of Jews was taken to a restaurant where, garbed in their prayer shawls, they were ordered to dance and sing for the amusement of the German diners. Similarly, just before the Nazis put the Vilna Synagogue in Lodz to the torch, they forced the renowned Lodz teacher, Rabbi Siegel, to put on his prayer shawl and phylacteries and, thus attired, to tear and desecrate the Scrolls of the Law. In contrast, on Yom Kippur eve in 1940, German officers appeared at Kol Nidre services held in a Lodz motion picture theater. They observed the services and behaved with perfect respect and dignity. It seems that they were motivated to do so in order to reassure and quiet the population. [48]

In addition, the Nazi authorities made it a practice to choose Jewish holidays as days for launching their *Aktionen* (mass deportations and killings). One such *Aktion* took place in the Vilna ghetto on Yom Kippur Eve of 1941. In Kovno, Jews were drawn out of the places where they had gathered to worship and rounded up for liquidation. [49]

But not even the danger of public insults, arrest, or deportation kept Jews in the ghettos from meeting in Minyan groups to repeat their prayers. (Jewish congregational worship requires attendance by at least ten males over the age of 13.) When synagogue worship was prohibited, Jews would meet in private dwellings, in hospitals, in ghetto workshops, and even in subterranean bunkers to pray or study together. Isaiah Trunk, a Lodz ghetto survivor, recalls one particularly moving demonstration of Jewish religious loyalty: When the ghetto Jews were forced to report for work as usual on Yom Kippur, they did so, wrapped in their prayer shawls or carrying them, hoping to be able to take time off from work for a few precious moments of prayer. Luckily the supervisor of that particular workshop was an understanding individual who permitted his workers to stand beside their machines and pray. [50].

In Judaism, religious study — the perusal of the Bible, the Talmud, and other Rabbinic literature — was always considered part and parcel of religious worship, so much so that, in Yiddish usage, the traditional synagogue is known as *shul*, literally "school." Synagogues, as well as private dwellings, became regular locations for study groups. In the ghetto, the *yeshiva bahurim*, (the boys and young men) who engaged in higher Talmudic studies at rabbinical academies prior to the war, viewed "learning" as the core of their very lives. Others, who were just as staunchly devout but had worked at secular occupations, cherished "learning" as spiritual recreation or as a fascinating intellectual exercise.

In the Warsaw ghetto, a group of yeshiva students set up an "underground yeshiva" at Nalewki 35, where they studied in makeshift classrooms under the guidance of prominent Talmudic scholars who fate had thrown into the ghetto. Reb Avremele Weinberg, one such scholar who headed his own yeshiva before the war, invited anyone who so desired to come to his home for lectures. His informal study group came to be known as "Rabbi Avremele's Group". [51] Other men took their holy books to the ghetto workshops where they were employed and studied alone or in pairs while they worked at their machines. [52] Still others gathered clandestinely in basements or attics after a day's work to study a *blat gemarah* (a folio of Talmud.)

In the Kovno ghetto, members of the two pre-war Orthodox organizations — the Beth Jacob movement, which trained young women as teachers, and *Tiferet Bahurim*, a prayer and study group for boys and young men — organized formal classes which met regularly. [53]

Religious Jews in the ghetto made every effort to observe all religious holidays as fully as possible. At Passover time, Jews somehow managed to bake *matzah*, the unleavened Passover bread, which must be prepared under special conditions and with carefully selected ingredients to prevent the dough from turning into forbidden "leavened bread." In the Kovno ghetto during the spring of 1942, hundreds of Jews lined up in front of a house on Linkova Street where *matzah* were baked for Passover. Each had brought with him a quantity of flour as his contribution. There was also a charge of 15 marks each to provide flour and *matzah* for those who could not afford to participate in the "operation." Rabbi Jacob Schmuckler organized a *Maoth Hittim* Committee to supply the penniless with such Passover foods as could be obtained under ghetto conditions. By the spring of 1944, the street of the *matzoh* bakery had been detached from the ghetto and the ovens and other special baking equipment had been lost. Some resourceful ghetto householders prepared ovens in the ghetto workshops to make them ritually pure and used them for baking the ghetto's supply of *matzah*.

In the Lodz ghetto, wheat flour was unavailable; corn meal was used instead for the *matzah*. Since it was impossible to obtain wine or even grape juice for the Passover Seder, beet juice — sweetened with saccharine — served as a substitute. Some of the extremely devout, who tended to be more meticulous about their Passover diets than ordinary pious Jews, fasted rather than partake of foods they would not ordinarily have eaten on Passover, even under ghetto conditions. [54]

The Seder ritual was observed despite most trying circumstances, including the Warsaw ghetto uprising, which coincided with the Passover season of 1943. It is said that one rabbi in Warsaw had some tiny *matzah* baked well before Passover that year and kept them on his person all the time so that he would have the required number of *matzah* on hand in order to celebrate the Seder properly no matter where he might find himself on Passover Eve.

The previous fall, the Warsaw ghetto Jews had found the heart to celebrate the Festival of *Simchat Torah*, the "Rejoicing of the Law," which comes at the end of the High Holiday season and marks the start of the annual Torah reading cycle. *Simchat Torah* is traditionally observed by *hakafot*, festive processions in the synagogue with the Torah scrolls, accompanied by lively singing and dancing, to demonstrate the Jewish love of *Torah*.

By the fall of 1942, the population of the Warsaw ghetto had been reduced by deportation and disease to 50,000 and many of the ghetto's children were no longer alive. Nevertheless, a small group gathered in the apartment of Rabbi

Menachem Zemba, one of the revered leaders of Poland's Orthodox Jews, for the traditional *hakafot*. A young boy entered the rabbi's room and joined in the dancing. Rabbi Judah Leib Orlean, an eminent Talmudic scholar, swept up the boy and a Torah Scroll in his arms and ecstatically whirled about the room, crying out, "*A klein Yidele mit der heiliker Torah*". (Just look at this little Jew and our great, holy Torah!) [55]

The writer and scholar Zelig Kalmanovitch, himself a victim, left behind a diary written for the most part in Hebrew with several entries in Yiddish. He described the spirit that inspired the celebration of *Simchat Torah* in the Vilna ghetto:

> There, in the midst of this tiny community, in this dingy remnant
> of a synagogue, we were one in spirit with the rest of the Jewish
> people . . . With our singing we hallowed the name of God, just as
> our forefathers had done for generations. And I, lost Jewish soul
> that I am, found my roots there . . . Now I know that the Jewish
> people will survive. For is it not written in the Bible that we shall
> endure "as the stars of heaven above the earth? . . . And even if we
> were indeed to be the last generation of Jews on this earth, we
> should give thanks . . . for having been privileged to be the
> children of such splendid forebears. Every added day which the
> Holy One, Blessed be He, will grant us is a precious gift. We shall
> accept it with rejoicing and give thanks to Him for it . . . [56]

Kalmanovitch, a rationalist and a non-Orthodox Jew, sensed the meaning of faith for Jewish survival.

Aside from the formal celebrations of the holidays, the pious Jews in the ghetto also devoted loving and painstaking attention to the observances of day-to-day life. Even after the Germans closed the *mikvot* (ritual baths), men and women found ways of visiting them secretly. In the Warsaw ghetto one year, Rabbi Kalonymos (Kalmish) Shapira, a famed Hassidic rebbe, led a group of followers to the *mikvah* to purify themselves on the eve of Yom Kippur. The men left their apartment block at 5 that morning after having bribed the Polish guard to open the gate of the house (which was supposed to be still locked for the night). Since the door to the *mikvot* had been sealed off by the Germans, Rabbi Shapira and his friends entered it through a basement window. Groping their way through the dark cellar, they found a hole in the wall through which they crawled into the *mikvot*. When they reached their destination, they found other men there too, waiting their turn to cleanse themselves in preparation for the Day of Atonement. [57]

When the Nazis issued edicts forbidding Jewish women to become pregnant, many couples not only defied the orders but also had the infant sons circumcised. One such incident took place in the Kovno ghetto early in May 1942. The Germans had announced that any woman in the ghetto who gave birth to a child would be killed along with her baby. Isaac Blau and his wife had their first child after five years of marriage; it was a boy. Since the apartment block in which they lived also housed an "officially permitted" vocational school, they hoped that the noise of the students would drown out the cries of the infant during the circumcision rite. The Blaus had secretly invited a small group of friends to attend the ceremony. Just as the *mohel* (circumciser) began the operation, a Gestapo car screeched to a halt outside the building. The *mohel* insisted on completing the circumcision; if the child had to die, he declared, at least let him die a Jew. Fortunately, the Gestapo agents who had come to inspect the school did not notice anything unusual in the apartment block, and the mother and child were saved. [58]

Pious Jews in the Kovno ghetto, as well as those in Lodz, organized societies to aid co-religionists in the observance of the Sabbath, the dietary laws, and even in the procurement of properly prepared *mezuzot* for the doors of their dwellings.

This intense preoccupation of the pious with religious observance even in the face of imminent destruction was motivated by the belief that meticulous adherence to religious law was a vital component of *Kiddush Hahayyim*, the Sanctification of Life. They believed that such adherence had to be continued as long as God would give them life; only death at the hands of their oppressors would free them of this sacred obligation. When that time came they would die *al kiddush ha shem*, as martyrs to sanctify the Name of God, but while they lived they would invest their lives with a spirit of sanctity that is *Kiddush Hahayyim* — even in the ghetto.

It was in the light of *Kiddush Hahayyim* that the religious leaders in the ghettos decided what constituted acceptable religious observance or the proper "Jewish" attitude and conduct in any given emergency.

The rabbis were called upon to decide such questions as to whether and under what circumstances pregnant women could be permitted to eat non-kosher meat; what food might be cooked on the Sabbath for those assigned to forced labor, and could peas and beans be eaten on Passover even though these vegetables were ordinarily prohibited for Passover use. In each case, the overriding consideration was *Pikuah Nefesh* — observance of dietary restrictions which would endanger the life of the individual involved. On February 27, 1941, all 15 rabbis in the Lodz ghetto signed a ruling permitting not only women in confinement but also anyone who was seriously ill or felt his or her strength failing, to eat non-kosher meat if no other meat was obtainable, and a physician would certify that the patient needed meat in order to survive. [59] The rabbis in the Kovno ghetto permitted the cooking of meals on the Sabbath for forced laborers who might otherwise not have enough food to sustain them. [60] In the spring of 1941, the rabbinate in the Warsaw ghetto declared it permissible to eat peas and beans on Passover because matzoth and other Passover foods were nearly unobtainable and eating these vegetables was preferable to eating outright *hametz* — leavened bread — in order to avoid starvation.

These "dispensations" were not lightly given. They were accommodations which enabled traditional Jews to survive physically without feeling that they had committed a sin by transgressing Jewish law. In this way the rabbis maintained, even under ghetto conditions, the spiritual foundations of Jewish religious life within a familiar framework, thereby helping to preserve morale and the will for meaningful survival.

Other rabbinical decisions involved questions of a more unusual order. A man who had managed to bring his personal Torah scroll with him into the ghetto went to a river in the dark of night. He submerged the scroll in the water, leaving it there in order to save it from being torn, trampled upon or soiled by the Germans. Was that man guilty of desecrating the Scroll and liable to the penalty of fasting that is usual in such a case? The decision rendered stated that the man had not transgressed by placing the Torah scroll in the water, though he had made it unfit for use. The man acted correctly; he protected the Torah from violation at the hands of the archenemy.[61] Then there was the problem of the young Kovno boy whose parents had been arrested and killed by the Nazis. His Gentile nurse converted him to Christianity, not out of any missionary zeal but solely with the intention of insuring his survival. When he realized that he had been converted, he fled into the ghetto, made himself known to one of the rabbis, and told him his story. The question was whether such an individual could be counted as part of a *minyan* once he had reached the age of thirteen. The rabbi ruled that he could. Since the boy had not knowingly submitted to conversion, he was not to be considered a renegade but a full-fledged member of the Jewish community.[62] Also, as regarded synagogue worship proper, was it not a contradiction for Jews in the ghettos to continue reciting, in the group of blessings in the daily morning service, the one giving thanks to God "Who has not made me a slave" when in reality they suffered the ultimate slavery of Nazi persecution? In his reply to this question, the rabbi pointed out the difference between physical and spiritual enslavement, observing that although the Germans had succeeded in enslaving the Jews in body, this did not mean that they had also gained mastery over the Jewish spirit. Consequently, the rabbi ruled that Jews in the ghetto were still duty-bound to thank God every morning for not having made them slaves (in the spiritual sense):

> ... therefore, I have responded to my questioner, God forbid that they invalidate this blessing bequeathed by our patriarchs of blessed memory. On the contrary, especially at such times, we are obliged to repeat this blessing. As we do, our enemies, our destroyers, will realize that though we are in their hands and subject to their every whim, yet we view ourselves as free people. Though we are illegally imprisoned and enslaved, our salvation is near, our redemption will come. [63]

Which consideration should have first priority: respect for the memory of the ghetto's dead, or the immediate physical needs of those who were still alive? According to Jewish law, clothes of people who had met a violent death cannot be used by the survivors but must be buried. The original intent of the law had been to make certain that garments stained with a victim's blood should be treated with the proper dignity, but some authorities had extended the law even to clothes that had not been on the victim's body at the time of his death. Did this mean that the clothes left behind in the ghetto by deportees who almost certainly had been murdered in the death camps could not be used by Jews who were still in the ghetto in desperate need of clothing? [64] To what extent was it permissible to endanger one's own life to save that of another, or conversely, to save oneself at the cost of the life of another human being? [65] Did Jewish law require one to risk one's life, not for any particular practical religious or moral observance, but simply for the purpose of study and prayer? In responding to the last mentioned queston the rabbinical authority consulted Maimonides' treatise, *Iggeret Teman*, which had been written in the 12th century, when Yemenite Jews had suffered persecution at the hands of the Arabs. The rabbis held that while it was praiseworthy to pray and to study the Law even at the risk of one's life, it was not a requirement of the Jewish faith; each individual was free to act according to the dictates of his own conscience and his own commitment to Judaism. [66]

In his endeavor to remain alive, was a Jew permitted to secure a Christian baptismal certificate? Was he permitted to save his children by placing them in Christian homes or institutions? It is interesting to note that the ghetto rabbis were inclined to answer the first question in the negative, but tended to take a more lenient view regarding the second. Those who forbade the securing of baptismal papers pointed out that *Kiddush Hahayyim* was based not only on physical survival but also on the maintenance of spiritual integrity. When a man traded his integrity for promises of physical protection he had sacrificed his spiritual integrity. There was a point, these rabbis said, at which mere survival loses its value and one must be prepared to sacrifice one's life for the sake of an ideal. [67] On the other hand, the rabbis did not see the placement of young children in Gentile homes as a renouncement of Jewish religious dignity or identity. It did not entail an official renunciation of Judaism on the part of the parent (or on the part of the child for that matter) as long as the Gentile host did not require the parents to have their children baptised in return for sheltering them; parents might also have a better chance to survive if they were unencumbered by little children; then after the war there was a good chance that they would be able to reclaim their children and raise them as Jews. If the parents did not return, Jewish organizations or institutions would make it their business to go to the Gentiles and seek out the Jewish children hidden in their homes or convents. [68]

Sex was also among those areas which were controlled by religious law. Briefly, in Judaism, sex is viewed as a normal and natural part of life. From the traditional viewpoint, while the sex act was designed to fulfill the biblical imperative "Be fruitful and multiply" (Genesis 1:29), it also viewed sex in marriage as a perfectly legitimate method of personal fulfillment and gratification. The sex act in marriage was holy. On April 7, 1942 the German Occupation authorities in Eastern Europe ruled that all pregnant women in the ghettos would be put to death. If one accepted the most stringent Jewish

religious ruling on artificial birth control, which forbade the use of any con-
traceptive method, it would mean that each marital sex act placed the wife in
danger of death. After a review of pertinent Rabbinic literature, the rabbis in
the ghetto of Kovno permitted the pratice of birth control. [69] Under certain circumstances, even abortion was permitted in order to save the mother from
being killed by the Germans. [70] (This was in accordance with the rabbinic
principle that an embryo could be aborted if it could be seen as the potential
"murderer" of its mother.)

In addition to giving their disciples practical guidance, the rabbis in the
ghettos sought to maintain morale by their sermons and their writings, some
of which have been preserved through the efforts of survivors. They continued
to preach the types of sermons to which traditional East European Jews had
been accustomed in their home towns, to help maintain a semblance of nor-
mality in ghetto existence.

These sermons included two classic types: the pilpulistic discourse and the
musar or moralist homily. The purpose of the pilpulistic discourse was to
elucidate some fine point in the rabbinic interpretation of Jewish law. (*Pilpul* is
the Hebrew word denoting sharp or "peppery" legal argumentation.) This type
of sermon reflected the traditional Jewish proclivity to study for the sake of
study, even if the subject matter is not relevant to everyday life. Rabbi Ephraim
Oshry, who survived the Kovno ghetto, presents three pilpulistic talks which
he himself delivered in the ghetto, [71] each given on the Sabbath preceding
Passover. Two of them, one delivered in 1943 and the other in 1944, dealt with
aspects of Jewish law that were relevant to the ghetto situation. In the former,
Rabbi Oshry discussed mixtures forbidden on Passover because they might
contain prohibited leaven. In the latter which he had prepared after a mass
deportation of children from the ghetto, he enumerated life-saving activities
for which Sabbath observance could be set aside. In the pre-Passover sermon
of 1941, on the other hand, Rabbi Oshry attempted to apply to ghetto life an
academic rabbinic debate on the implications of slavery, namely, the Biblical
status of individuals who were regarded as half slave and half free.

A typical *musar* sermon from the ghetto (delivered during Adar 5702, the
month preceding Passover 1942) was recorded in a handwritten version by
Rabbi Yehudah Aaronson who, together with the congregation from his
home town of Sanok, was deported to the Konin labor camp, where all
perished. In this sermon delivered in Yiddish, as was the custom, the preacher
blamed the sufferings of the Jewish people on the fact that the Jews had drifted
away from God by accepting the defective morality of modern civilization.
Their present plight was but another vindication of Divine justice. Rabbi
Aaronson pleaded with his congregation to hold firm to their human dignity
as creatures of God. God, the rabbi held, was using the Nazis as his scourges,
but eventually the Germans would go down in defeat and Israel would be
saved. He writes:

> Dear brothers, let us turn back to our Heavenly Father. Let us
> repent from the depths of our hearts, we must not succumb to the

depths of degradation that the enemy wishes to impose on us. If we can not save our bodies; at least let us save our souls — remaining faithful to the Divine image within us!

We are the faithful who believe in Your Providence and we know that the enemy is a punishing rod which ultimately You will shatter and destroy. We acknowledge our sins, we affirm our faith. We fulfill our religious responsibilities. We express our love of God and the people of Israel. [72]

Among the documents discovered in the Ringelblum archives were handwritten copies of sermons delivered in the Warsaw ghetto by Rabbi Kalonymus (Kalmish) Shapira. Known from childhood as gifted with a prodigious Talmudic mind, "Reb Kalmish" had been the author of several rabbinic works and had founded a yeshiva of his own soon after World War I. When the Germans took Warsaw in 1939, he refused to leave the city and, though by then a man of 60, he was put to work in one of the factories set up by the Germans in the ghetto. After the liquidation of the Warsaw ghetto, he was taken to a concentration camp where he died.

In his sermons, which were published posthumously in Israel, "Reb Kalmish" sought to give perspective and meaning to the sufferings of the Jews, not only in the light of past Jewish history, theology, ethics, and practice, but also as a reflection of the contemporary struggle. He called upon his listeners to sustain Jewish life, no matter what the cost, to hold their heads high as Jews and as human beings even in the face of persecution and brutality. His sermon in 1940, on the weekly portion of *Shalach L'Kha* (Numbers 13:1-15:41) deals with the lack of faith shown by the Children of Israel in the wilderness when they heard the adverse reports of the twelve spies who had been sent out to explore the Promised Land. They reported that the inhabitants were too strong to be conquered. To "Reb Kalmish", faith in a God Whose ways are inscrutable is vital. Faith that moves beyond the rational is the only path toward ultimate salvation. It is not an easy faith, but one based on total commitment in evil times as well as in good days. He applies this to the Biblical narrative and to the predicament of his people:

> Particularly at such moments when he sees no possibility of salvation must the Jew have faith in Divine Deliverance. At such times, it is best not to attempt to intellectualize, for this can destroy faith and place obstacles in the way to salvation. It is imperative to recognize the truth of the spies' report, that the dwellers in the land are strong and their cities are fortified. Yet with our belief in the Supreme God, who will save us, we will inherit the land. It is such faith and trust which will herald our salvation. [73]

For Kalmish this same faith was to hold good also for his people in their hour of trial and time of doubt. Such a faith is not an abstract thing, he notes in his commentary (1940) on the weekly portion of *Vayeshev* (Genesis 37:1-40:23), the story of Joseph's sufferings first at the hands of his own brethren and then among the Egyptians. The faith of the Jew must be expressed in religious observance and truly Jewish behavior even in the face of Nazi destruction. [74] The plan of the Germans was not only to annihilate the Jews physically but also to destroy them spiritually. The Jews were being persecuted because they were Jews; hence, their only proper response would be to strengthen their lives as members of the Jewish people. Suffering became a touchstone of one's faith in God. By standing erect before his oppressors, the Jew demonstrates his faith and thereby strengthens his own spirit.

Suffering, "Reb Kalmish" pointed out, was not new to the people of Israel; all of Jewish history is the epic of a people's suffering without losing faith in God. While he saw little gain in "intellectualizing" he attempted to establish a rationale for preserving one's faith even amidst suffering. He interpreted the agony of the Jews under the Nazi yoke as *Hevlei Mashiah*, "the birth pangs" that must precede the coming of the Messiah. Through its sufferings, Israel would hasten the advent of the Messianic age for all mankind. Without Israel's sufferings, mankind could not attain deliverance. Consequently, the Jew did not suffer for himself alone but for the rest of mankind; this was the eternal mandate for which Israel had been chosen.

> According to our understanding, such are the birth pangs of the Messiah. Redemption and salvation are the evidence of Divine revelation, God's revelation through the people of Israel. All redemption depends on Israel. In this way, we may interpret Isaiah 66 . . . we recognize that through Israel the light of the Messiah will be revealed. [75]

But how could the Jew best meet the challenge of persecution? By leading a Jewish life no matter what befell him, "Reb Kalmish" explained. One response to oppression was prayer, difficult though that might be practically and psychologically in the ghetto.

> What can we do if we are not permitted to gather in prayer and cry out to God? At such times each individual must pray alone from out of the depths of his own heart. [76]

In addition to prayer, the study of Torah was a basic way of reaching out to God; therefore, it had to be pursued regardless of the difficulties and dangers involved. Together, prayer and study strengthened the individual and brought God and man closer to one another. [77]

Kalmish admonishes his people to confront their difficult times with *Betachon* — faith in God. He warns them that God in His wisdom may delay salvation, yet His redemptive power will ultimately act to save His people. One must accept one's current sufferings as a manifestation of *yeshurim shel ahavah*,

> The classic Jewish idea "though He flay me, though He slay me, yet will I trust Him." When Almighty God wishes to punish us, this too we must accept with love and hope that He will not aban-

79

don us and will bring us close to Him . . . For when one bolsters his hope for deliverance with an acknowledgement of God's omnipotence, then the bitterness of this pain and suffering is alleviated. Under such circumstances he can withstand suffering even if the hope for salvation is delayed. [78]

Kalonymus Kalmish's message, distilled from Jewish tradition, is clear. Its elements are hope and faith in the face of suffering and unspeakable hardship. It encouraged the people not to give up, but to live with dignity and pride in the face of destruction. Kalmish was motivated by a desire to elevate and to encourage, and his words were life-directed. He stood among those who offered spiritual resistance to the Nazis rather than surrender.

Sermons like those of Rabbi Oshry, Rabbi Aaronson and "Reb Kalmish" did much to help the traditional Jews in the ghettos persevere with dignity until the end. The ideal of these and other spiritual leaders in the Nazi ghettos was not *Kiddush Hashem*, the hallowing of God's name through martyrdom, but *Kiddush Hahayyim*, the hallowing of God through the maintenance of meaningful lives for as long as possible. In the case of the religious Jews in Hitler's ghettos and concentration camps, the experience of *Kiddush Hahayyim*, in its broadest expression, can be defined in terms of their determination to center their lives around Judaism as they saw it. By their firm belief in Divine Providence and their scrupulous adherence to Jewish law even in the ghetto, they saw themselves as living witnesses to the sanctity of human life. To the religious Jew, the sanctification of life even in the face of death was the ultimate act of heroism, a hallowing of the Name of God before the eyes of all mankind.

Chapter Six

Zionist Activities

Political Zionism, both in theory and practice, affirmed the reality of the restoration of Jewish nationhood in its ancient homeland. It was committed to the realization of this goal. For Zionists, no matter what their other religious or social ideals, the principal aim was national revival, national restoration and the restructuring of Jewish life in *Eretz Yisrael*, the Jewish homeland. Adherents of Zionism persisted in pursuing this aim even in the ghetto, when it might have seemed that there was no future for the Jew as an individual, let alone as a member of a Jewish national entity. Such activity in the ghettos of occupied Europe is yet another manifestation of *Kiddush Hahayyim*, the will to live and affirm one's intrinsic identity even in the holocaust era.

Zionism in the ghetto served as a focal point for those segments of the community committed to Jewish national survival. Jews, as individuals, would die at the hands of the Nazis, but the Jewish people would continue to live. Motivated by this perception, the leaders who were active in the Zionist movement prior to their internment in the ghettos continued to train their followers in the intellectual attitudes and practical skills they felt best suited for a life of building and pioneering in *Eretz Yisrael*. "We will be able to preserve our pride as (Jewish) individuals and as members of the Jewish nation," Shmuel Breslau, a leader of the left-wing *Hashomer Hatzair* declared in a 1941 report of Zionist activities:

> There is no need for us to run away from our uniqueness . . . We must plan . . . with the help of our intellect . . . to cast off the slave mentality.
>
> With the help of our intellect, we must build a basis for this profound realization which will enable us to survive in pride and strength. [79]

The Zionists never doubted that the war would end in victory for the Allies, the forces of justice and right. As part of this victory they envisioned the establishment of an independent Jewish state in Palestine, the only viable, permanent solution for the age-old problem of Jewish homelessness. In the ghettos they urged the young people not only to strengthen their sense of

Jewish national pride in theory and train for life in the Jewish state that would rise after the war, but to also initiate organized resistance against the Nazi overlords. In this manner, the young would be able to help hasten the day when the yearned-for Jewish state would come into being.

Zionist activities, carried on by Zionists of all stamps in the ghettos, centered around two focal points: their present situation and their future home. They planned, studied, and prepared for life in *Eretz Yisrael*, while actively working to meet the physical, moral, and intellectual needs that confronted their people trapped in the ghetto. Their objective: to insure the survival by building their inner defiance.

The various parties within Zionism managed to set up *Hakhshara* centers for training the young in practical skills that would be needed in *Eretz Yisrael*. Prior to the war, much of *Hakhshara's* activity had been conducted in the countryside on farms established for this purpose. This practice continued during the war under Nazi occupation in the Warsaw area, where *Hakhshara* activities continued through the spring of 1942. In the initial period young Jews, by and large members of various Zionist groups, were recruited by Toporol (an organization established to encourage agriculture among Jews in Poland) and were assigned to work on farms owned by Germans and Poles. They came as individuals, yet they managed to work as groups, following *Hakhshara* discipline. During 1941-42 two specific *Hakhshara* centers were set up. One was Lublin, for Warsaw's young revisionist Zionists of the Betar Group, the other at *Tchernikov* for *Dror Hekhalutz*, where 170 were in training by the spring of 1942. [80] Jews in the urban ghetto, particularly in Lodz and Vilna, [81] also were given similar vocational training (agricultural training, of course, was impossible) clandestinely in private apartments and other "unofficial" places. During the war years there were instances of individuals managing to escape from Nazi-held Europe and making their way via Hungary and Rumania (when these countries were neutral) to Palestine. Correspondence smuggled out of the ghetto to Zionist centers in Palestine and elsewhere obliquely refer to *Hakhshara* training and to an attempt at "illegal" migration to Palestine (Aliyah). The words *Hakhshara* and *Aliya*, defining two aspects of Zionist activity, were used as names of members of the correspondent's family.

Warsaw, March 29, 1940

Dear Mordecai,
Surely you have already received my letter, but I want to give you some news about my beloved family . . . all of us are longing for our dear relative, Aliyah . . . [82]

In December 1941, three months after the establishment of the Vilna ghetto, the leaders of Vilna's *Hashomer Hatzair* held a clandestine executive meeting at a convent of Benedictine Sisters seven km outside of the city. They found a haven there through the efforts of a non-Jewish Polish sympathizer, Yedwiga Dudzec. Abba Kovner, a Hebrew writer and poet who was to take a leading role in organizing the Vilna ghetto's resistance fighters, opened the meeting with a situation report. Ruz'ka Korczak, one of the future ghetto fighters, recorded one of the statements made in the discussion which followed:

> All our education to date, indeed, all our lives have been directed toward Eretz Yisrael. European Jewry is now engulfed in a holocaust . . . We have remained here in its vortex, a handful of guardians, but in fact our being here is only accidental, for our place is really in the land of Israel, which is our goal. Even now, immigration to Eretz Yisrael is the cornerstone of our existence. We must do everything possible to save the largest possible number of our comrades for this purpose . . . [83]

Ghetto Zionist groups managed to maintain close ties with their counterparts in Palestine. As late as November 15, 1943, the Polish branch of Po'ale Zion, the Labor Zionist movement, succeeded in sending heartfelt greetings to the Po'ale Zion World Federation:

> We send greetings to our brethren who are fighting and working for a better tomorrow for all of us in a reborn *Eretz Yisrael*. We say to them, "Be strong and of good courage."

> Even in the abject depths in which we find ourselves today we derive strength from the knowledge that you (in Palestine) are toiling ceaselessly for our free Socialist *Eretz Yisrael*. [84]

Among the signers of this letter were Itzhak Zuckerman and Zivia Lubetkin, who were to play a key role in the partisan movement. They survived the ghetto, married each other, and settled in Israel on a kibbutz founded by former ghetto fighters.

As already mentioned, the Dror Zionist youth movement carried on extensive educational and cultural activities in the ghettos. In the Warsaw ghetto, Dror leadership held underground seminars to train new cadres of leaders not only for Warsaw but also for other ghetto communities. Dror's underground press published valuable educational materials under the direction of the Hebrew educator, poet, and playwright Itzhak Katzenelson. The Dror publications included older works as well as new ones created in the ghettos by Katzenelson and others. According to report, Katzenelson, who was then in his mid-fifties, "wrote a great deal during this period. Perhaps he had no other period so creative as his period in the ghetto." [85] Dror, like the other Zionist groups, carried on traditional Zionist activities. In January 1942 they demonstrated their love for Palestine by conducting a fund-raising campaign in the Warsaw ghetto on behalf of the J.N.F., and in this way they observed the 15th day of Shevat, the New Year for Trees, when fund collections traditionally took place to aid Palestine's reforestration program.

Gordonia, a pioneer scouting movement also linked to Labor Zionism, sought to perpetuate its own interpretation of Jewish and human values in the Polish ghettos.

As in peacetime, so in the days of the ghetto, too, the Zionist movement was divided into many parties — from the extreme right to the extreme left in politics and religious beliefs. Aside from the Labor Zionist, there was the Orthodox Mizrachi and its religious-socialist sister organization haPo'el haMizrachi, the right-wing Revisionist movement (the party of Menahem Begin, Israel's sixth Prime Minister), and the middle-of-the-road General Zionist party. Though each of these groups operated independently in the ghettos as they had prior to the war, at various times they all cooperated. Thus, almost from the very first day in the Vilna ghetto all work of all Zionist parties was coordinated under the leadership of Mordecai Tenenbaum-Tamarof. Before long, the "Committee of the Seven," a coordinating committee which included representatives from all Zionist groupings in the ghetto, was developed. This committee became an umbrella organization for such cultural activities as a Hebrew theater, a Hebrew scientific institute, and a Hebrew choir. In addition to its educational endeavors, it found places of work for young Zionists and distributed funds of the American Jewish Joint Distribution Committee (which was permitted to aid many East European ghettos until America's entry into the war in December 1941). There was also similar cooperation among Zionist parties in the ghettos of Kovno and Warsaw.

In Kovno there were two Zionist coordinating bodies: *Matzok*, a name created from the initials of *Mercaz Tziyonam, Vatolo, b'Kovno*, represented the four major Zionist groups in Kovno. This body was established in April of 1942 by representatives of the General Zionist A and B, the Revisionist as well as the *ZS Studenten Farband* (Zionist Student Federation). Der Altester of the ghetto was an ex-officio member of the group, which secretly coordinated underground Zionist activity. It maintained contact with the Aryan world beyond the ghetto walls as well as with other ghettos seeking to insure the survival of Zionists wherever possible.

During the same period the Young Zionist also developed a coordinating body called *Irgun Brit Tziyon*, (Zion Federation of Youth). This was an outgrowth of the work begun during the period of Soviet occupation in the early part of the war. Its objectives were articulated at an ideological conference held early in 1942. It built its activities on *Shelilat Hagalut*, the negation of the diaspora, and pledged itself to work for *Aliyah*, immigration to the land of Israel. It clarified for itself the nature of the Jewish homeland that it wished to see built on nationalistic and socialistic principles. *Irgun Brit Tziyon* conducted cultural projects which focused on educating the young in Zionist thought, Palestinography, and basic Judaism. All of these activities were conducted in Hebrew. It initiated rescue efforts and ultimately shared in anti-Nazi resistance. The *Irgun* gathered a library of Hebrew books and published a handwritten periodical *Nitzot* (Sparks) of which thirty issues appeared.

One member of the group summarized its goals as follows:

> . . . we must awake and not live passively. We must not deteriorate, despite the awful circumstances. We must guard our

Zionism and attract the youth to us in order that they will not be swept into the corrosive stream of ghetto life . . . degradation and demoralization . . . let us gather to study the history of Zionism and of the Jewish people. [86]

One of the most interesting groups associated with the *Irgun* was *Irgun Shemirah Laganim* (Guardians of the Gardens), organized in the summer of 1942 to protect the vegetable gardens planted by ghetto inhabitants.

The youngest of the Zionist groups affiliated with the *Irgun Shemirah Laganim* was *G'dud Hama-apilim* (The Strivers), a well-organized group that kept handwritten minutes and records in a notebook recovered after the war's end. The group's objectives were set down by its leader, A. Ben Avner on January 1, 1944:

> During the time when the sword of war hovers over all the world; and blood is being spilled like water upon the earth; at a time which brings annihilation to European Jewry in general and Latvian Jewry in particular, we the youth, remnants of the Jews of the ghetto that has become the Concentration Camp of Kaunas, Slobodka
>
> *Proclaim*: We have not abandoned our hope
> *We believe*: Israel is Eternal
> *We are certain*: Our Liberation and Salvation will come! [87]

In addition the group set forth the following ten commandments to guide their activities:

1. *Hama-apil* believes in the justice and sanctity of the ideal of a Jewish State for the Jewish people and pledges to struggle until the last moment to realize this ideal.

2. *Hama-apil* is a pioneer struggling for the rebirth of our people and its homeland. He will spread this idea among the masses. In the ghetto he is devoted to the task of preparing the youth. To this end he will develop his abilities and knowledge in all areas.

3. *Hama-apil* guards the national culture and the Hebrew language which he speaks and spreads among the populace.

4. *Hama-apil* believes that the people of Israel are eternal. He strengthens this belief and the hope of our future within the people as he struggles against despair.

5. *Hama-apil* will guard our secrets even in the most difficult of circumstances.

6. *Hama-apil* knows that his group is his family. He loves it and is loyal to his friends, sharing openly with them.

7. *Hama-apil* fulfills without any doubts the commands of his superiors.

8. *Hama-apil* is a well integrated person, ready to work for national causes and prepared to protect his national dignity under all circumstances.

9. *Hama-apil* is truthful and compassionate to all in his thoughts, his words and his deeds.

10. *Hama-apil* will always remember his brother's spilled blood and will avenge his people. He will remember the cursed existence of the Hebrew people in Europe and will arouse the people to end the European diaspora. He mourns the loss of his sainted brothers and pledges not to take part in joyous celebrations.[88]

In some cases the activities conducted by the Zionists were supported even by the ultra-Orthodox Agudath Israel which before the war preferred not to collaborate with Zionist organizations.

As already mentioned, Zionist leaders were prominent in the Jewish partisan units. Many escaped from the ghettos to the woods, where they joined the partisan fighters, and, of course, all Zionist factions were represented in the planning and execution of the Warsaw ghetto revolt in April 1943. Following the war, those Zionists who had survived the ghettos of Eastern Europe helped lead other survivors, often at the risk of their own lives, to the West, from where they made their way to Palestine.

Though the various Zionist factions differed greatly in their world outlook — and these differences were by no means blurred by ghetto existence — the overall objective of Zionism, the national renaissance of the Jewish people, was an expression of Jewish dignity, of the sacredness of life in general, and of Jewish life in particular. By creating a structure of positive Jewish activities in the ghettos, each Zionist grouping in its own way applied the principle of *Kiddush Hahayyim* to the struggle for survival in the Nazi Holocaust. As Israel Gutman noted:

> ... Members of the youth movements (Zionist) succeeded in guarding and developing during the war period the idea that they belonged to human society which exists beyond the borders of the Nazi conquered lands and the enslavement ... through the press of the movement as well as correspondence, the tie with the land of Israel becomes clear, the tie that sustains faith in the future. [89]

It is in this way that the Zionist movement reacted to ghetto life. It created a response pattern of positive Jewish activities with which the Jew confronted the tragic realities of living behind the ghetto walls. The Zionist movement, rejecting resignation and despair as a way of life, built for the future even as life was being destroyed day by day in the ghetto. Zionism offered tangible options for its adherents. As Avnon notes:

> ... We wished to perpetuate the spiritual world as well as the ideological struggle of the Gordonia members imprisoned as they were in the middle of the 20th century behind the ghetto walls. While their world, the world of youth, grew dark around them, their spirit did not break; rather they rose above their trouble and misfortunes and they found the strength to go on living — though confronted by the dangers of death and finally death itself. They called upon the youth to guard their humanity — at a time when the enemy sought with all his means to destroy it. They educated them to sustain their national pride and their faith in the eternal Jewish people ... They infused them with a Messianic hope that the day of redemption was close at hand, and pleaded with the Jewish community: "Stand on guard, be stalwart, stand forth, remain alive — the end of the Nazi hell is at hand ... [90]

Chapter Seven

The Underground Press

One of the most important means of pursuing a semblance of communal structure in the ghettos of Eastern Europe during the Holocaust was the maintenance of contact between the groups and individuals in the ghetto communities. This function was performed by ghetto newpapers and periodicals which were clandestinely published. These were not the "official" bulletins of the Germans or the *Judenrat*, which served only to promulgate the orders of the Nazi occupation authorities, but rather the publications which developed secretly within the ghetto communities themselves.

This "illegal" press was yet another concrete expression of a commitment to survival — not only physical but also intellectual and spiritual. Many of the underground newspapers originated with various youth organizations that had flourished before the war and continued their activities in the ghettos. At first, they were simply outgrowths of pre-war house organs, directed only to the members of the organization that published them. But before long, many of these periodicals expanded their scope to appeal to the entire ghetto community. Written in Yiddish, Polish or Hebrew, some appeared only sporadically, but a great number of them were issued regularly in the form of monthlies, weeklies or even dailies. Generally, they were printed or mimeographed and frequently boasted eye-catching art work which carried the message the paper sought to convey. The length of their publishing life varied, as did the size of their circulation.

Some underground papers were in great demand. *Yediot*, the Yiddish-language weekly published by the Dror youth movement in Warsaw between March and July, 1942, started out with a circulation of 60 copies, but during its short life managed to increase its circulation to 1,000 copies per week. [91] The editorial committee which produced this mimeographed paper consisted of Eliahu Gotkovski, Mordecai Tenenbaum-Tamarof, and Itzhak Zukerman.

In Warsaw, ghetto newspapers first appeared in the early months of 1940 and continued during the great deportation of July 22, 1942. Even during the ghetto revolt in April — May 1943 single-sheet bulletins appeared and Ringelblum archives include examples of forty-nine periodicals in Yiddish, Polish, and Hebrew. From time to time periodicals changed their names as a protective device; the Bund's periodical called the "Bulletin" during 1940-41 became "Der Vekker" (The Awakener) in 1942.

All underground newspapers maintained high journalistic standards in keeping with their common aim — to combat despair and to keep their readers informed as accurately as possible about developments in ghetto life. The newspapers described not only life in their own particular community, but also what was happening to Jews in the rest of occupied Europe. In addition, they provided their readers with as detailed and as accurate information as possible on the course of the war. They secured such information through their contacts with the Polish underground or by way of their hidden radios which enabled them to tune in on Allied broadcasts. Several newspapers also culled Polish and German presses for the benefit of their readers and from time to time printed detailed reports and evaluations of Allied economic and political activities. It was through such reporting that these papers sought to break the sense of isolation that engulfed the embattled Jewish communities.

Each underground paper, in its own way, also sought to inculcate the firm belief that the Jews would outlive their would-be destroyers. As one paper put it:

> These human shadows refuse to vanish. They grasp life as with a vise. The will to live ... holds sway in every heart. To live, despite everything, to go on living until the end of the war, to outlive, by at least one day, those who had brought death with them. [92]

For the most part, the underground press was not parochial in nature. Many conceived the future of the Jewish people in universal terms. They spoke of deliverance within the framework of a bright future which would come for all mankind after the end of the war. They never seemed to doubt that the war would end in an Allied victory, and they prodded their ghetto readers to prepare for the dawn of a new day. Publications associated with communist and socialist organizations viewed the plight of the Jews as part of the ongoing class struggle to elevate all mankind. May Day became a focal point in the press for expressions of Jewish solidarity with world proletarianism in its conflicts with both fascism and capitalism. Jewish survival in Europe as well as in the *Yishuv* (the Jewish community in Palestine) was linked to the victory of socialism. The editors of Dror marked May Day, 1941 with the following editorial:

> ... May Day in the ghetto — a frightening dissonance. May First expresses freedom and the heights of human progress, while the ghetto is an expression of the darkness of the Middle Ages. But there is no strength in the world that can separate us, the Jews, from the rest of humanity. From the other side of ghetto walls we send this May First heartfelt greeting to all the workers and the socialists imprisoned by the fascists or waging war against them ...

On this May First in the ghetto, we express more than usually our strong ties with the *Yishuv* in the land of Israel, its people and its pioneers . . . Just as there is no power on earth that can cut us off from the battle for a new social order in the world, there is no human power that can destroy our connection with the land of our ultimate hopes . . .

We invite everyone to observe May First. It is unthinkable that in the chorus hailing the new world that the voice of the most downtrodden of people will not be heard. Carry in your hearts the ideals of socialism and *chalutziyuth* (the pioneer spirit). Drive out despair and apathy from our streets, spread hope and faith in the hearts of Jewish youth. Be strengthened in the faith that the hour of liberation is close at hand. [93]

This theme recurs in other publications such as *Neged Hazerem*, *Yunge Shtimeh*, and *Partezaner Gedank*. [94]

In some newspapers there was a sense of the mystical in their approach to May Day. May Day, as it symbolized the rebirth of the human spirit and the concomitant yearning for freedom, was linked to springtime, the moment of nature's rebirth:

Nature awakens. The air is fresh. The sun caresses like a mother. The trees blossom and the river's waters are misty with ancient mysteries. Princely man walks between forest and river, staring quickly at the sun, pondering the beauty of a tree . . . What can he feel on such a day? Feelings become thoughts, thoughts that demand a curse . . . Cursed is nature in all its beauty . . .

No, not curses rather blessings. Blessed is nature in all its radiance and its glory, cursed its captors.

. . . May Day symbolizes man's freedom, while springtime expresses nature's freedom.

Man and nature are interdependent, for man responds to its call. Man is part of nature and there is a mutuality that binds them. When man senses the stirring of spring, the spirit of freedom is aroused in him, it flames, it explodes . . . With renewed, youthful exuberance joyously he battles for the freedom of man and nature.

Today we live in a time when society's spring tarries, still caught in winter's freezing darkness. Spring has as yet not burst forth on the calendar. Man's spring is unlike nature's spring. It does not awaken on its own. However when it finally arrives, it is unlike nature. It does not fade quickly. Rather it heralds a worldwide summer for all humanity. [95]

In the ghetto, newspapers served as catalysts, calling upon Jews to prepare themselves for the post-war revolution in which they would be expected to play an active role. As one Bundist Yiddish newspaper put it in the summer of 1941:

> Every major social change that has come into this world was accompanied by thunder and lightning... The world is now in the eye of the storm... Let us believe that the day is not far off when a new chapter will begin in the history of mankind. The proletariat, which until now has been oppressed, will ascend to the stage of history and institute the new world, the world of justice. We must prepare for this day. We, the young activist avant-garde, have the great duty to be ready... to receive the new day which is about to dawn... We must therefore make good use of the present time to arm ourselves spiritually. [96]

For the Communist the concept of the sanctity of human life was as real as it was for the religious. Many non-Communist papers, too, interpreted the struggle for human dignity. "We are not alone," the Hebrew language paper published by the Gordonia Zionist youth movement in the Warsaw ghetto proclaimed. "Our suffering is part of everybody's suffering."

> Our hopes are part and parcel of the hopes for freedom and equality cherished by all nations and by all humanity. They are the hopes of all those suffering people who cannot stand alone against the power of those stronger than themselves, who constantly threaten them with destruction...
>
> Our eyes are looking to the future, a future in which we believe with all our might. We shall weave our thoughts of such a future against the background of our present gloom...
>
> We do not view these pages as a closed, completed book... on the contrary; we are ready to continue and to weave our dreams, to deepen our thought, to surround ourselves with life, to prepare for the future, the future of all mankind and of our people. [97]

Regarding the future of the Jewish people as an entity, the underground Zionist Press looked to *Eretz Yisrael*:

> We must energize the spirit of the Jew so that it will seethe with a strong yearning for a new life, the life which is emerging in *Eretz Yisrael*... At that point he will take the rudder of his own fate into his own hands in order to clear his own path...
>
> This is not just an ideological pronouncement. It is our way, our reality and the quality of our lives. [98]

All Zionist newspapers circulated in the ghetto stressed the need for Jewish creativity, particularly in the education of the young, and called for the strengthening of Jewish identity through adherence to the prophetic promises and ideals of Jewish national rebirth. The secularist Gordonia newspaper, as an example, contained a section entitled "*Mimkorot Tarbuteynu haAtikah*"

(From Our Ancient Cultural Sources), which cited biblical passages stressing faith and hope side by side with commitments to the Zionist ideal stated by Theodor Hurzl, the poet Chaim Nachman Bialik, and Aaron David Gordon, the ideological leader of the Labor Zionist movement for whom Gordonia was named.

The ghetto's underground press served not only as a repository of the Jewish spirit, but also sought to harden the will to live as it built a defense position based on firm Jewish spiritual and cultural foundations. In one instance, *Neged Hazerem* devoted pages 1 and 2 of its first issue of February-March 1941 to an attack on assimilation and polonization, a danger engulfing the ghetto. It is interesting to note that this issue was written in Polish except for these two pages. The article entitled "On Guard" deals with the question of "Yiddish or Hebrew" as the *lingua franca* of the ghetto. The point of departure for the discussion is the question of national survival or assimilation and which language contributes most to survival:

> We oppose assimilation . . . A nation that assimilates perishes and it is not our intent to prepare the way for the nation's demise or to allow for its assimilation . . .

> We are not opposed to Yiddish. Yet we do not acknowledge its primacy. Yiddish is the language of the present, Hebrew—the language of the past and the future. We are building bridges that unite two shining periods of our history, our people's bright past on its own soil and its future, returned to its homeland.

> Yiddish is dear to the nation, expressing its suffering persecution, wandering and fear. Our goal is to enable the people to experience joy and creativity. In the homeland—Jews live, work and tire but they are filled with creative song. Here they are bent and powerless, pain and fear fill their eyes bursting forth . . .

> We must meet the ghetto prisoners not with moments filled with sorrow and despair, not with broken spirits—shadowed We must cleave the darkness with light, arousing hope in the future, healing the wounded Jewish soul, kindling a spark that will ignite a life-giving fire!

> . . . Ghetto life is difficult . . . loss of hope, despair gnaws at the heart, saddened eyes filled with pain.

> Yet an ember glows, to flare enkindling strength-giving flames.

> At such a difficult juncture, when despair and assimilation walk hand in hand in a dance of destruction, we know how to guard our roots and our values.

> We weave dreams of a bright future woven of a vision of the nation's redemption, the Zionistic socialistic vision by which we live.[99]

Generally speaking, the underground newspapers in the ghettos covered most of the following areas:

1. Reports of Nazi depredations, and of conditions in other ghettos, with emphasis on Jewish resistance activities. These reports were intended to create closer links between the various ghetto communities, and to lessen the sense of isolation which sometimes prevailed in the ghettos.

2. Analyses of military and political developments in the world outside, with stress on Nazi defeats.

3. Reports of Jewish organizational activities in the ghettos, with emphasis on positive accomplishments.

4. Material from traditional Jewish literary sources that stressed courage and hope.

5. Literary works created in the ghetto.

6. Editorials intended to encourage physical and spiritual resistance against the Germans.[100]

In January 1941, the Yiddish language bulletin *Yediot Fun Land* noted British military activities in North Africa as well as British bombing raids on the German heartland. Analyzing German press reports against the background of its own information which it had obtained from authentic sources, *Yediot Fun Land* reported that it sensed the beginning of a breakdown of German morale.[100] In an editorial in February 1942, the left-wing Yiddish publication *Der Vekker* described a speech delivered by Hitler on January 30, 1942 as a *Yaush Rede*, a speech of despair.[101]

Among the "house organs" published in the Warsaw ghetto was *Korespondentziah P'nimit*, the Hebrew language paper of the Dror Zionist youth movement. This publication, whose final issue appeared in mid-1942, discussed among other subjects Jewish education, Hakhshara training and "illegal" emigration to Palestine.[102]

A small and rather unusual publication which seemed to be the work of one individual, Alter Shnur, appeared briefly in the ghetto of Lodz. It was published in two separate sections: *haMesapper* ("The Reporter"), and a literary supplement entitled *Min haMetzar*, ("From Out of the Depths"). From material found in the rubble of the ghetto, it seems that these publications were bi-weeklies and came out in editions of 120 each. *Min haMetzar* was handwritten and featured a variety of offerings including articles, poetry written by ghetto inmates, an art column, a column entitled "A Moment of Laughter", current events, legends of the ghetto, and even advertisements.[103]

An indication of the spirit which inspired the editor-writer-publisher of *haMesapper* may be found in one of his editorials describing the significance of Kislev, the Hebrew month in which the miracle of Hanukkah is commemorated:

The Name of the Month, Its Meaning and Its Implications

This is the month during which miracles were wrought for the people of Israel . . . For this reason, it should stir praises and thanksgiving within us. It is written (in the Book of Psalms,) "Not the dead shall praise the Lord." Therefore man must live a life of saintliness as symbolized by the flickering light of the Hanukkah candles.[104]

The underground publications of the ghettos were more than mere bulletins or information sheets. By creating a sense of cohesion among their readers and strengthening their morale, they encouraged Jewish resistance and creativity, thus making their own contribution to the will to live during the Holocaust.

It is fitting to underscore the thrust of the ghetto press with the explanation offered by the editor of the supplement *Min Hametzer* for the genesis of this title. It is a play on the verse in the Book of Psalms (118:5) *Min Hametzer* – Out of the Depths, *Karote Yah* – I called upon the Lord – *Ananee B'Merchav Yah* – He answered me through the breath of Divine relief:

We cry out from the depths, God, May it be acceptable in Thy sight that all we have written, we will be privileged to retell and publicize, that we shall live, we shall see and relate – as Thou dost answer our call within the breath of Divine relief.[105]

1. Nachman Blumenthal, *Mi-bayot Ha-hinuckh Biymei Hashoah* ("Educational Problems During the Holocaust, Children and Youth During the Holocaust") *Hayeled Vehano-ar Bashoah* (Jerusalem: Hotza-at Kiryat Sefer, 1965) p. 273.

2. *Ibid.*, p. 274.

3. Trunk, *Op. Cit.*, pp. 198-199.

4. Kruk, *Op. Cit.*, pp. 464-465.

5. Dworzetsky, *Op. Cit.*, pp. 223, 226-227.

6. *Ibid.*, p. 210.

7. Blumenthal, *Op. Cit.*, p. 276.

8. Arye Bauminger, Nachman Blumenthal and Joseph Kermish, eds., *Hayeled Vehano-ar Bashoah U-vagevurah* (Jerusalem: Hotza-at Kiryat Sefer, 1965) pp. 55–56. In addition to listing the objectives, activities the author carried on to implement objectives are also noted.

9. Dworzetsky, *Op. Cit.*, p. 225.

10. Bauminger, Blumenthal and Kermish, eds., *Op. Cit.*, pp. 106-107.

11. Zvi Shner. *"Letoldot Hahayyim Hatarbutim Bageto"* ("Cultural Life in the Ghetto") *Beyt Lochamai Hageta-ot Dapim L'chayker Hasho-ah V'hamered*, April 1951, p. 100.

12. See Appendix V.

13. See Appendix VI.

14.   ,   "Korespondenziyah P'nimit," *Beyt Lochamai Hageta-ot Dapim L'chayker Hasho-ah V'hamered,* April, 1951, pp. 155-156.

15. David Gottesfurcht, Hayyim Hadari and Aharon Reichman, eds., *Sefer Dror* (Ein Harod, Israel: World Organization of Dror-Hechalutz Hatzair, 1946) pp. 461-462.

16. *Ibid.*, p. 463.

17. Dworzetsky, *Op. Cit.*, pp. 246-247.

18. Aharon Eisenbach, "Vissenshaftliche Forshungen in Varshever Ghetto," 2 vols. *Bleter Far Geshikhte, Varshe Historisher Institut fun Yiden in Polin*, Vol. I, No. I, January-March 1948, p. 121.

19. Wolf Yasney, *Di Geshikhte fun Yiden in Lodz in den Yoren fun Deutscher Oisharg* ("The History of Lodz Jewry During the Period of German Murder") 2 Vols., (Israel: Y. L. Peretz Press, 1960) Vol. I. p. 322.

20. Abraham Sutzkever, *Ghetto Vilna*, trans. by Nathan Levanah (Tel-Aviv: Sechvee, 1946) p. 90.

21. Melekh Neistadt, *Hurban un Oifstand fun di Yiden in Varshe* ("Destruction and Revolt of Jews in Warsaw") 2 vols. (Tel-Aviv: Eydut Bleter un Hazkarah, 1948) Vol. I, p. 308.

22. Sutzkever, *Op. Cit.* p. 89.

23. Ruzika Korczak. *Lehavot B'afar* ("Flames in the Ashes") (Israel: Moreshet Sifrei Poalim, 1965) p. 352.

23a. *See*: Appendix VII.

24. Trunk, Lodzer Ghetto, *Op. Cit.,* p. 395.

24a. *Ibid.*, p. 397. *Also see*: Appendix XII for a typical concert program.

25. Yasney, *Op. Cit.*, p. 279.

26. Trunk, *Op. Cit.*, p. 397.

27. Dworzetsky, *Op. Cit.*, pp. 248–252.

28. *Ibid.*, p. 250.

29. *Ibid.*, p. 252.

30. Jonas Turkov, *Haya Haytah Varshe Hayehudit* ("Warsaw Jewry That Was") (Tel-Aviv: Tarbuth V'chinuch, 1969) pp. 85-93.

31. Berg, *Op. Cit.*, p. 56.
    See also: Appendix IX.

32. *Ibid.*, p. 56.

33. Turkov, *Op. Cit.*, p. 96.

34. Trunk, *Judenrat, Op. Cit.*, p. 221.

35. Trunk *Lodzer Ghetto, Op. Cit.*, p. 400.

36. Rachel Auerbach, *B'Hutzot Varshe* ("In the Streets of Warsaw") (Tel-Aviv: Am Oved, 1951) pp. 168-170, *passim*.

37. Isaac Greenbaum ed., Enzyklopedia Shel Galuyot, Diaspora Encyclopedia 12 vols., (Jeru-salem: Hotza-at Enzyklopedia Shel Galuyot) Vol. 6, pp. 521-524, *passim*.

38. Kruk, *Op. Cit.*, pp. 179-181.

39. Yitzchak Rudashevski, *The Diary of the Vilna Ghetto, June 1941-April 1943*, trans. by Percy Matenko (Beit Lochamei Hagheta-ot, 1973) p. 106.

40. Sutzkever, *Op. Cit.*, p. 92.

41. *Ibid.*, p. 92.

42. Rudashevski, *Op. Cit.*, p. 134.

43. Dworzetsky, *Op. Cit.*, p. 230.

44. *Ibid.*, p. 273.

45. Yeshayahu Aviad Wolfsberg, *"Hayahadut Hane-emanah B'milhamah"* ("Traditional Jewry in Wartime") *Areshet, Sefer Shanah Shel Agudat Hasofrim Hadate-em*, 1953-1954, pp. 16-17.

46. Sarah Nishmit, *Ma-avako shel Ghetto* ("A Ghetto's Struggle") (Beit Lochamai Hageta-ot: Hotza-at Kibbutz Meuchad, 1962) p. 53.

47. Moshe Prager, *Eleh She'lo Nikhne'u* ("Those Who Did Not Surrender") 2 vols., (B'nai Brak: Hotza-at Netzach, 1960) Vol. II, p. 106.

48. Trunk, *Op. Cit.*, p. 403.

49. Kruk, *Op. Cit.*, pp. 86-88.
    See Also: Mordecai Eli-Av, *Ani Ma-amin* ("I Believe") (Jerusalem: Hotza-at Mosad Harav Kuk, 1969) p. 55.

50. Trunk, *Op. Cit.*, p. 404.

51. Mordecai Eliav, *Ani Ma-amin* ("I Believe") (Jerusalem: Hotza-at Mosad Harav Kuk, 1979) p. 147.

52. Menashe Ungar, *Der Geistike Vidershtand fun Yidn in Getos und Lagern* ("Jewish Spiritual Resistance in the Ghettos and Camps") (Tel-Aviv: Farlag Menorah, 1970) p. 116.

53. *Ibid.*, pp. 118-119.

54. Trunk, *Op. Cit.*, p. 405.
    See also: Rabbi Elhanan Piesrson, "Fun Letzten Hurban" ("From the Last Destruction") *Zeitschrift*, Munich, September 1948, pp. 47-48.

55. Ungar, *Op. Cit.*, p. 228.

56. Zelig Kalmanovitch, *"A Togbuch fun Vilner Ghetto"* ("Warsaw Ghetto Daybook") Yivo Annual of Jewish Social Science, Koppel Pinson, ed., Vol. VIII, 1953, pp. 30-31. This and all other citations from Kalmanovitch's diary are given as translated by the editors of Yivo Bleter.

57. Eli-Av. *Op. Cit.*, p. 88.

58. *Ibid.*, p. 93.

59. Zonneband Collection (New York, Yivo Archives) Document 1268.

60. Ephraim Oshry, *Mi-ma-amakin, Sefer Sh-elot U'tshuvot* ("Questions and Answers From Out of the Depths") 3 vols., (New York: By the author, 1959) Vol. I, pp. 39-44.

61. *Ibid.*, Vol. 2, pp. 109-112.

62. *Ibid.*, pp. 16-24.

63. *Ibid.*, Vol. 3, pp. 56-58.

64. *Ibid.*, Vol. 2, pp. 31-35.

65. *Ibid.*, pp. 7-15.

66. *Ibid.*, pp. 59-68.

67. *Ibid.*, Vol. I, p. 102.

68. *Ibid.*, Supplement, *Kontros Emek Habachah*, p. 102.

69. *Ibid.*, Vol. I, pp. 111-114.

70. *Ibid.*, pp. 126-127.

71. *Ibid.*, Vol. 2, pp. 226; 240; 254.

72. Yad Vashem Archives, Jerusalem, *Mezichronot Yehudeh Aaronsohn*, Number 56.

73. Rabbi Kalonymus Kalmish Schapira, *Sefer Or Kodesh* ("Book of Sacred Light") (Jerusalem: Hav-ad L'hadpasat Sifrei Ha-admor m'Piastzenah, 1960) p. 55.

74. *Ibid.*, pp. 84-85.

75. *Ibid.*, pp. 106-107.

76. *Ibid.*, pp. 62-63.

77. *Ibid.*, p. 179.

78. *Ibid.*, p. 166.

79. Levi Dror and Israel Rosenzweig, *Sefer Hashomer Hatzair* ("Shomer Hatzair Chronicles") (Merhavia, Israel: Hakibbutz Hameuchad, 1956) p. 505.

80. Israel Gutman, *Yehude Varshe 1939-1943* ("Warsaw Jewry 1939-1943") (Jerusalem: Hebrew University and Yad Vashem, 1977) pp. 172-173.

81. Gottesfurcht, Hadari and Reichman eds., *Op. Cit.*, p. 452.

82. Dror and Rosenzweig, *Op. Cit.*, p. 452.

83. Korczak, *Op. Cit.*, p. 50.

84. Melekh Neishtadt ed., *Op. Cit.*, p. 224.
See also: Yad Vashem Archives, Jerusalem, Israel, B18-2 06/39. The following greetings were sent on May 24, 1944 by survivors of the Warsaw Ghetto Uprising to the *Histadruth Haovdim* in the then Tel-Aviv, Palestine:

Separated by oceans of blood and continents strewn with corpses we send you our brotherly greetings.

There are not many of us left. We live, work and struggle overshadowed by the threat of death. In this situation in which we are likely to part with our life at any moment, we want you to know and to deliver the message to the Palestine worker that the Jewish workers in Poland have done their duty to the letter. They rose in arms in the defense of the dignity of the Jewish nation and fell in an unequal struggle. The faith in a future Jewish, working socialist Palestine animated them.

In the name of the workers and the heroic youth still alive we join you in the fight for freedom and liberation.

Adolf, Cyvia, Itzaak, Joseph

85. Gottesfurcht, Hadari and Reichman, eds., *Op. Cit.*, pp. 400-406.

86. Tzvi Baron and Dov Levin, *Toldoteha Shel Machteret* ("Chronicles From the Underground") (Jerusalem: Yad Vashem, 1962) p. 85.

87. Yad Vashem Archives, Jerusalem, Israel, 0-48 B/12-5.

88. *Ibid.* The Almanach Hamaapilim was brought from Lithuania through Poland to Germany by Mina Kaminski (now Shafir) under extremely dangerous conditions. Mina Kaminski was a member of the 'Maapilim' and one of the authors or the Almanach.

89. Gutman, *Op. Cit.,* p. 175.

90. Aryeh Avnon, *Itonut Gordonia B'machteret Geto Varshe* ("Gordonia's Press in Warsaw's Underground:) (Hulda: Hotza-at Archion Gordonia Maccabee Hatzair, 1966) p. 7.

91. *Itono Shel B'machteret Geto Varshe* (Dror's Press in the Warsaw Underground") *Yediot Bet Lochamai Hageta-ot,* No. 22, 1960, p. 5.

92. Aryeh Avnon, *Ha-ayarah Bitkufat Hamilhama* ("The Village in Wartime") September, 1941 *"Stow Mlodoch"*, Vol 4, Nos. 20-21. *See also:* Appendix X.

93. Kermish, Joseph and Bialotsky, Yisrael, *The Jewish Underground Press in Warsaw* (Jerusalem: Yad Vashem, 1979), Vol. 2, p. 269.

94. *Ibid.,* pp. 163; 276; 290.

95. *Ibid.,* pp. 274-275.

96. *Yunge Gvardie,* No. 1, July 1941 (Jerusalem: Yad Vashem Archives, Underground Press, Microfilms Dm 2675) p. 1.

97. Avnon, *Op. Cit.,* pp. 33-34.

98. Bauminger, Blumenthal and Kermish, eds., Op. Cit., p. 236. The quotation is taken from *Neged Hazerem,* a ghetto underground newspaper of *Hashomer Hatzair.*

99. Kermish and Bialotsky, Op. Cit., p. 28.

100. *Buletin Yediot Fun Land,* January 1941 (Jerusalem: Yad Vashem Archives, Underground Press, Microfilm JM 68).

101. *Der Vekker,* February 1942 (Jerusalem: Yad Vashem Archives, Microfilm JM 68).

102. "Korespondentziyah P'nimit," *Dapim L'cheker Hashoah V'hamered,* April 1951, pp. 148-156.

103. "Min Hametzar" ("From the Depths") *Dapim L'cheker Hashoah V'hamered,* April 1951, pp. 115-147.

104. "Hamsaper" ("The Reporter") *Dapim L'cheker Hashoah V'hamered,* February 1952, p. 90.

105. "Min Hametzar", *Op. Cit.,* p. 116.

Part Four

Kiddush Hahayyim
in
Ghetto Literature and Art

Chapter Eight

Individual Creativity

The previous section of this study reviewed a series of communal activities developed in the ghettos from the perspective of their role in building the morale of those trapped there. This capacity to erect a structure that strengthened the inner defenses of the people with the resolve not to succumb to dehumanization even in the face of death flows directly out of normative Judaism. In this construct it is an approach to human existence which places a premium on the quality of life beyond the physical. It is a lifestyle that sanctified the human being to which the term *Kiddush Hahayyim* has been applied. In order to probe this further we now turn to individuals who responded to the Holocaust experience with determination to live meaningfully and with dignity. We deal with the individual as a creative human being who did not allow his creativity to be stifled and destroyed by the tormentors.

A wealth of ghetto literature and art has been discovered in the rubble of the ghettos and concentration camps; apparently some of this material had been carefully hidden by the artists and writers themselves in the final days of the ghettos. [1] Other material was brought to light when the Allies liberated the death camps in the closing days of the war.

The most important repository of ghetto creativity was the Ringelblum archives, a part of which was found after the war in the ruins of the Warsaw ghetto. It represents the *Oneg Shabbat* project, mentioned earlier, which was created to preserve for posterity the record of the last days of Polish Jewry. One part of the Archives was discovered in 1946, another in 1950, buried in milk cans hidden under the rubble. Among the materials in this collection were copies of literature created in the Warsaw ghetto.

Other similar ghetto archives are the Wasser and the Sutzkever-Kaczerginski Collections. Hirsch Wasser was one of the archivists who had worked with Ringelblum in Warsaw; the materials he assembled are now in the YIVO (Yiddish Scientific Institute) in New York City. Abraham Sutzkever, a poet, and Shmarya Kaczerginski, a poet and short-story writer, were forced by the Germans in the Vilna ghetto to select books from the YIVO headquarters for shipment to Germany, presumably to be exhibited as relics of the "extinct" Jewish race. In the process, the two men (Sutzkever was then in his late 20s, Kaczerginski in his early 30s) succeeded in hiding a great amount of material to keep it from the Germans. After the war, they returned to the ghetto, recovered the books and documents and shipped them to YIVO in New York City. (Sutzkever eventually settled in Israel, Kaczerginski was active in Argentina as executive secretary of the Congress of Jewish Culture until his death in a plane crash in 1954.)

We will probably never know the full extent of the literary and artistic creativity of the ghettos and concentration camps, but it is possible to draw some conclusions from the materials which are available to us today.

It is important to note that the poets, writers, and artists who were active in the East European ghettos during the Holocaust period fall into two categories. In one category there were known writers, poets and artists who had been engaged in artistic and literary pursuits before the Holocaust; they simply continued their activities in the ghetto until the end of the war or until they lost their lives. Then there were others who had never written, painted or created before, but were moved to do so in the ghetto by the urge to defy the enemy and by a desire to leave behind a record of what they had endured. Much of the work by the artists in this second category has come down to us anonymously. Moshe Prager, the literary critic and ghetto anthologist, was to write:

> The folk poetry of the ghetto, understandably, was by and large anonymous. It is the creation of the unsung, common people ... These poets came from the masses. They never considered themselves as poets, they did not even know what poetry was. It was when the pressure of events moved them ... that they first sang their songs.
>
> (Some of) this primitive poetry found its way into the heart of the masses ... Most of the ghetto poems, however, were the fruits of the creativity of poets who remained unknown ... It was not their literary worth that determined their success ... The value of this folk poetry lay in the fact that it reflected the ghetto period and its upheavals ... [2]

As one reviews the extant material it is logical to conclude that a basic motivation behind both literary and artistic individual creativity in the ghetto was a desire to provide the audiences, and the artist himself, with the spiritual incentive required for survival. Alexander Bogen, an artist who survived, observed when interviewed in New York:

> I think that in the final analysis, creativity in the ghetto represented a form of spiritual self-protection, an armor — a spiritual armor — against the Nazi oppressor. When you are creative, you will not allow your spirit to be broken ... The art of creativity then, was a way of combating the Nazis ... [3]

In a study of the literature and art created in the ghetto during the Holocaust one can identify certain recurrent themes: life in the ghetto; accounts of personal suffering; recollections of the past before the war; love between man and woman or parent and child; calls for revenge and resistance; loss of belief and, conversely, a persistent faith despite suffering; hope for a better future after the war; Zion and national rebirth of the Jewish people.

What concerns us here is not the quality of these works as literature, poetry or art but primarily the manner in which they reflect ghetto life and the response of the individual to the ghetto experience.

Such artistic and literary expressions were in effect an active manifestation of a basic characteristic of Judaism: the will to live and the determination not to succumb to dehumanization, but rather to do everything possible to remain human:

> A dying community stubbornly proclaimed its will to live, emaciated faces, wild eyes cry out their protest, their will to live . . . [4]

All forms of literary and artistic creativity expressed the will to withstand and to hope:

> It can be said of the strong influence of these folk creations, that they converted the masses inured and silenced by pain into articulate beings, enflaming them to stand with pride against the cruelty and degradation that engulfed them. [5]

Chapter Nine

Poetry and Song

What poetry and song meant to the Jew in the Nazi ghettos of Eastern Europe can best be understood from the words of a Hassid who insisted on remaining in his Succah instead of hiding when the Nazis chose the Feast of Tabernacles to initiate a mass deportation of Jews to Treblinka:

> What could the Germans possibly take from me? Perhaps my body, that bag of bones. But they have no control over my soul ... Our Jewish soul will not surrender; our soul is still free, and so is our song. 6

Moshe Prager, who recounted this incident, added:

> The first command expressed in the songs of the camps and ghettos was: Do not cry! Laugh in the face of the enemy! ... These folk songs accurately reflect the war of nerves which the Nazis waged on the Jewish masses even before the hangman built his houses of death ... He employed every device in his power to break the resistance of the Jews, to destroy their will to survive ... But the Jews were determined to surpress the pain within them and gathered their strength to confront the catastrophe ... 7

The poems and songs that emerged from the ghettos reflect an important component of *Kiddush Hahayyim*; an abiding optimism which the teachings of Judaism have instilled in Jews through the ages. It is this optimism which has helped Jews survive centuries of persecution by seeking ways and means of coping with the forces of disintegration and destruction instead of succumbing to them. Jewish tradition teaches that the responsibility for Jewish survival rests not on an elite of high priests, prophets or rabbis but actually upon every Jewish individual — man, woman and child. 8 In the Nazi ghettos the Jewish masses utilized every possible means to preserve their humanity in the face of Nazi efforts to turn them into non-persons. Faced with destruction though they were, Jews in the ghettos of Eastern Europe fought to maintain a meaningful life as long as that life would last.

Poetry and song served to promote this goal. The very act of composing songs and poems was an act of commitment to the future and an affirmation of life. But even more important, these creations helped the ghetto Jew build his inner defenses, encouraging him to strive and struggle for the survival of his people even if he felt that he would not live to see the end of Hitler and Nazism.

The ghettos of Nazi Europe produced a veritable torrent of poems and songs. Blumenthal notes:

> ... wherever there were Jews, songs were born. Chased from place
> to place they were accompanied by song ... even to the death
> camps and the crematoria, songs followed them. [9]

In the Kovno ghetto, Lerke Rosenblum poked fun at this proliferation of creativity. It seems, he wrote in a four-verse poem, that everyone in the ghetto was moved by the literary urge. "Everybody thinks he's a poet," he complained, and suggested with some sarcasm that if things continued in this way, the officials of the ghetto's administrative agencies would soon be talking to their constituents in rhymes. [10]

Like other forms of art, poetry and song are the works of individuals expressing their personal reactions to the events that shape their lives. But at the same time — and this was true particularly in the ghettos — the songs and poems not only expressed the mood and the feelings of their creators themselves but also captured the hopes and fears of the society in which the authors lived.

Though some of the ghetto poems and songs expressed fears, doubts, and at times despair, ghetto poetry generally conveyed a positive message of courage and hope, [11] directed both to the individual in his personal plight and to the harassed ghetto community as a whole.

While we know the origin of many poems and songs, a great number of the literary and musical creations which survived the war are of unknown authorship. In fact it is sometimes difficult to determine even the ghetto where they originated. Works which were discovered in the ghetto ruins after the war will arbitrarily be presumed to have been composed where they were subsequently found and are interpreted as portraying ghetto life in general.

The Faith Motif

In terms of faith, ghetto dwellers manifested a variety of reactions as a result of the persecution and suffering that the Holocaust brought. Many did not deviate from their pre-Holocaust pattern of faith reflecting a pre-existent broad spectrum of religious attitudes ranging from fanatical devoutness to confirmed atheism. Yet in contrast, as a result of Nazi atrocities, there were those formerly devout who lost their faith. Their rejection of the concept of an all-righteous God ultimately led them to deny God's existence and His effectiveness in rescuing them. Both the religionist and the atheist lamented their existential predicament, a dilemma that was expressed poetically in what was later characterized as "*Eicha* (Lamentation) poetry."[12] Tangentially, while it is acknowledged that poetry and song were literary vehicles expressing both faith and doubt, for the purpose of this study we focus on those themes which elicited resolve to resist and persist.

Eicha (Lamenations) refers to the biblical volume attributed to Jeremiah the prophet. In it he describes the destruction of the First Temple and the sacking of Jerusalem that he witnessed, constituting a graphic description of the anguish of his people and their almost indescribable sufferings in ancient days. Traditionally, the book of Lamentations is recited in a dirge-like chant in the Synagogue on Tisha B'Ab, the day which marks this early tragedy. The horrors of the Holocaust could only be described in the same terms.

In some cases, by contrast, the experience of the Holocaust served to strengthen faith. [13] This attitude, too, was recorded in the form of poetry. Without faith, these poets wrote, life would be devoid of whatever meaning it still held. As one anonymous poet put it:

> If I have no faith
> In God, blessed be He
> What will be the good
> Of anything I do?

> If I have no trust
> In His deliverance,
> Life would not be worth living
> For even one moment. [14]

Abraham Sutzkever, the Vilna ghetto poet and descendant of Hassidic rabbis, expressed his personal need to voice his anguish, his fears, and his doubts in a poem written as a prayer on January 17, 1942. Here Sutzkever conveys his questioning and frustration. In a poem written sometime in 1943,[15] however, he professes his yearning for God and his feelings of personal dependence on Divine protection. He implores God to stretch forth His hand from heaven that it may become possible for him to commit his body and sould to God. Thus, through his faith in God, he sought security and salvation.

> From Thy starry skies above,
> Stretch forth to me Thy lambent arm;
> For my words to tears are turning,
> Seeking peace within Thy palm.

> See, their sparkle fast is dimming
> In my wary, mournful eyes,
> And I have no secret corner
> Whence to Thee my tears could rise.

> Dear God, grant me my desire
> To walk with Thee all my ways,
> For there is a fire within me,
> Which consumes my earthly days.

Only in dark holes and cellars
Is the graveyard's silence now;
But I soar up, higher, higher,
And I seek Thee, where are Thou?

It's a strange chase through the ghetto
Through its streets without a name,
Like a broken string I dangle,
But my song is sill the same.

From Thy starry skies above,
Stretch forth to me Thy lambent arm;
For my words to tears are turning,
Seeking peace within Thy palm. 16

The same longing for faith in God is voiced by Yitzhak Katznelson, the poet laureate of the Warsaw ghetto (1886-1944). A Hebrew school principal by profession, he wrote prolifically in both Hebrew and Yiddish. His Yiddish dramatic poem, *Al Naharot Bavel* (By the Rivers of Babylon), written during the winter of 1941, recounts the sufferings of the Jewish people during their Babylonian exile following the destruction of the First Temple in 586 B.C.E. He relived those tragedies in terms of his own agony in the ghetto. (After the fall of the Warsaw ghetto, Katznelson was deported to Vitel, France, and from there to Auschwitz, where he perished.) Before he was deported to Vitel, Katznelson buried this poetic work as well as his play "Job" in the cellar at 34 Dzelena St. with the Hechalutz archives. Just before being sent to Auschwitz, he told his friends Berl Katzenelson and Isaac Tabenkin where he had hidden his work; they found them there in April 1945. Shavneh, one of the protagonists in the poem *Al Naharot Bavel*, is sitting by the rivers of Babylon when he is urged to sing the songs of Zion. As he strums his harp, quoting Psalm 137 ("By the rivers of Babylon, we sat and wept . . ."), he declares his faith even in the face of oppression and calls upon his people to retain their trust in God.

O Israel, Hope, Hope
Keep your trust in God,
Place your trust in Him now and forever! 17

An unknown poet of the Kovno ghetto concludes his traumatic description of ghetto living conditions with a proclamation of faith that God will restore him and his people to their former homes and to their former lives, which now seemed so tranquil in contrast.

But God's goodness is sure; He will let us endure
To return to our homes, never to part,
Each one to his room, to his hammer and loom,
To his kitchen, his bed and his hearth.

110

And we'll have elation, a big celebration
When the reign of the ghetto will cease,
And we, all together, forever and ever,
Will dwell in quiet and peace. [18]

There is a sense of simplicity here, a sense of certainty matched by a call of determination to hope.

Even as they called for faith in God, the ghetto poets pleaded with Him to come to the rescue of His people and to avenge the crimes that had been committed against them. [19] The ideas and the language of this body of poetry reflect the content and literary style of the Bible and traditional Jewish liturgy. God is called upon to prove His omnipotence and His justice by demonstrating His special relationship with the Jewish people for all mankind to see. One poet paraphrases and elaborates upon classic passages from the traditional High Holiday prayer book in which God is adjured to look down from heaven, to see how His people are being led to the slaughter and to swoop down to their aid. The style is biblical and liturgical, but the message applies to the poet's time.

Oy, habet mi-shamayim u'r'eh,
Look down from heaven and see,
Ki hayyinu le-loag ve-kales
Le-loag ve-kales bagoyim,
How we have become a mockery among the Gentiles,
Nechshavnu ke-tzon le-tevakh,
Canst Thou look on while we are led to the slaughter,
We are never permitted to rest,
They herd us like lambs to our death.

Refrain:

Therefore we pray to Thee without fail,
Help us, O *shomer Yisrael* (Guardian of Israel)
And give heed, O our God, to our tears,
For there's no one else who will hear.
Do we not proclaim *Sh'ma Yisrael?* (Hear O Israel, the Lord
    our God is One)?
O hear us, *shomer goy echad*! (Keeper of the One Nation)
Show to the nations that Thou art our God!
For we have none, except Thee alone.
Whose Name is God, Who is One!

The others say, *En tohelet ve-tikvah,*
The nations say that there is no hope for us,
It is safe to chase us,
It's safe to debase us,
For we've no one to champion our cause.
But whatever they say,

We know that Thou art there, in heaven above,
Of Thee it is said: *Hine lo yanum ve-lo yishan.* (Behold the
    Keeper of Israel neither slumbers nor sleeps.)
Thou must guard and keep us,
Thy children on earth,
— For Thou art in Heaven —
With miracles and wondrous works.

Refrain: Therefore we pray to Thee without fail, . . .

Husah, HaShem Elohenu
Ve-al titenu bi'y-de-hem
Have mercy, do not permit us
To fall into their hands,
Lamah yomru ha-goyim: (Why should the nations say:)
Ayeh Elohehem? (Where is their God?)
That's what they say all the time —
Jew, damned Jew, what are you doing here?
Pack your bags and go to Palestine!
We'd like to oblige,
But the doors are all closed,
Why dost Thou let them torture us so? [20]

There were those among ghetto poets who sought to strengthen their trapped brothers as they focused on the reality of God and His association with the Jewish people. Thus they admonished their people to meet despair with hope and trust in Divine intervention on their behalf. These poets, driven by the power of God, pleaded with Him to act with merciful dispatch in order to end His people's tribulations, (but this is not to imply that other poets questioned and rejected such faith).

One poet, in despair, summarily "orders" God to delay no longer but to dispatch the Messiah to earth now and save His people. Through such a saving act the world will know at last who is truly God:

Have pity, O Father, and send
For our sufferings the long-yearned-for end,
Let our sufferings finally cease,
And give us freedom and peace.
Ribbono shel olam, with the might that You hold
See how they chase us; it's rainy and cold,
Homeless and barefoot we're prey for the foe,
They beat and they torture us: where shall we go?

We'll be good, O God, do You hear?
Just let the Messiah appear,
Let the world see with all speed,
That the Lord is God indeed! [21]

These poets reflected their people's faith and yearning for godly intervention to bring an end to their unbearable suffering, verbalizing their people's response to the agony they experienced and articulating a faith which was not vain. Through poetry and song they defied oppression and challenged despair.

The Survival and Restoration Motif

Many other ghetto poems did not deal with religious issues or dependence on Divine providence, but affirmed faith in the historic survival capability and restoration of the Jewish people. For them, even if individual Jews are killed, the Jews as a people will live forever, because they are eternal. They will outlive all of their oppressors and be vindicated by the restoration of their national existence in their ancient homeland.

Even in a world aflame, the people of Israel will not be denied the right to life. For some this conviction has mystical overtones which emerge out of the reality of the historical experiences of the Jewish people. Their hopes for the future were based on the implications of the Jewish past.

> We'll live forever, though the world's in flames!
> We'll live forever, without a cent to our names!
> We'll live despite the burden of our woes!
> We'll live despite the slander of our foes!
> We'll live forever, each hour and day!
> We'll live forever, let come what may!
> We'll live, we'll live and persevere —
> We'll live forever, look — we are here! [22]

In the Warsaw ghetto, Katzenelson affirmed his conviction of Jewish indestructibility in his lengthy Hebrew poem *Avoy Lekha* ("Woe Unto You"). Scornfully, he admonished his people's tormentors. They will be destroyed, while the Jewish people will be resurrected to mock their present tormentors. We may sense the substance of this poem as freely translated:

> ... See, you murderous people,
> Eternal, indestructible Jerusalem,
> Now, take aim at my heart,
> Fire your final shot ...
>
> Woe to you, your hour of doom has come
> Your end is near —
> On all the highways and byways, we pursue you
> We arise from our graves, an avenging army.
>
> Our women, our children, our elders
> Sinless, causeless, you executed them.
> The nation you buried will arise
> To fill you with awe and fear.
>
> Listen, our song overflows and swirls,
> With love, with faith, it bursts forth,

It lives. Hear its sound, strong, free uplifted
In the chorus of nations this eternal people sings.

Hear the whirling tornado,
Come to grind you to dust
You, your elders, your children.
You remain without a trace, — a memory —
Only a horror-filled dream, swept away in a whirlwind. 23

Side by side with the conviction that Israel, as a people is indestructible, the ghetto poets were prophetic, envisioning the rebirth of the Jewish people in their ancient homeland, *Eretz Yisrael*. Typical is a Yiddish poem, *Mein kleyner martyerer*, (My Little Martyr), in which a mother sings her baby to sleep with the dream that he will grow up to be a good *halutz* (pioneer) in *Eretz Yisrael*:

From now on its name will be "Eretz Yisrael"
It will be a Jewish land.
And to it will go young children
Who've known nothing but misery and pain.

I hope that my son will join the ranks
Of the brigade of pioneers;
You'll become a loyal *halutz*;
Sleep, my little boy, sleep. 24

This poem became a lullaby in the Kovno ghetto.

Katzenelson's *Al Naharot Bavel*, as distinguished from other poems, concludes with a prophetic note based on the Prophet Ezekiel's vision of Israel restored:

I will protect them, guard them and favor them,
And rescue them, My long-tormented sheep.
From all the places where they have been scattered
In the day of clouds and thick darkness.
And I will bring them out from the peoples,
And gather them into their own land,
And I will feed them upon the mountains of Israel,
By the streams,
And in all the habitable places of the land . . .

And I will raise up unto them a plantation for renown,
And they shall no more be consumed with hunger in the land,
And they will no longer wither on the earth;
No longer will they have to bear
The insults of the nations
And they will know that I, their God, am with them,
And that they, the House of Israel, are the children of My
   people —
Says the Lord God. 25

114

The yearning for national restoration is expressed by both the religiously oriented and the secularists. It reflects not only Jewish nationalism but also the belief that, as a human being, the Jew is entitled to the same rights and dignity which all other human beings claim. [26] The poets of Jewish renaissance urge their people to meet physical torment and degradation with dignity and fortitude. This attitude is expressed in such poems as *Moishe Halt Zich*, (Bear Up, Moishe,) written by Katriel Broido in the Vilna ghetto [27] and *Yidishe Brigades*, (Jewish Brigades), composed by Abraham Akselrod in the Kovno ghetto in 1941. [28] The act of remaining alive despite the atrocities perpetrated by the Nazi overlords was in itself an act of defiance and preparation for the future.

But if one could not live with dignity, one should know how to conduct oneself in such a manner than even in death life should have some meaning. This is the main theme of Katzenelson's *Hashir Shel Shlomo Zalechowski* Ballad of Shlomo Zalechowski), based on the heroism of Zalechowski, a simple Hassid in the town of Zdonska-Vola. On Purim, 1942, the Germans hanged ten Jewish men (the quorum traditionally required for public worship). Several months later, on the eve of Shavuoth (the festival which celebrates the giving of the Law on Mount Sinai), the Germans selected another ten men for execution and ordered the town's entire population, including the Jews who still survived, to assemble at the gallows to witness the proceedings. Zalechowski, who, before the war had lived in the town of Pabianicze, was one of the victims. As he took his place on the gallows, he addressed the crowd, urging his fellow Jews not to lose their courage but to remember that he considered it a privilege to die, with head held high, for his community, his faith, and his belief in his people's restoration under God:

> Why are your heads bowed, Jews?
> Why are your faces so full of gloom?
> Why stand as if you were stricken dumb?
> Take heart from the faith whence courage shall flow,
> Lest you descend into the depths of despair.
>
> "Remember, Jews, it's Shavuoth tonight!
> Our eternal Torah, a comfort now, as of old, is given us
>   anew:
> And we, we in particular, who will no longer be able to
>   receive it
> Must not permit sadness to overtake us now.
>
> Rejoice, Jews! Fortunate we to die in this manner!
> Giving our lives for others, sanctifying the name of God!
> Fortunate we, to die on the scaffold, to die such a death!
> Jew, Let us sing out; let joy be proclaimed."
>
> Saying these words, it seemed that a weight had fallen from
>   his heart;

115

He raises his splendid head skyward,
Singing a song of Jerusalem within the gates of
   Zdonska-Vola:
"O Jerusalem, eternal city!
I remember God, and I weep . . ."

"City of God, City of our God . . .
Our holy city —
Desolate!
Alas! Woe!
Profaned by villains and laid low!
To the depths of hell!"

And yet — nevertheless —
We belong to God!
We are his to the innermost core of our souls;
Our eyes turn to God,
Raised to Him forevermore."

And so he sang to Jerusalem a torrent of words,
His head erect, throat white.
His impassioned song was balm
To the Jews of Zdonska-Vola.
Broken-hearted they listened
And they were consoled.
Thus he sang and their souls grew calm. [29]

Katzenelson ends his ballad with the statement that Zalechowski deserves praise and is worthy of emulation because he remembered the importance of pride and self-respect, finding the strength to inculcate his attitude in his fellow Jews even as he himself was about to die.

A number of poems from the ghettos voice the conviction that all is not lost, a new day will dawn in the future which is at hand. Katriel Broido expresses this hope:

The hour strikes,
And we are here!
We're looking to the future.
The skies are turning blue again;
A new day is coming.
Today it is still dark,
But we are patient, we can wait,
Until the day, until the hour
When the guilty will be cast to the ground. [30]

Even from the darkness of the Vilna ghetto, Broido can see a distant beacon of hope shining with the light of a new day, and he admonishes his fellow Jews to keep their eyes directed to this faint beam of light which will bring with it a world reborn. Of this he is certain.

116

When life is bleak and heavy,
When storms sweep over the earth,
It's no use shedding tears,
Or sighing, "This is how it was meant to be."
This is a wind which tears us limb from limb,
A wind which penetrates our bones;
We're bent, but we intend to rise again
And we shall go on.

We look to a better tomorrow;
We march on to better days;
And though our joy may still be withheld,
Our paths leads us toward it.
A new world reborn
Smiles at us from afar —
Enchanted, blossoming, in full bloom —
We are believers
In this magic,
For this we know for certain;
It will come. [31]

This hope is a recurrent theme, taking on different guises. In the Kovno ghetto, the poet Abraham Akselrod concludes his description of the massacre of Jews in the Ninth Fort near Slobodka with a plea for courage and strength linked to the healing power of hope and sustained by the vision of vengeance which is at hand.

Don't weep, mothers!
Cease your wailing, brothers!
Though the wound is deep and the heart is bleeding . . .
Heal it with hope that we will take revenge
For all those in their graves —
    revenge for everything! [32]

Abraham Chipkin, in his poem *Hafenning*, (Hope), also counsels his people not to despair, for notwithstanding the agonies of the present, a better day will dawn:

Just don't weep Jew!
Better days are coming;
I can see the song from afar,
Soldiers on horseback coming toward us,
The banner is waving on high. [33]

Elsewhere, Chipkin bids the "eternal Jew" not to lose hope, for neither suffering nor slavery can last forever:

Just remain strong, O eternal Jew;
Lose neither faith nor hope!

Evil and servitude do not last forever,
Neither will your sufferings. [34]

Moshe Prager quotes a lullaby by Katcherginsky promising the child a new day of freedom when darkness will come to an end. [35] The theme of survival and hope is articulated also in the famous "Hymn of the Partisans" (Never say that this your journey is the last") by Hersh Glick.

Never say that this is the last road,
   the final way,
Though darkened skies blot out the light of day,
The longed-for hour shall come,
Oh never fear!
Our tread drums forth the tidings —
We are here!

From greenest palmland to the land of whitest snow
We are present with our pain and our woe.
And there where every drop of blood was shed,
There will our courage lift its head.

The sun of dawn will yet light our way,
The tragic past will yet fade away,
But if the light should fail to rise for us
Then this song shall tell all ages of our trust.

We wrote this song in blood for all to sing
It is not the carol of a gay bird on the wing.
But amidst crashing walls and fiercely flaming brands
We sang it holding grenades in our hands.

Never say that this is the last road, the final way,
That this is the last time that we shall see the day.
The longed-for hour will come,
Oh never fear!
Our tread shall roll like thunder —
We are here! [36]

For the poet, such themes as hope, revolt, human dignity, ultimate victory, were more than words. For the poet they were catalysts that served to strengthen the will to live and to reach out to freedom. [37]

For the ghetto Jew these interrelated themes were part of a whole which stressed freedom and righteousness through which the Jew will survive. This motif is crystallized in a call to revolt, to break the chains of slavery; only slavery itself is not forgiven. [38] The poetic message is clear — no surrender. Even in the depths of torment, there is dignity and meaning to life and one dare not give up. In poetry we find that *Kiddush Hashem*, rather than stressing martyrdom like *Kiddush Hahayyim*, is life oriented. In the face of seemingly insurmountable odds it requires a struggle by the individual to maintain the existence of both Jew and Judaism.

... In our generation the term *Kiddush Hashem* acquired a new definition, unique in its time. *Kiddush Hashem* may now be defined not as martyrdom, but rather guarding zealously the continued existence of the Jew and Judaism ... [39]

Katzenelson articulates this overpowering theme in his *Al Naharot Bavel.* We find those who were exiled to Babylonia after the sacking of Jerusalem by the Babylonians in 586 B.C.E. gathered on the banks of the river, mourning the destruction of the Beth-Hamikdash (Jerusalem's Temple). Even as they mourn, they ponder how they will live and survive exile in Babylonian captivity. Katzenelson, in this poetic epic drama, suggests the response of his forebears, but he really conveys a message to his people, in his time trapped in the ghetto.

Kolyah:
Hear now —
I am already old
Live!
In freedom
Or in Suffering
Live!
Whether in joy
Or in slavery —
Live with *will*, free, right
Or even if by strangers enslaved
Live! Live!
Be free in one's own land,
Heedless of enemy or shame —
With God's mercy and grace!
You live!
"You shall live"! — For a Jew, a commandment!

Shemayah:
I live, I remain alive — but ...

Kolyah:
And when the enemy wild, wide-mouthed
    curses and spits? —

Shemayah:
I live ... I live and — Suffer! [40]

Inner Defenses

Poetry and song served not only to summon others to hope and courage, but also to express the mood of the ghetto populace as well as to mold its morale. They not only reflected but in fact also shaped the psychological reactions and spiritual responses of the ghetto Jews to their sufferings as individuals and as members of the Jewish community at large.

119

Most of the ghetto poets did not seek to escape from their tribulations into a world of fantasy. They wrote against the background of ghetto realities, describing the suffering and the torment, the anxiety and despair in graphic detail. They do not spare us the horrors of hunger, disease and deportation, yet in many instances they inject a note of hope and encouragement into even these grim tales.

One outstanding case in point is a classic of the Lodz ghetto, the epic poem *Lekh Lekha*, ("Go Thou Forth")[41] by S. Shayevitch. Dated February 23, 1942, this poem was written at the time of the first deportation of Jews from Lodz, and takes the form of a father's parting words to his daughter Blimele.

The father tries to prepare his young daughter for the ordeal she is about to face. In language partly tender, partly bitter and sarcastic, the father describes the pain and anguish that the Jewish people have experienced in the past, comparing them with their contemporary terrors. The poem ends with the father pleading with his daughter to be brave and not to cry so that the enemy will not win the ultimate victory over the Jews. If we must die, the father declares, then let us die with that pride and personal dignity born of boundless faith which also characterized the forebears of the Jewish people:

> Only let us not weep and wail;
> Let us spite all our foes;
> Let us smile and keep smiling;
> Let them marvel at how strong we Jews can be
> They cannot understand that there courses in our veins
> The strength of our forefathers,
> Who in every generation
> Went forth to make the final sacrifice.
>
> Even if we walk with steps unsure,
> Like a blind man before a door not his own
> Our steps carry the echo of the feet of our fathers
> As they trod the path to Siberia.
>
> Even though terror may cause us to tremble
> Like animals captured and caged,
> Our flaming eyes reflect the look of pride
> Of our fathers on their way to the gallows.
>
> Only let us not weep and wail;
> Let us spite all our foes.
> Let us smile and keep smiling;
> Let them marvel at how strong we Jews can be.
>
> They cannot know that the archangels of old
> Are with us now, too, on our way;
> At our right hand Michael, at our left Gabriel,

Before us Uriel and behind us Raphael.
Though with every step — Below — death —
Above — God's providence —
The child went forth to Martyrdom
(Strengthened) by the Hallowed *Echad*. [42]

Shayevitch's appeal is echoed also in the words of other poets, all of whom express the same central idea: Enough of weeping and wailing. They bring only humiliation and with it a fear worse than death. This is the time for courage, not for confusion and despair:

Stop quaking about the bitterness of life;
This is ten times worse than death;
Abandon the way of wailing and whining,
Of spiritual humiliation.

Stop bowing and scraping; rather look the hangman
Of freedom and right straight in the eye.
Too long have you cringed like abject slaves
Before the rulers of the world.

Victory will come with freedom and joy —
Peace and freedom: let these be our motto!
Let this motto sound forth, and soon
the mighty, bloodthirsty monster will topple and fall to his
knees. [43]

Poets encouraged the people to withstand spiritually, to defy their Nazi tormentors through Jewish will and courage, their hope to create a model for spiritual defiance and to shore up the sagging morale.

In a handwritten, partially illegible manuscript, the poet Bliecher of the Vilna ghetto vows that he will travel on the road of suffering with his head held high, without cringing or trembling. Determined to laugh even in the face of death, he will continue to sing songs of hope and dream audacious dreams about the eternal destiny of his people:

No matter where my journey will take me,
My feet will not totter on my final path;
My head will not be bowed in despair;
My hands will not be seen trembling;
My spirits . . . will not falter.

My song will send forth rays of light;
My song will overflow with hope.
I shall spin our wonderful dreams
Of my eternal destiny.

My foot will hang above you
And I will laugh at death.

Ah, thou fate which awaits me:

I will stand erect upon thy threshold
And sing my own song of life . . .
And through the mists of my final agony
My last look will not be upon thee
But upon the worlds of my future,
Upon my splendid visions
Which rise up to meet me with shouts of joy,
With the music of victory . . .
And the last words to come
From my dying lips shall be:

"I am eternity;
I know of no death . . ."
And all the future generations
   which I bear within me,
Will whisper through my lips:
"We know no death." [44]

As for the Germans, they will ultimately reap their just deserts. An anonymous poet from the Warsaw ghetto expresses this thought in a playful quasi-doggerel style:

Why should we weep or why feel dismay?
We'll live and for Frank Kaddish we'll say,
Biri-bi, bom, bom, bom.

Let's be merry and have some fun,
We'll still be alive when Hitler is done,
Biri-bi, bom . . .

Let's take comfort, our troubles forget,
The worms will eat Adolf Hitler yet,
Biri-bi, bom . . .

They took us to Treblinka, the enemy,
But the ground will swallow them up, you'll see,
Biri-bi, bom . . .

If God wills it, He rescues and saves,
And we'll join hands and dance on the Germans' graves,
Biri-bi, bom . . . [45]

Another young man in the Warsaw ghetto, of whom we know only his last name — it was Rubinstein — puts it in even simpler terms:

Let them go to hell!
Let them go to hell!
Let them go to hell!
Let them go to hell!
We will live to see it —
We'll outlive them yet! [46]

What we have here are poems, often set to music, which expressed inner faith. They elaborated a message of self-respect, articulating a demand to face the Nazi tormentor without obsequiousness. They demanded of the ghetto inhabitants as they faced death not to do so with crying and pleading in despair, but to frustrate their oppressors by standing tall even as they faced them. If they responded in this way their people, oppressed and downtrodden, would emerge the victor in fact.

Notwithstanding all that has been said in this chapter, the poets of the ghetto did not concentrate on the Holocaust to the exclusion of normal everyday human emotions and experiences. One aspect of their determination to survive is reflected in their tender, almost idyllic descriptions of the beauties of nature and of human love.

When they expressed love in all its forms, the poets implied that they, as well as their readers, were still human beings. Through love, they clung not only to the past but looked to the future, withstanding dehumanization. They were not stripped of emotions and feelings. They were not converted into automatons, but were human beings, each of whom was sacred.

That the inhabitants of the ghetto should have given any thought at all to nature is remarkable, for trapped in the wretched warrens set aside for Jews, they hardly ever saw a patch of green; the few trees that grew in the ghetto were almost bare. Typically, Hersh Glick, the author of the Partisans' Hymn, was moved to set down his longing for the outdoors which he enjoyed as a child and now missed. Behind the ghetto walls, he glorified nature and expressed the longings of many for things denied them by the Nazis. Perhaps he romanticized the past, the world he yearned for, to prepare for the future, but in so doing he offered a vision to cling to:

> Sunlight on the beach sands shining,
> Honey-like from blue skies beams,
> Castles in the sand are shrouded
> In a veil of silver dreams.
>
> In the air hang sounds of music
> Notes so brilliant, clear and true;
> Songs of birds perched on some wires,
> And above, the sky of blue.
>
> Garlanded with snowy blossoms
> One lone cherry tree does rise;
> Evening casts its first grey shadows
> And the stars pour from the skies. [47]

Glick has also left us a love poem. The love poems created by Glick and others in the ghettos represented an act of resistance in their own right, an attempt to foil the design of the tormentors to turn the Jews into unfeeling creatures and beasts of burden. Love bears within it the seeds of survival; the ability to love implies the ability to remain human and to anticipate a brighter future. Glick's poem is a song of a man and a maid pledging their eternal love to one another without any reference to the terror and sufferings that were the daily companions of the ghetto Jews.

> Your hair is flaxen like an ear of corn,
> Beautiful like the sunset
> Lead me over hills and valleys . . .
> Till we will have to part.
>
> If you should see them part
> In the pink sunset,
> Lips golden
> Eyes full of tears —
> Better not to speak of it.
>
> Listen, girl, to my desire
> In the sunset red with fire;
> Swear to me as the sun does shine,
> That you forever will be mine —
> And she promised what he asked.
>
> She promised what he asked,
> And his face turned red as fire,
> Red as fervent heart's desire,
> Like the setting of the sun
> Behind the yellow corn.
>
> The moon was followed by the stars,
> Rising above the two below,
> The man and the maid,
> With the trees around them standing like poles
> Of a bridal canopy. [48]

Other love poems voiced similar emotions but against a bachground of anguish, pain, and German oppression. These poems include *Ikh Vart Oyf Dir* (I Will Wait For You) and *Azoy Vet Es Zeyn* (This Is How It Will Be) by Meir Getman [49] and *Tzu A Fremder Froy in a Tzerissen Kleyd* (To an Unknown Woman in a Tattered Dress) by Isaiah Spiegel. [50]

The subjects of the poets' creativity bear witness to the determination of at least a segment of the Jews in the ghettos not to allow the enemy to break their spirits, to reduce them or to dehumanize them.

As Abraham Axelrod of the Kovno ghetto put it:

> You will not hear us weep and wail,
> Not even if you beat and kick us;
> But you should not take this to mean
> That you have broken our spirit. [51]

Poetry and song written and composed in the ghettos, read and sung by ghetto inhabitants, reflected life-affirming values and focused on the will to survive. They testify to the Jewish view which places a premium on the holiness of the human being, the sanctity of each individual human life and the innate will to live. Despite the darkness that engulfed them, the poets responded with a resounding *"Lechayim!"* To Life!

Chapter Ten

Short Stories and Essays

As distinct from poetry, only a relatively limited amount of prose literature from the ghettos has survived. To date only one full-length fictional work written in its entirety in the ghetto has been discovered: the Yiddish novel *Der Hakenkreitz* (The Swastika) by Zelman Skalow. Skalow was already well known in Warsaw Yiddish literary circles during the 1930s as a short story writer. His works dealt mostly with characters who were dissatisfied with the capitalist system and with the old world order in general. In the Warsaw ghetto, he participated in the work of the Ringelblum Archives, writing reports about ghetto life and deportations for posterity. Though his reports are factual, their style is artistic and reveals a great deal of feeling. He was among those ghetto authors whose writings became increasingly radical as the period of Nazi occupation wore on. Ringleblum wrote that Skalow "Showed extraordinary endurance during all the (ghetto) blockades. He would wander about in the streets even during periods of great danger . . . I helped him and some other deserving individuals obtain employment in a brush factory. It seems that he was arrested at his place of work and deported . . ." [52] In *Der Hakenkreitz* Skalow attempted to portray the fate of the Jewish masses locked in the ghetto and to sketch a variety of ghetto characters.

The principal forms of prose to emerge from the ghetto, however, were the essay and the short story. [53] Among the short story writers whose works survived the Holocaust are, in addition to Skalow, Yehuda Feld, Leib Goldin, Joseph Kirman, Joshua Perle, S. Shinkinder, Yehezkiel Wiltshinsky, and Israel Winick, all of whom were murdered by the Nazis. Among the writers who were spared are Isaiah Spiegel, survivor of Auschwitz, and Rivkah Kviatkovsky-Pinchasik. Both eventually settled in Israel; Spiegel in Tel Aviv and Kviatkovsky-Pinchasik in Kiryat Hayim.

As with other creative endeavors in the ghettos, prose writing was motivated by several distinct considerations. To begin with, the human urge to create could not be repressed, not even amidst the incredible hardships of ghetto life. But beyond the motivation of individual creativity, there were also group imperatives which reflected the will to survive spiritually as well as physically.

Through literary endeavors they sought to deny brutalization and affirm human worth and dignity. This latter aspect is discussed by an anonymous author in an essay entitled *Vi A Bahaltener Vasser Kval Fun Unter Der Erd*. (As a Hidden Spring Beneath the Ground). The unknown writer refers to a literary evening held in the Warsaw ghetto in memory of a writer named Weissenberg. Evidently this was the first of a series of cultural evenings designed, in the words of the writer, to strengthen the will to live. This short essay, dated November 13, 1941, concludes with a call to the young people of the ghetto to strive to emulate Weissenberg's literary activity as a manifestation of their own will to survive and to maintain their humanity even in the face of Nazi barbarism:

> And yet we have not forgotten that we are human beings, not degenerate, primitive creatures . . .
>
> We want to go on living and remain free, creative human beings. This will be the test of our lives. If our life will not be extinguished even beneath the thick layer of ashes that now covers it, this will signify a triumph of humanity over inhumanity. It will be proof positive that the fiber of our vitality is stronger than the will to destroy and that we are capable of overcoming all the forces of evil which seek to swallow us up . . .
>
> Jewish youth! Perhaps there are potential Weissenbergs among you even now. But even if not, I urge you to muster your strength so that you may endure until the sun will rise again for all the children of the earth, with no exceptions. Then new Weissenbergs and other creative talents will arise also in our midst, and then we will honor not only the memory of departed writers but also the living young artists who will be creative in every area of culture and civilization. [54]

Like poetry, short stories from the ghettos depict life against a background of persecution, suffering, hunger, and death. They do not seek to provide an escape from reality but present a portrayal of how individuals imprisoned in the ghettos attempted to come to terms with their existential predicament. Some of the characters succumbed to despair, but others sought to meet their agony not only with personal dignity but also with compassion and concern for others. Short stories provide qualitative evidence of *Kiddush Hahayyim* as an active ingredient, a catalyst in ghetto life.

The works of each author reflected the particular conditions that prevailed in the ghetto where he lived. Obviously, the nuances of life in the ghetto of Lodz under Chaim Mordecai Rumkovski, who sought a *modus vivendi* with the German authorities, differed from those in Vilna, which was close to the centers of partisan resistance. Yet all ghettos shared in common certain basic problems and hopes, and these are reflected in the short stories and the essays that have survived. These individualized accounts, though clothed in fiction, afford us a faithful picture of life in the ghetto.

Even as they portrayed the terror of the Holocaust, these authors often isolated a moment, an event, a feeling, an experience, a belief or a conviction that stressed meaning and determination in the face of catastrophe. They fictionalized reality without losing the sense of urgency. Their works were not vehicles of escape or submission, but rather a means to express their confrontation with grim reality. This confrontation was based on a system of Jewish values and experiences of the ordinary individual, *Amchah*, the common man. If suffering and even death was their fate, they called upon their sisters and brothers to accept suffering and die with Jewish dignity, refusing to grovel before the Nazis. Even in death there must be the sanctity of human dignity, of Jewish self pride.

The short story writers of the ghetto succeeded in conveying the responses of the others who lived with them because they were not merely observers; they themselves experienced the trauma and shared in the suffering. They treated not only one-time heroic deeds but also the acts of quiet heroism that characterized day-to-day living in the ghettos, in effect depicting the actual application of *Kiddush Hahayyim* to life, for they stood for human dignity and meaningful living.

One dominant theme in ghetto short stories was the spiritual resistance of ghetto inmates against the Nazi efforts to dehumanize them, and to break their spirits as they destroyed their bodies. The protagonists in these stories proclaimed in word and deed that even if their bodies could be broken, their spirit could not. This nuance is captured in a number of moving short stories. One such story by Joshua Perle (1888-1943) is entitled *4580*. Perle, a Yiddish novelist who before the war worked as a bookkeeper in Warsaw, had published his first book, *Unter Der Zun* (Beneath the Sun) in 1920. It was an anthology of realistic short stories dealing with Polish-Jewish village life. *4580* was written in the Warsaw ghetto during the final months of 1942. (Though he had forged American papers, Perle was to vanish the following year, his fate unknown.) In *4580* Perle enters into the realm of psychology; he focuses on the depersonalizing Nazi tactic of assiging numbers to people to identify them in place of their personal names. Perle traces what a given name means to an individual in terms of his identity as a person, his integrity as a human being. He then assesses what the individual loses when he surrenders the name which was given him at birth. According to Perle, one's name implies the will to exist, the will to retain personhood.

> In order to turn me into a number, they first had to erase all my fifty-three years in blood, erase them, ridicule them and shame them. In order to turn me into a number, they first had to destroy my house, destroy it, uproot it. Beneath my number lie three hundred thousand Jewish martyrs, three hundred thousand Jewish lives which Amalek slaughtered with the full consent of the head of the (Jewish) community and his lackeys. From beneath my lucky number there rise the bitter cries of tens of thousands

of poisoned Jewish children...lucky me...I'm a number now. [55]

To have one's name taken away and to be turned into a number is the antithesis of personhood; it signifies anonymity. Hence the individual is prepared to suffer and struggle in order to keep his name as long as possible; it is part of his identity, of his very being and humanity.

> A man regards his name like a living limb of his body; it has flesh and blood, one doesn't feel his name but without it you can't live. I actually wore it, this name of mine, like a beautiful woman wears a string of pearls even more beautiful than she herself is. It was mine, mine alone...

> Is it possible to forget one's own name?... For fifty-three years it has grown with me... For fifty-three years it has blossomed, taken root and was passed from father to child to grandchild. Anyone with even a little learning knows that a name is capable of destroying an entire world. On the other hand, a name can suffice to build up a whole new world. The Law of the Jewish people is called the Law of Moses; it bears Moses' name. And the Iliad bears one name — that of Homer. [56]

The reality that the quest for human dignity is a focal point of life rests upon several kinds of meaningful relationships that the individual creates for himself. Among them we find the determination to maintain an ongoing commitment to a set of religious beliefs, practices and sacred objects. Such a relationship provides the individual with a framework in which to live and grow. It provides him with an anchor of strength to be able to keep his perspective as it assures him that life in all circumstances has meaning and is worthwhile. Through such a relationship, the Jew links himself to those aspects of Jewish tradition which demonstrate the message of Jewish fortitude and survival through the ages. In this way the Jewish individual simultaneously becomes part of his people's past history even as he participates in his people's present and shares its hopes for the future.

In a number of short stories these sentiments are expressed by such things as the determination of the protagonists to observe the Sabbath and the other Jewish holidays as much as possible.

The Sabbath candlesticks, the challah cover, emerge as symbols of this determination, underscoring the victory of the Jewish spirit over oppression. If only for a brief moment, the Jew raises himself above his existential present difficulties to become a human being again.

Rivkah Kviatkovsky-Pinchasik describes such a moment in the life of Leah. Her husband and two sons gone, she is left alone. Her life destroyed, she is yoked to a wagon like an animal with two young girls to plod the ghetto's alleys at dawn. Broken and beaten she carries on disheveled, grimy, covered with rags. At dawn one morning, her dull eyes brighten, her mind clears, "Today is Friday," she calls out. "Today I refuse to pull the cart, they can drive me out, if they wish, today is Friday. I must prepare for the Sabbath." With irrepressible energy she cleans the hovel that is her room, finds a lost tablecloth, improvises candles, bathes and dresses. Then sitting beside the table with a yellowed prayer book, she whispers ashamedly, "Sabbath, my Sabbath, how quickly I have forgotten you." [57]

By cherishing the sancta of Judaism, the Jew in effect affirms the meaning of his existence, that of his people, and the determination of both to survive. This feeling is expressed also in observances that signify the fulfillment of one's religious responsibilities, individal and communal alike, no matter what the consequences. It is the ordinary individual acting heroically without counting the cost. It means, for instance, reciting one's prayers even under the most inhospitable circumstances. Spiegel describes such a moment of prayer in a hospital ward, where to complete a *Minyan* (quorum needed for prayer), nine sick elderly Jews stand beside the bed of one who has just died. Though they know that their hours are numbered, they pray as they wait for their end. [58] Others risked their lives in order to save Jewish religious objects from desecration and destruction. [59]

Another moving illustration of such heroism is presented in Isaiah Spiegel's *A Yid Fun Beys-Oylem* (The Cemetery Caretaker), written in Lodz in 1942. This short story deals with the final symbol which reaffirms the sanctity of the human being at the time of death. The sanctity to which the Jew is entitled after death is accorded the individual by *taharah* (the ritual cleansing of the body before burial), which the Nazis had prohibited. In Spiegel's story, Yehiel, the caretaker of the Jewish cemetery, enlists the help of his niece, Mindel, to perform at least a partial *taharah*, which though only symbolic, would impart dignity to the victims of Nazism even in death. [60] A similar theme is treated in a story entitled *Der Hessedfun A Shtillen Toyt* (A Peaceful Death), [61] written in December 1941 by Joseph Kirman (1903-1943), a member of the Left Po'ale Zion who was active in the Warsaw ghetto underground until his death at the hands of the Germans. Kirman describes the plight of the children, trapped in the ghetto, abandoned and homeless. Here he sketches the desperation of a 12-year-old boy outside the ghetto hospital, naked, cold, and hungry on a rainy windswept November day. Sick with dysentery, he pleads with the attendant to admit him, for if he is to die, he begs that he be permitted to die in bed as a human being with dignity, not as a beaten, driven animal.

All these stories capture the yearning of the ghetto Jew for human dignity even in the face of death. It was a cry that could not be silenced, not even by the imminence of physical destruction. In Spiegel's *Nikki*, written in 1943, [62] this commitment to personal dignity is displayed by the dowager Anna Yakovlevna Temkin in her bearing, in her belated identification with her people, in her relationship with *"Hoykhe Royze"* (Tall Rosa), the prostitute, and in their relationship to Nikki, the dog.

This over-arching attitude may well be summarized by citing the passage from Zalman Skalow's novel *Der Hakenkreitz* in which Skalow notes that "a Jew must not give up. As long as he has any energy left, he must behave like a human being and have only utter contempt for any evil that may befall him." [63]

Since no one in the ghetto could escape the realities of ghetto existence — hunger, starvation, persecution, disease and, ultimately, death — it was only natural that the short stories, vignettes and sketches which emerged from the ghettos should treat these conditions as their underlying themes. The tragic facts of ghetto life were presented in all their horror, together with the frustration and despair they engendered. Yet there were writers who could see beyond their contemporary tribulations and visualize a better future, even if only a few of the ghetto inmates would survive. They viewed the intolerable situation in which they found themselves as a dark night, a transient phenomenon that precedes the dawn of a new day, and they were determined to live to see the hour of liberation. Thus when Zalman Skalow, wandering through the ghetto streets, is stopped at a Jewish refugee hostel by one Mayer Medzinski, he says to him:

> I don't know why a man like myself should want to continue bearing the burden of life under these circumstances . . . But yes, I do want to go on living, to survive the horror, so that I may behold with my own eyes the bright dawn at the end. [64]

It should be noted that here is reflected more than a desire for physical survival; it implies a commitment to spiritual imperatives which move beyond concern for the body to the soul. In addition, the authors of these works universalize their message and their concerns.

Thus in *Der Hakenkreitz* Skalow relates how the ghetto Jew for the most part viewed his own liberation as the beginning of a freedom for all mankind.

> Now Moishe began to believe firmly in his own future and in the future of the whole world. He was no longer touched by tyranny and cruelty because he and the world had become one. A joyous wave streamed from his heart and lifted him high into the air. [65]

The ghetto writers took new courage particularly when the German forces began to retreat on the Russian front. In a vignette, *Nehnter Varshe Brent*, part of a series of descriptions written in February and March 1942 entitled *Ikh Red Tzu Dir Offen, Meyn Kind*, Joseph Kirman calls his child to watch Warsaw burning in the distance. It is too early to put out these flames, he tells his child, because *Rishus* (anti-Semitism) has not yet been uprooted from the hearts and minds of the oppressors of his people.

> My son, I want to show you a fire that is burning in Warsaw. I don't know who or what started this fire; whether it was planes flying west from Russia, or the "birds" from the other side of the canal, or perhaps incendiaries inside the city itself . . . But never mind who did it. Look how the sky is turning red, how beautiful is all this red over the snow covering the city! It is evening, but the

light is bright as the day. And over there, from beyond the frozen-over Vistula, you can see them rising higher and higher, almost into the sky: giant tongues of fire and smoke. Wherever we turn we will see vast expanses illuminated by the fire. The ice is thick, and the snow is heavy on the walls and housetops, but you can smell the brimstone, my child, and feel the flaming heat.

How beautiful it is, my child, this winter night. There, look, near the Vistula River, something big — I do not know what it is — but it is in flames.

You say you're sorry, my child, that you can't put out the fire, that you can't be a Polish fireman with a trumpet that goes toot, toot, toot?

Never mind, silly boy! You'll be a fireman some day. But not just yet, my child, not just yet. The time has not yet come to put out the fires! Let the fires go on burning, let them keep on burning for a while yet, my child.

Come, children, let's make a circle, let's clap our hands and dance: Tra-la-la, tra-la-la!

The fire is getting smaller, what a pity! . . . They're asking me in the street, "Tell me, Mister Jew, maybe you know, what was that big fire? What was it?

It was *rishus, rishus* that was on fire; at least that's what I think.

"Oh, really?" The woman begins to understand. [66]

In his description of that same conflagration, Joshua Perle proclaims that the most significant act of defiance a man could perform was that of survival in the face of an implacable foe who spared no effort to destroy him.

If one really and truly wants to go on living, with every limb of his body, then one puts up a fight. Especially now, when death haunts you at every turn, when death shares your bed and you ingest death with every bite your eat. Slowly, slowly, like a sleep-walker, you emerge from your hiding place and look around. And people ask each other what news there is from this street and that. Already people are selling a piece of bread here, an onion, a box of matches. Already smoke is rising from the chimneys; it's a sign that people are cooking food again. A cat appears, a dog barks — all these things are signs of life. In some places there is weeping and wailing: entire families have been lost. And in other places people are falling upon each other's necks: We're here! We didn't get killed! We're alive!

And so one day passes, a second day, and a third. The gutted streets are coming alive again. At first it is just here a person, there

133

a person. Later it is dozens of people, then hundreds and thousands ... Danger is lurking at every turn, but the power of life has won the day. [67]

Some of the stories of anguish and heroism are suffused with a yearning for vestiges of normalcy and the ability to express human emotions such as love which would effectively help confront the realities of ghetto life. This, too, is a way of clinging to one's humanity, a refusal to degenerate into a groveling animal. One of Spiegel's stories, *Mekhele*, tells of the tenderness between the deformed, stammering *Mekhele* and the unnamed young woman who befriends him when his mother dies. [68] Faith through love is the theme of another story by Spiegel, *Der Himel Fun Onkel Teodor* (Uncle Theodore's Heaven), written in the Lodz ghetto in 1944. [69] It is a special kind of love that is shared here, the love of the sixteen-year-old Faigelle for the Viennese Jew who came to be called Uncle Theodore. Miraculously he brought a telescope into the ghetto and at every possible moment he searched the heavens to find solace and escape reality, Faigelle hovering over him with the tenderness of young love. They stayed behind when the Nazis drove the inhabitants out of the building, hiding in the cellar. When Faigelle's mother died, he stood beside her consoling her. Finally, when their hiding place was discovered by German bloodhounds, they went to their death, hand in hand, heads held high.

In the ghetto, the routine activities of everyday life took on new significance as symbols of personhood, of resistance against dehumanization. Rivkah Kviatkovsky-Pinchasik, in her story, *Hamesh Dakot Le-ahar Sheva* (Five Minutes Past Seven), originally written in Yiddish and translated by Ben Eliezer into Hebrew, has a young girl in the ghetto combing her hair and primping before going to her job at the public soup kitchen. The shadow of fear and despair is in her eyes but she attempts to drive these spectres away by concern for her personal appearance. [70] Kviatkovsky-Pinchasik goes on to contrast the mood of workers and clients in two soup kitchens; the atmosphere in the one place is filled with joking, singing and conviviality, while that in the other is one of unmitigated gloom. The author protests that pessimism is no way to respond to trouble. Problems, she insists, cannot be made to disappear by constantly dwelling upon them. [71]

In some ghetto stories the protagonists give expression to their faith in Divine Providence and deliverance. Kviatkovsky-Pinchasik portrays this mood also in a conversation between the potato peelers in the ghetto soup kitchen. Instead of giving way to despair, these helpers declare their faith in God as devout Jews with a simple faith. They picture the deliverance of the Jewish people in the form of the coming of the Messiah, the scion of King David. [72]

Isaiah Spiegel captures the mood of ghetto inhabitants. He understands and shares their inner feelings, their concerns, their dilemmas, their fears and their doubts, as well as their hopes and their convictions. In several of his short stories, he muses on such critical concerns as faith in God when faced by the death of a beloved one in such monstrous times. He deals too with the determination to hold fast to life, the meaning of death with dignity in Jewish terms and the validity and reality of revenge. In his vignette *Halom* (A Dream), written in Yiddish in 1943, Spiegel conveys the yearning for a death with dignity as he describes the last moments of the bedridden Hirsch-Leib. [73] In contrast Spiegel turns to such eternal questions as life and death and God's avenging power in his *Kinah Al Bitti Hamaytah*, (Elegy Over My Dead Daughter), written in Yiddish in 1941. As he laments and mourns his daughter's death, the bereaved father ponders the mystery of God's omnipotence and proclaims the justice of God's avenging power.

> ... (O God) is it possible that you can no longer guide me? I always felt your breath on my face ... Omnipotent God won't You turn to me again? ... Has Satan's black spirit vanquished You?

> My lips refuse to curse. Can man curse Your greatness? My heart refuses to desecrate You ... Is my inner soul prepared to follow your spirit? My heart, a human heart, is weak: Why does a consoling light still burn in its melancholy and sadness? Our life is all but ended. Yet You shall return to straighten our people's bent backs, as well as those of all the world's people. Your spirit bears within it healing for our ills. You shall destroy Satan's grasp of death with avenging justice. My God, You shall avenge! The vengeance of the weak, embittered by tears, beseeching, imprisoned, moaning from the depths. You shall avenge every sigh, every tear, every poisoned breath. You shall avenge every infant in its crib ... You shall avenge every happy child, every old one with hands outstretched to You — hands torn from their arms ... You shall avenge the death of every Jew, sudden death, prolonged death ... death with eyes open, death with eyes closed. With Your light You shall forever uproot Satan from Your land. O my God, sometimes blinded, sometimes aware! ... [74]

By no means do all the characters portrayed in ghetto literature come to us in larger than life dimensions. Some are depicted in all their human weakness. They are portrayed as reacting to persecution by becoming self-centered or even selfish, concerned only about themselves and their own survival.

One such poignant moment of utter dehumanization is depicted in Kviatkovsky-Pinchasik's *Beyn Sh'te Halukot* (Between Two Food Distributions). It is the story of Golde, her husband Mordecai, and their children. When the first Germans appeared, Mordecai gave up all hope. Despondent, he took to bed and for three years he neither lived nor died, but wasted away. Golde and her children became the providers. Mordecai came to life only when there was some food. After each official food distribution, Golde would hide some pieces of bread in a sack under her pillow for the future. One night, ravenous, Mordecai crawls out of bed thinking that he is unobserved by his sleeping wife and children. But he is observed by his two sons who watch in sadness and horror as their father, animal-like, crawls to their mother's bedside, slips the bag from under the pillow and devours the bread. He crawls back to his bed only to collapse and die soon thereafter. [75]

Other stories focus on such individuals and particularly the inner tensions and conflicts that become manifest. In several we experience their moments of truth, the instant when they realize that their egocentricity has resulted in inhumanity and immorality. In true-to-life situations, they feel remorse and try to mitigate the effects of their self-centered behavior upon others and upon themselves. Some cry out in protest, while others make atonement by desperate acts which in many instances cost them their lives. By such acts of mad remorse and atonement, they seek to re-establish the fact of their humanity and the reality of their morality.

It is Spiegel who raises this problem in his depiction of Baileh in *Goldine Yoch*. She is left along to support her three-year-old daughter, Chavahle, when her husband disappears. Fiavish, a ghetto policeman is attracted to her. As a result of their illicit relationship he provides her with food. In her heart Baileh is haunted by the feeling that this relationship is immoral and sinful, but justifies it to herself that through it she can save her daughter. But then the dreaded order comes: all infants and young children must be surrendered to the Germans. It is Faivish who collects the infants and children. When Baileh refuses to give up Chavahle, he tears the child from Baileh's arms. After handing over the children to the Germans, Faivish returns drunk to Baileh's room. Maddened, she disrobes partially and as they are locked in a feverish embrace, she plunges a knife into him. Baileh flees the room running insanely towards the barbed wire. A German soldier calls out to her, "Where to you, witch, to the heavens . . . to the stars?" "Yes," she mumbles hysterically, "To the heavens . . . to the stars," as she impales herself on the wire where she hangs in death. [76]

On the other hand, there are many uplifting stories of compassion and humanity shown by the protagonists to those even less fortunate than themselves. These stories depict the realities of ghetto life. They portray those who did everything possible to alleviate the physical and emotional anguish of their fellow sufferers in the ghetto. Several stories deal particularly with the well-known antagonism that existed between Eastern European and German Jews. In these stories the protagonists rise above these feelings to help German Jews who found themselves in the ghetto. Their psychological and emotional trauma was even greater for they were so much a part of German life that they could not understand or accept their persecution in the light of their past and their weakened Jewish links.

In the story *Yehudim*, Spiegel in a few broad strokes underscores this dilemma It is the story of Yitzchak-Ber and his wife Sarah-Leah, who occupy one of two rooms in an abandoned and partially demolished building. Soon after they set up housekeeping, a group of German Jews arrive. They are completely Germanized in dress, speaking no Yiddish. Sarah-Leah wants to drive them out, while her husband implores her to let they stay, for they are Jews. Grudgingly she allows them to stay in the stripped second room. At dusk Yitzchak-Ber begins to pray. As he does so, singing is heard in the other room, singing in a German idiom. To Sarah-Leah this is sacrilege, to Yitzchak-Ber it is evidence of their Jewishness, their way of prayer. He prevails on his wife to prepare some warm food for them from her meager supplies, which she does reluctantly. As she serves them, the leader of the group haltingly says to her: "Dear brother . . . dear sister . . . thank you, thank you . . . indeed all of us we are Jews, Jews, Jews." [77]

In numerous ghetto stories, acts of unselfish heroism to help or protect others place the hero in grave personal danger, but he is willing to take that risk with little or no concern for himself. Yehuda Feld (1906-1942), a Yiddish writer who embraced Communism and was active in the anti-Fascist movement even in the Warsaw ghetto, wrote several stories describing such behavior. Noteworthy among them are *Fuftzen Minut Nokh Finf* (Fifteen Minutes After Five), *A Holem Fun A Mamen* (A Mother's Dream; dated May 3, 1941), and *Gayrush P'K* (Expulsion; dated November 5, 1941). Shelomo Feltsher and his wife Chana, the protagonists of *Gayrush P'K*, may be considered archetypes of this kind of self-sacrifice. The story tells not only what the Feltshers did for their fellow Jews when they where expelled from their homes, but also how Chana, with her husband's consent, aided a Gentile woman in labor even though the Germans had forbidden Jewesses to act as midwives for "Aryan" mothers. [78] Feld himself suffered a tragic fate. In the Warsaw ghetto he founded and edited a Yiddish language Communist newspaper *Morgen Frei* (later known as *Morgen Freiheit*). He attacked not only the Germans but also the *Judenrat*, whose members he regarded as collaborators with the Nazis. In August 1942, he left the ghetto and moved over to the "Aryan" side of the city. A month later he was captured and murdered by the Germans.

At least one story by a ghetto author deals with the sympathetic response of Polish Gentiles to the sufferings of their Jewish neighbors. In Spiegel's *Di Mishpokhe Lifshitz Gayt in Ghetto* (The Lifshitz Family Moves Into the Ghetto; 1941), Marianne Schweik, the Lifshitz's Polish maid, not only moves into the ghetto with the family but also dons the yellow badge. As she begins to understand the sufferings and the tragedy of the Jews, she interprets it in her own terms by identifying the head of the family, Isaac Lifshitz, with Jesus, whom she regards as the ultimate symbol of suffering. [79]

The short stories written in the ghetto shed a new and significant light on the emotional and spiritual climate of the times. One may conclude that the short stories written in the ghettos of Eastern Europe during the Holocaust period are a significant primary source for the understanding of that tragic era in Jewish history. A blend of fact and fiction, they reflect the full spectrum of ghetto life and the responses of the authors and their fellow sufferers to the Nazi terror. Most importantly, this ghetto literature points again and again to the efforts made by ghetto Jews to maintain a semblance of human dignity in line with the traditional Jewish concept that man was created in the image of God; *B'tzelem Elohim*. This is a conviction many Jews did not reject, not even in the terror that characterized Hitler's ghettos and concentration camps. As the Israeli author Dov Sadan notes in his introduction to the Hebrew version of Spiegel's short stories, *Malkhut Haghetto*:

> Note how the stories in this volume reflect not only the ultimate tension of maintaining mere physical survival, but also the quality of that survival. Thus it can be concluded that every consistent effort made to preserve not only the breath but also the meaningfulness of life was in itself an act of continuous revolt . . . [80]

Chapter Eleven

Eyewitness Accounts

When analyzing the eyewitness accounts that have survived from the ghettos of Eastern Europe, a clear distinction must be made between two categories. One category includes accounts which received the official sanction of the German occupation authorities and of the leaders of the ghetto "establishment"; other accounts came from sources considered unofficial or quasi-legal, if not altogether "illegal." The "official" category includes such documentary material as the records kept under the direction of Mordecai Rumkovski, the *Judenaelteste* of the Lodz ghetto. These accounts describe life in the ghetto as it was perceived by the German-approved ghetto leadership and tend to be self-serving, to praise and justify the activities of Rumkovski and his associates. Documents of the "unofficial" or underground category were discovered after the war in various archives that survived amidst the ruins of the ghettos; prominent among these are the archives of Ringelblum, of Sutzkever and Katcherginsky, of Sonnebend and of Wasser. This chapter is limited to this second category, which is most meaningful for the contemporary reader who seeks to understand the mood of the people.

A perusal of the eyewitness accounts found in the ghetto archives reveals that they are the work of many individuals and that they were intended neither as literary works nor as statements of self-justification. They served as straightforward records of the responses of individuals and communities to the horrors perpetrated against them and as indictments of the Nazis and their cohorts. Death could not still their voices. They spoke through the words they left behind. The victims were guaranteed that the reality of their struggle for life would not be lost in the anonymity of statistical abstracts. Each diarist who told his personal story or expressed his feelings, as well as those of his confreres, became more than a cipher; he emerged as a human being.

Like other literary material from the Holocaust ghettos, these eyewitness accounts represent a manifestation of the spiritual strength that is part of the traditional Jewish ethic. They serve as documentary evidence against the Nazis and as a frame of reference for events portrayed in ghetto art and fiction. Most important, however, they bear witness to the vitality and spiritual stamina of the Jews, reflecting in turn the intrinsic sanctity of life that is an integral concept of Judaism.

It is important to note that the writers represented in the surviving accounts came from all ages and from almost every walk of life; they were men, women, and teenagers. They wanted to chronicle what actually happened to the individual, his family, his friends, his community. They gave voice to the attitudes, emotions, hopes and feelings of the ghetto population, reflecting immediacy and urgency — the immediacy of the participants, the urgency of their struggle for survival. Some of the chroniclers were known even before the war as writers, scholars or educators; others were previously unknown and still others have remained anonymous. To this day some of their reports are merely fragmentary notes; others are minutely detailed. They were composed not only in Yiddish, Hebrew or Polish, but also in Russian, German, and even English. Some of the writers used more than one of these languages. One interesting example of such linguistic versatility is the diary kept by an anonymous writer in the ghetto of Lodz. The entry for July 18, 1944 is written in English; the entry for the next day is in Polish; the next entry is in English again, while the two entries that follow are in Hebrew and Yiddish respectively, all in a cramped handwriting on the same page. The two English entries (exactly as set down by the author) read as follows:

> July 18, 1944
>
> A new order reached today the Getto Authorities according to which a register of the number of the Getto population is to be compiled! ... What mischief are they up to, these Godforsaken creatures with this new demand of theirs? How disgracefully abominable they are, our German fiends; they don't even want to inflict us the ultimate coup de grace but to (one word illegible) in this horrible blood-sucking, in this gradual massacre of children and women, in this annihilation of a whole getto nation!

> July 19
>
> We have some (?) good times in the Getto. We can get some cabbage with what to lessen our mortal hunger. The only care is about our future, the nearest future, because every one is convinced that the war is decidedly approaching its end. Fears are aroused by rumours according to which the G. destroyed tens of thousands of Hungarian Jews. When will this question of "to be or not to be" be taken off our shoulders.? [81]

The reports appeared not only in the form of diaries (composed of daily or weekly entries) but also as periodic summaries of events, journals, biographies or fictionalized accounts of actual events. Writing materials, particularly paper, were in short supply, forcing the authors to improvise and use whatever materials came to hand. Thus, the anonymous diary from the Lodz ghetto was written in part in the margins of the pages of a French book. [82]

Another Lodz ghetto diary, kept by one Menachem Oppenheim, was written in the margins of the pages of a prayer book, *Derekh Hayyim*. [83]

These "unofficial" accounts of ghetto life may be divided into two categories: the factual and the reflective. The former reported Nazi activities and documented the Jewish response to them in terms of political, economic, cultural, religious and mutual aid endeavors carried on to nullify the German restrictions in order to make survival possible. The latter were not so much reports of actual occurrences as they were expressions of emotions, feelings, thoughts and attitudes stimulated by these events.

These first-person accounts provide graphic evidence documenting the premeditated program of annihilation. It is difficult to conceive of positive responses to the horrors that were described. Nevertheless the words of the victims themselves inspire awe and admiration. So often their words represent a triumph for the Jewish elan — a spirit which refused to abandon hope, a spirit built on intrinsic Jewish values — the sanctity of life in all circumstances. They expressed the will to live and the determination to survive. This mood is expressed by Herman Kruk (1897-1944) in his *Togbukh Fun Vilner Ghetto*, published in the original Yiddish in the United States after the war:

> Nevertheless, life is stronger than everything else here. Life has begun to pulse again in the Vilna ghetto. From beneath the cover of Ponar (the execution site) there has emerged a new life which pushes forward to a better tomorrow ... And although we cannot visit the graves of our loved ones, we cling to them in spirit and cherish the hope that while we may be physically weak, we will be able to hold out and to survive ... The masses live in hope and are sure that deliverance is near, very near indeed ... [84]

The above entry dates from the Spring of 1942. The Kruk diary, dictated by the author to Mrs. Mandelsund-Kowarsky in the Vilna ghetto, covers the period from June 25, 1941 to July 14, 1943. Formerly the director of the Grosser Library in Warsaw, Kruk had come to Vilna after the outbreak of the war. In the ghetto he soon became prominent in cultural activities. He opened and expanded the library of *M'fitze Haskalah*, adding to it a reading room and a small museum. Eventually he was drafted into the group of ghetto inmates ordered by Hitler's racial "expert", Alfred Rosenberg, to assort Jewish books for eventual shipment to Germany to serve as a record of the extinct Jewish people. He was murdered in Klugs in 1944. In 1948 Abraham Sutzkever discovered 380 pages of Kruk's diary scattered on the floor of the Vilna bunker where the diary had been buried. Another 130 pages were discovered in 1959 among the documents in the Yad Vashem Archives in Jerusalem.

Other diarists from the Vilna ghetto included the Yiddish philologist and translator Zelig Kalmanovitch (1881-1944), and the teen-aged Yitzchak Rudashevski (1927-1943) who has been mentioned earlier in this study. Kalmanovitch was a founder of Yivo (The Yiddish Scientific Institute) and was also editor-in-chief of Yivo Bleter and director of the Vilna ghetto's

Kulturhaus. Like Herman Kruk, he was drafted by Alfred Rosenberg to serve on his staff of experts on Jewish life. In September 1943, he and his wife were deported to an Estonian extermination camp where they died. Kalmanovitch's diary is one of the most remarkable and most poignant human documents of this period. It was preserved almost miraculously. Found by Herman Kruk after Kalmanovitch was deported, it was hidden in the ghetto library. When the ghetto was liquidated, the janitor of the building used the libraries' books and materials to heat the building. In 1945 the poet Abraham Sutzkever salvaged the remains, including Kalmanovitch's diary, which was written in Hebrew with a few Yiddish passages interspersed in it.

The 204-page notebook diary kept by Yitzchak Rudashevski, who had been active in various youth movements, was discovered in 1944 by his cousin, Sara Voloshin. It covers the period from June 6, 1941 until April 7, 1943, the date of his death.

The Warsaw ghetto yielded a wealth of material by many individuals, including Emanuel Ringelblum (1900-1944), architect of the Ringelblum Oneg-Shabbat Archives; the well-known educator Chaim Kaplan (1880-December 1942 or January 1943); the journalist and writer Peretz Opotinsky (1895-1943) and the educator and Zionist leader Abraham Levin (1893-?). Ringelblum, a noted historian who wrote in Yiddish, was able to produce in the ghetto a 237-page work which was published in English in New York in 1972 under the title *Polish-Jewish Relationships During The Second World War.* In addition to his historical and archival activities, he actively participated in mutual aid and relief work. As early as 1938 he had coordinated, in the name of the American Jewish Joint Distribution Committee, a relief program for 17,000 Jews stranded in the town of Zbaszyn. While in the ghetto during World War II, he headed the Coordinating Committee of Jewish Aid Organizations. In fact, the data he collected in the course of this work became the basis for the Ringelblum Archives. Ringelblum and his family were murdered by the Nazis on March 7, 1944, in Warsaw's Pawiak Prison.

Kaplan, another diarist, founded a pioneering Hebrew elementary school in Warsaw and served as its principal for 40 years. He began a diary in 1933; his wartime entries start on September 1, 1939 and continue through August 4, 1942, approximately six months before he was murdered in Treblinka. Portions of his diary were smuggled out of the Warsaw ghetto by a Jew named Rubinsztejn, who was employed at forced labor outside the ghetto. Eventually, the diary passed into the hands of Wladyslaw Wojeck, a friendly Pole.

Opotinsky, an active Labor Zionist who had worked on the staff of the Yiddish newspaper *Dos Vort,* made his way to the Warsaw ghetto in 1943.

In the ghetto, he participated in Ringelblum's archival group, *Oneg Shabbat,* while working as a letter carrier. His reports of ghetto life, described from the perspective of the apartment compound in which he lived as well as from that of a letter carrier making his rounds, were discovered with other fragmentary diary notations after the war.

Abraham Levin continued his educational work in the Warsaw ghetto, teaching at one of the ghetto's underground schools and in a *komplety*. His diaries, written in Yiddish and Hebrew, were discovered in the Ringelblum Archives, which he had helped assemble. In his writings he viewed Nazi bestiality in a broader perspective, symptomatic of the moral breakdown of all mankind.

A significant surviving eyewitness account of life in the ghetto of Lodz is provided by the well-known Yiddish journalist Joseph Zelkovitch. As a social worker for the Lodz ghetto administration under Mordecai Rumkovski, Zelkovitch visited homes and workshops and witnessed the deportation of children and old people. His "unofficial" reports are graphic descriptions of the tragedies which he observed daily in the ghetto. He probably died in Auschwitz.

Zelig Kalmanovitch, as he reflected on life in the Vilna ghetto community, sought to maintain a sense of balance and historical perspective in his descriptions and interpretation of Jewish suffering. In his assessment of the ghetto situation, he stressed his conviction that the Jews were capable of surviving the efforts of the Nazis to dehumanize them. If the Jews could maintain their humanity despite the incredible sufferings they endured, they would emerge as the physical and spiritual victors in the end. In one of his reports published after the war, he wrote:

> I have already implied why this should be so in principle. The ghetto was conceived not as a dwelling place for humans but as a shelter for low forms of life, for primitive creatures without soul or intellect. There was no room in the ghetto for such a thing as the spirit. But the struggle which the ghetto inmates waged and which, to a certain extent, they won by winning back their human personality was in fact the struggle for the survival of the spirit . . . This was the clear-cut victory of spirit over matter. Let us hope that it will give us the strength to pull together our shattered nerves and to celebrate the final victory, the fulfillment of the wish of all the people in the ghetto: to survive until the Happy End. [85]

Though not Orthodox himself, Kalmanovitch was among those who perceived the existential reality of the ghetto from a religious perspective. This implied coming to grips with the spiritual integrity of the Jewish people, their suffering and ultimate vindication. These were all viewed in relationship to the Jewish concepts of God and Torah, which together with Jewish peoplehood form the triad of classical Judaism.

In his diary, Kalmanovitch recounts a story told him by a teacher of religion in a ghetto school. He tells of a class in which children, total strangers to their people and their tradition, eagerly listened to bible stories. When discussing the weekly portion *Toldot*, they learned about Jacob and Esau. One child called out, "Teacher, we are descendants of Jacob and they (i.e. those who wronged us) are descendants of Esau. Right? It is good this way. I want to be of the descendants of Jacob and not of the descendants of Esau."

Kalmanovitch, fascinated by the child's instinctive choice of his Jewishness, reflected on this incident and its religious implications. He repeated it in his diary entry, dated April 30, 1943, during the Passover season. He responded there to a gnawing question that had occupied ghetto residents for a year, a question propounded by some circles of ghetto intelligentsia, "What is a Jew, who is a Jew?" In his entry, Kalmanovitch interpreted Passover as the symbol of Jewish survival through faith in God, the Torah, and Jewish peoplehood. This type of spiritual defiance of the German overlords, exemplified by the child, lent an aura of sanctity to Jewish existence in the Nazi ghettos. Kalmanovitch wrote in his diary:

> To be a Jew means in every instance to be in an exalted position. The temporary suffering and blows that descend upon the Jew have a meaning, are not merely oppressions, and do not degrade the Jew. For a Jew is a part of the sacred triad: Israel, the Torah, and the Holy One, blessed be He. That means the Jewish people, the moral law, and the Creator of the universe. This sacred triad runs through the whole course of history. It is a reality that has been proved countless times. Our grandfathers clung to the triad, lived by its strength. And now, too, the Jew who does not cling to this triad is to be pitied. He wanders in a world of chaos, he suffers and finds no rationale for his suffering; he can be severed from his people, i.e. he can wish to change his self. But the Jew who clings to the sacred triad need not be pitied. He is in a secure association. To be sure, this is a stormy period in history. A war is being waged against the Jew. But this war is not merely directed against one link in the triad but against the entire one: against the Torah and God, against the moral law and Creator of the universe. Can anyone still doubt which side is the stronger? In a war it happens that one regiment is beaten, taken captive. Let the Jews in the ghetto consider themselves as such prisoners of war. But let them also remember that the army as a whole is not and cannot be beaten. The Passover of Egypt is a symbol of an ancient victory of the sacred triad. My wish is that all of us should live to see the Passover of the future. [86]

In an earlier chapter we have quoted a passage from another diary entry, Kalmanovitch's description of the spirit which sparked the celebration of *Simhat Torah* (the Festival of the Rejoicing of the Law) in the Vilna ghetto. There he justified such rejoicing not only as an act of present-day sanctification, but also as an affirmation of Israel's link with the past. He viewed it as a demonstration of Jewish thanksgiving to God for every day of survival. Observing Simhat Torah became a defiant act of hope, an authentic Jewish response to the tragedy of ghetto life. In another entry, dated December 23,

1942, he broadens this theme by observing that though individuals may be sacrificed, the Jewish people will not be deterred by fear and despair. They will emerge strengthened as a people from the Hitlerite ordeal.

In this manner, by distinguishing between individual survival and that of the people, he responds to the tribulations of eastern Jewry after the outbreak of the Russo-German war.

> ... Eventually the Jewish people itself will forget this branch that was broken from it. It will have to do without it. The healthy trunk will bring forth branches, blossoms and leaves. There is still strength and life. Dried up and decayed — this happens to every tree. There are still thousands of years ahead. Lamentation for the dead, of course: that is natural, particularly if they are your own near and dear ones. But the people must not be confused. The mourning for relatives — some people bear their sorrow for a long time; the largest part takes comfort. This is the nature of man, such is the world. Whatever the earth covers up is forgotten. Here in the ghetto we see how people forget. It cannot be otherwise and it certainly deserves no censure. The real motive in mourning is after all fear of one's own end. Wherein are we better than those tens of thousands? It must happen to us, too. If we only had a guarantee of survival! That we don't have, and one cannot keep on in constant fear, therefore, the sense of fear is projected into mourning for the fallen and sorrow over the destruction of Jewry... Refrain from sorrow! The nation will not be hurt. It will, we hope, come out fortified by these trials. This should fill the heart with joyous gratitude to the sovereign of history. [87]

Thus, Kalmanovitch affirms that though the individual Jew or even perhaps a whole branch of the Jewish family tree may be sacrificed, the Jewish people as an entity will survive, emerging with renewed strength, revivified from its most recent descent into hell. Oddly, Kalmanovitch objected to the activism of groups which he regarded as "extremists," including what he called the "extreme nationalists." Drawing on Jewish history he equated extremism with tyranny, which ran counter to the faith one should display in the ultimate victory of God and of the Allies, the bearers of morality against the forces of evil. He viewed extremism, whatever its form, as a sign of despair which could end in suicidal acts. Hence, it was not the Jewish way. [88]

In contrast, Kalmanovitch reacted with enthusiasm to every manifestation of positive activity among ghetto inmates. Thus, for instance, he hailed the clearing of space in the ghetto for an athletic field. Some condemned the very idea of an athletic field in the ghetto as a frivolous, almost sacrilegious act in the face of imminent death. For Kalmanovitch, this was not an act of desecration but an act of sanctification, demonstrating faith in life and faith in God. To him it was a manifestation of humanity in a world plagued by de-

145

humanization. This feeling is revealed in a diary entry dated August 21, 1942:

> The athletic field is most active, not to speak of Sundays, when there are games. Over 1,000 people, mainly youth, fill the field. Gymnastic exercises are carried out. The games are cheered loudly — as if we were free. A road to man. My pious friend laments: "So many mourn, so many died, and here merriment and celebrations!" Such is life. But live we must as long as God gives life. He knows best! Jewish children devote themselves to sports; may God give them strength. [89]

He expressed a similar reaction some months later in a visit to a children's home on December 13, 1942. He was impressed with the activity he saw there. For him it was added evidence of the vitality of the Jewish people.

> This morning I was in the children's nursery. Women who work leave their children from 7 to 6. There are 150 children between the ages of three months and two years, (one group) from two to three years, (one group) from three to six and another group that studies reading and writing. Speeches, dramatic presentations, the children march in line. But the Jewish flavor is missing. In ghetto circumstances the order is missing. In ghetto circumstances the order is remarkable. What vitality in this people on the brink of destruction! [90]

Kalmanovitch praised the role of discipline, order and cleanliness as acts of resistance against dehumanization and as means of survival. After a group of German newspapermen had visited the ghetto to provide their readers with their version of how the Jews lived, he wrote on August 21, 1942:

> There is still excitement about the exhibition. Visitors come to see it, and the journalist prepares tidbits for his readers or for these who sent him, and constantly describes what is about to please them. Let us hope that the wheel of the universe will return everything to its position and that our miserable work will also help a little in making the crooked straight. The "masters" visited the ghetto and found that all was well and orderly. "There is no ghetto like it among all the ghettos." So! After depriving us of all opportunities for a human life we have nevertheless not given up hope. The dweller in the ghetto has strength in his soul and might of hand and a will to live that conquer all difficulties. And when the day of peace comes — do not their hearts prophesy to them the coming end? [91]

A similar spirit of faith and confidence is evident also in other first-hand accounts of ghetto life. In the 204-page Yiddish diary of Yitzhak Rudashevski covering a span of two years (June 1941-April 1943) and written on ledger paper, this attitude is recorded from the perspective of youth by a 15-year-old adolescent. He succeeds in articulating not only his own confrontation with the atrocities around him, but also the fortitude of other young people in the Vilna ghetto facing their Nazi oppressors. Rudashevski finds his faith in the future reaffirmed by the many ghetto events he witnessed and shared, such as studies and school activities, [92] the celebration marking the circulation of the 100,000th book in the ghetto library, the exhibit arranged by the Literary Club in memory of the Yiddish poet and Bible translator Yehoash. His accounts of the two latter ghetto happenings have been quoted in an earlier chapter. [93]

Many times the teenager is so profoundly moved by the cultural activities he sees and is a part of in the Vilna ghetto that he forgets he is a prisoner within the ghetto walls. As a teenager caught up in the hustle and bustle of youthful life which obscures the reality that surrounds him on all sides, Rudashevski can note with complete candor in his diary on March 18, 1943:

> I am busy for hours at a time. It is so hard to accomplish some-
> thing at school and in the club, and at the same time to be
> involved with cooking and cleaning. First of all, reports sneaked
> up on us. At school we are now covering the theme Vilna in
> geography. I am preparing a report 'On Jew(ish) Printing in
> Vilna.' For several months now there is no light in the evenings.
> In the evenings we lie around in the workroom, the reading room.
> I often reflect, this is supposedly the ghetto yet I have such a rich
> life of intellectual work: I study, I read, I visit club circles. Time
> runs by so quickly and there is so much work to be done, lectures,
> social gatherings. I often forget that I am in the ghetto. [94]

The cruel realities of ghetto life could not destroy the natural energy and optimism of youth which marked this young man's view of life and his convictions about the future. He was convinced that as an individual he would outlive the ghetto. He built his inner defenses on the conviction that with his own eyes he would witness the end of his people's suffering. Thus with faith and hope, Rudashevski could observe in his diary on December 1, 1942 as he wrote of his school work:

> At school today we had a class composition of the theme: 'Scenes
> of Deprivation.' I wrote at great length. I found topical parallels to
> Reyzen's stories. I connected them and concluded that our ghetto
> is the finale of generations of want. We shall be those who, emerg-
> ing from the ghetto, shall cast off the affliction which has
> oppressed the Jewish people for generations. [95]

Like so many other young people, his spirit could not be broken. Rudashevski refused to submit to frustration or succumb to despair. He appreciated the value of time and would not allow himself to be overwhelmed or give way to inertia, frustration, and boredom. He was convinced that there was a life to be lived even within the ghetto walls that surrounded him. On December 10, 1942, realizing that this day marked his fifteenth birthday, he wrote in his diary in triumphant tones:

147

It dawned on me that today is my birthday. Today I became 15 years old. You hardly realize how time flies. It, the time, runs ahead unnoticed and presently we realize, as I did today, for example, and discover that days and months go by, that the ghetto is not a painful, squirming moment of a dream which constantly disappears, but is a large swamp in which we lose our days and weeks. Today I became deeply absorbed in the thought. I decided not to trifle my time away in the ghetto on nothing and I feel somehow happy that I can study, read, develop myself, and see that time does not stand still as long as I progress normally with it. In my daily ghetto life it seems to me that I live normally but often I have deep qualms. Surely I could have lived better. Must I, day in and day out, see the walled-up ghetto gate, must I, in my best years, see only the one little street, the few stuffy courtyards?

Still other thoughts buzzed around in my head but I felt two things most strongly: a regret, a sort of gnawing. I wish to shout to time to linger, not to run. I wish to recapture my past year and keep it for later, for the new life. My second feeling today is that of strength and hope. I do not feel the slightest despair. Today I became 15 years of age and I live confident in the future. I am not conflicted about it, and see before me sun and sun and sun . . . [96]

Rudashevski in his words conveys the glow of youth, the warmth of conviviality of young people expressing their joy through song, through study, and through togetherness. This is not to imply that they did not understand or were blind to the abject conditions of ghetto existence. Despite all, as young people, they pulsed with life, with zeal, and with conviction. They sanctified every possible moment with meaningful living and soaring spirits. Our diarist captures one such moment as he describes the evening of December 11, 1942 that he shared with his friends:

Today we had a club holiday in the kitchen of Rudnitski 6. We felt like having a little fun. So we wangled 100 kg. of potatoes out of the administration and we have a baked pudding. This was the happiest evening I have spent in the ghetto.

At nine o'clock we met in the kitchen. People are already sitting at the tables. Many, many guests came. And here we sit crowded together. I look around at the crowd, all of our kind teachers, friends, intimates. It is so cozy, so warm, so pleasant. This evening we demonstrated what we are and what we can accomplish. Club members came with songs, recitations. Until late into the night we sang with the adults songs which tell about youthfulness and hope. Very beautiful was the living newspaper in which the club with its chairman and speakers was humorously criticized. We sat at the meager tables and ate baked pudding and coffee and we were so happy, so happy. Song after song resounded. It is already 12 o'clock. We are, as it were, intoxicated with the joy of youth. We do not want to go home. Songs keep bursting forth, they simply will not stop. We disperse late at night. We have demonstrated that we are young, 'within walls yet young, forever young. Our slogan with which 'we go to meet the sun.' Today we have demonstrated that even within the three small streets we can maintain our youthful zeal. We have proved that from the ghetto there will not emerge a youth broken in spirit; from the ghetto there will emerge a strong youth which is hardy and cheerful.[97]

In a similar vein a year later, on December 9, 1943, young Rudashevski comments on another evening event at the youth center. He notes the banner headline over the wall newspaper, "Within The Walls Yet Young," and observes that the mood is exalted. Then he quotes the words of his beloved teacher, Rokhl Broydo, who observed:

. . . When a people has a young generation it is a sign of its progress. We have a youth, its flag is drenched in blood, it is red, but we hold it firmly; the youth in the ghetto, that is the firm bridge to the future![98]

In his own insightful and incisive way Rudashevski echoed his teacher's comment. He summarizes not only his mood but also that of his contemporaries:

. . . We are young, the young hall is saturated with youthful joy and work. Our spirit, which we bear proudly within the ghetto walls, will be the most beautiful gift to the newly rising future . . . long live youth!—The progress of our people.[99]

Young Yitzchak Rudashevski bears witness through the medium of his diary to the vitality, dynamism and hope that moved many ghetto young people. He, like they, understood the enormity of the tragedy that was their life and death yet they created positive attitudes. These they expressed through multiform activities that they carried on. They were restless young people and he expressed their moments of spiritual grandeur, the moments that sanctified time. His diary as it conveys a picture of youthful vitality breathes life into the prophetic words: *Bachuraychem Chezyonot Yeru* (Joel 3:1), "Your Youth Shall See Visions".

Herman Kruk follows the same pattern. In his *Togbukh*, which covers the period June 23, 1941–July 14, 1943, he meticulously details the crimes of the Nazis. His dated entries record such events as the mass killings of aged Jews, deportations to the execution site at Ponar and the actual executions, starvation, slave labor, and inventories taken by the Nazis of furniture and other belongings to be confiscated from the Jews.[100] However, he balances his report of the tragedies with sketches of the institutions and activities organized to counteract the dehumanizing effects of the Nazi acts. In this way he reflects the will to live that was part of the ghetto scene. Thus, he summarized the cultural activities in the ghetto, the ghetto's libraries, the ghetto's musical and dramatic programs, religious life and the ghetto's school system in great detail.[101]

In his entry for January 1, 1942, Kruk reveals his hopes for the future despite the terrors of the past and present:

> Nevertheless, I am filled with faith and with hope for the great new era which the new year of 1942 will bring . . . What we wish is that we may be able to hold out, survive and live to tell our story.[102]

Perhaps the most detailed first-hand accounts and personal diaries have come to us from the Warsaw ghetto through such representative works as those of Abraham Levin, Chaim Kaplan, Peretz Opotinsky and Emanuel Ringelblum. Their accounts date basically from the earlier period of Nazi occupation, before the "Final Solution" was implemented in its grim entirety, while it was still possible for the ghetto Jews to put their ideas and feelings on paper. Most of the Warsaw materials that have survived were written in the middle of 1942, when the Nazi intentions had already become obvious to the Jews but had not yet been fully implemented.

In his diary, written principally in Hebrew with a number of Yiddish inclusions, Abraham Levin, the educator, attempted to set down the basic mood of the people in the Warsaw ghetto as he perceived it. On June 11, 1942, he sketches the reaction of the populace to an incident in which two Jews were shot down in the street for smuggling:

> . . . Today, despite the terror unleashed against smugglers and despite the many victims of the past two days, smuggling continues full steam as if nothing had happened. This proves that under the present conditions, smuggling means survival itself and that life is stronger than death. In these sad days life and death walk hand in hand and death seeks to destroy life. But in the end life will triumph over death and emerge victorious.[103]

Here Levin suggests that Jews tenaciously hold on to life as a means of outwitting their oppressors.

In an entry from the preceding month (May 3, 1942), Levin cites this determination to survive as one of the reasons for the minimal incidence of suicide in the Warsaw ghetto:

> One of the most remarkable phenomena of this war has been the determination to survive, the near-absence of suicide . . . One does not escape from life of one's own free will. On the contrary, one clings to life with all his might: one is determined to remain alive and to survive the war no matter what the cost. The tension

of this historic world conflict is so great that everyone, young and old, wants to live to see how it will end and what new order will emerge afterward. (Even) the old have only one desire: to live to see the end and to outlive Hitler. [104]

Levin notes a wry comment by a man of 80 whose only son died of typhus:

'I would like to live to see the end of the war, and after that, I would like to live just for one more half-hour.' One might ask what an old man like that would have to live for. And yet, even he wants to survive the war, even if it is only 'for one more half-hour' after the last shot has been fired. This is the passionate desire of every Jew. [105]

Reduced to simplest terms, one might say that this old man wanted to justify his own existence in the face of his son's death by demonstrating his ability to outlive his tormentors. In this context life had meaning, not merely as physical survival but as an act of defiance. By outliving the enemy, even if it would be for only one half-hour, the Jew would affirm the sanctity of Jewish survival.

Chaim Kaplan, another Warsaw diarist, stresses the philosophical basis of Judaism which he sees as the foundation for Jewish creativity and survival. Against the background of Nazi atrocities that he does not hesitate to report in detail, Kaplan summarizes the spiritual factors that constantly infused the survivalists in the Warsaw ghetto with renewed courage. They were motivated and strengthened by the Jewish mystique, a mystique which has enabled the Jew to survive age-old persecution. It is the basis of the will to life expressed by the individual Jew and the people as a whole. Like Levin, he points to the almost complete absence of suicide in the Warsaw ghetto:

March 10, 1940

But even at this time our response does not follow natural laws. There lies submerged within us a kind of hidden, secret strength which maintains and sustains us despite the laws of nature . . .

This secret strength is working wonders for us. One proof of this is that we have no suicides . . . Say what you will: the lust for life even amidst such horrible circumstances as the ones which surround us now is the result of some hidden, secret force whose nature we still do not quite understand . . .

The reality is that we have been stripped naked. Yet as long as this secret strength lies hidden within us we will not despair. This strength is hidden within the existential source of Polish Jewry; it is rooted in our external heritage which commands us to go on living.

Together with our poet (Chaim Nachman Bialik) the Jews of Poland proclaim:

151

A spark is hidden within the rock of our heart;
A small spark, 'tis true, but mine alone;
Neither borrowed nor stolen,
It is mine, for it comes from me alone.[106]

Kaplan notes, too that the Jew is able to endure because he is able to transpose his will to live into activities which make survival possible. This inventive genius enabled the Jew to withstand persecution and pogroms in the past, and it will enable him to cope also with this most dismal period in Jewish history. In an entry dated June 17, 1942, he describes ghetto activities as they continued even after the Jews had become fully aware of the fate the Germans were planning for them:

> June 17, 1942
>
> . . . Nazism has marked us for death. In its arrogance and stupidity it does not even seek to hide this fact, and it is clear to us that if at all possible, it will carry out this death sentence it has meted out to us. Therefore we are expecting death —
>
> However, as long as we remain alive we are in need of all the necessities of life. We eradicate from our hearts not only the dead but also death itself. There can be no life without activity, without goals, without desires, and once you have desires and expectations you are immersed in all the vanities of life. Death is thrust aside by life . . .
>
> Oh, I almost forgot the most important thing: the kindergartens. and the komplety where the older children can study — in short, all those things that are thorns in the eyes of the Nazis. Our lifegiving pulses never stop beating. We are wise in the skills of survival; we are craftsmen in the arts of living. It is as the prophet Isaiah wrote, "You shall not be burned by fire, neither shall you be consumed by flame."[107]

Kaplan feels that the Jews in the Warsaw ghetto were motivated by an inherent optimism which, for some, was founded on the conviction that the God of Israel would not abandon his people. This faith, tested throughout Jewish history, would not fail now. As in the past, it is still valid, providing substance and direction. Thus he writes on September 5, 1940:

> September 5, 1940
>
> . . . Within the people of Israel there is an obstinate optimism. We all believe that the days of the murderer are numbered. that he will fall, never to rise again . . . We have experienced many difficult periods in our history. The God of Israel will not betray us; He will not forsake us.[108]

More than a year later, as the ghetto faced raging hunger, rampant disease, and massive deportations, he wrote on January 25, 1941:

> January 25, 1941
>
> Will we be able to survive? This question is on everyone's tongue.

As a rule it is asked in tones of resignation, because most people feel that there is no hope but that you do want to have the opinion of others, just in order to be sure. But the answer of the believers, as can be expected, is always the same, "God knows best."

At times like these there is no more useful and healthy remedy than religious faith. The believer, first and foremost, is able to accept the concept of yesurim shel ahavah, that one must accept suffering because one loves God. The believer is confident that God will not forsake His people, His heritage. This certainty is one of the foundations of the believer's faith . . . Our ancestors settled down in the ghetto but even though they were hated and despised, they never ceased to create cultural values. We will do as they did.[109]

Over and over, Kaplan states the conviction which nonbelievers, too, could accept as justification for faith in Israel's capacity for survival: the inherent strength of the Jewish people. On January 26, 1941 he reports that hundreds of families have been uprooted from their homes and are making their way to Warsaw on foot. Warsaw, he indicates, is thus to become one of three concentration points for Jews making the General Government Judenrein and simplifying the process of destruction for the Germans. Yet he begins his entry and concludes it with a profession of his faith in Israel's indestructibility:

January 26, 1941

He who does not believe in the eternity of the Jewish people could say that the end of Polish Jewry is at hand. But even the Gentiles are awed by our life giving strength . . . Even those of us who do not believe in miracles admit that there is deep within us a primeval force that supports and enables us to survive . . .

But the guardian of Israel neither sleeps nor slumbers, and good news comes from the dunes of Africa. The Jews continue in their belief that the downfall of the Germans is at hand, that their troubles are greater than ours. Their incompetent partner is already on his knees and will not rise again. It is the beginning of the end.

It is obvious to us that we will end in joy and redemption, while they will end in doom and destruction.[110]

These beliefs were not mere intellectual rationalizations for a refusal to give in, but formed the foundation on which the entire network of ghetto institutions was built. While the Jews lived, they intended to live in a structured, meaningful fashion.

Peretz Opotinsky, less given to philosophizing than his colleagues, strove for the same objective, exhorting his people not to surrender to despair by portraying the feelings of amkha (literally, "Thy, i.e. (God's) people") personified by the simple, ordinary Jews whom he saw every day on his rounds as a letter carrier. His writings document all the reasons for despair, but they also single out acts of defiance born of the conviction that while the flame of the Jewish

153

spirit might flicker, it would never go out. Much as Kalmanovitch hailed the new athletic field in the Vilna ghetto, so Opotinsky cited the dedication ceremony held to inaugurate a children's playground in the ghetto of Warsaw as evidence of the Jewish will to survive. [111]

Describing the day care centers set up by the various ghetto organizations, Opotinsky, Zionist activist that he was, had little patience with those who stressed the Polish language and Polish culture rather than strictly Jewish interests. The institutions he singled out for praise were those based on Jewish national values. He lauded particularly the founders of the underground Zionist youth groups for sensing the Jewish national needs of the ghetto children and responding to them. [112]

He paid tribute to the extraordinary courage of one Jew who was shot by the Nazis:

> His name will remain in the annals of German murder as something out of the ordinary . . . Before he died, he rose to his feet and made a speech to the Germans. Among the things he said to them was that they should not think that by slaughtering the Polish Jews they were going to achieve their goal and win the war. 'No!' he shouted, 'You will lose the war and you will not be able to put an end to our existence. The Jewish people will outlive you!' Thereupon the Germans, infuriated, aimed their rifles at him and stopped his words with a hail of bullets. [113]

Like Levin and Kaplan, Opotinsky emphasized the insignificant suicide rate among Warsaw's Jews:

> Jews have not been taking their own lives in this war, (except in Galicia). This fact is a natural reaction of the Jewish urge of self-preservation which countered the extermination program of Hitlerism and the Germans' endeavors to make their lives bitter (the allusion is to Israel's slavery in Egypt under the Pharaohs) with a mighty determined resolve to live and to endure. [114]

He envisaged the emergence of a new type of Jew who would be infused with a sense of Jewish dignity and committed to the redemption and reconstruction of the entire world:

> As of this moment the ghetto's wide-ranging program has not been crowned with success. But even if the enemy should become so savage, so bloodthirsty, so demented that he will place our masses under cannon fire as he did the Jews in the parts of Russia occupied by Germany, and if he should destroy us like so many rabid dogs — even then our victory will be complete.

> The last surviving son of the people of Israel will raise the coming generation, the new Jew — proud, clean, pure and refined in all the furnaces of our age. Within the heart of this new Jew there will burn a yearning for the redemption of all mankind, a longing to

cleanse the shame and infamy from his people and to uproot from the world this plague, this hatred between nations. [115]

Finally we turn to the master diarist of all, Emanuel Ringelblum, who has left us his own voluminous diary written in both Yiddish and Polish covering the period from 1939 to 1942. Though his main concern was to document the enormity of the German crimes against his people, he also recorded the reactions of the ghetto population to the Nazi terror. He wrote against a background of rampant starvation; of children dying in the streets from hunger or cold; of newspaper-covered frozen bodies left on the street to be carted off to the cemetery; of individuals smuggling food in an attempt to keep themselves and their families alive, and of people seized in the ghetto streets for deportation or death. Yet from time to time in the light of such conditions, Ringelblum focuses on efforts to resist German dehumanization. In an entry in which he summarizes various events during the period January 5-April 20, 1940, he quotes approvingly from the lead editorial of the publication, *"Neged Hazerem"*:

> ... The war transforms men into beasts. We have become accustomed to declaring: 'We never wanted war and we shall not be transformed into wild beasts. We were and we shall remain human beings.' [116]

On another occasion, Ringelblum points out a strange paradox: the worse conditions in the ghetto became, the more he could discern a refusal on the part of the Jews to surrender. Instead he sensed a renewed hope for survival and for a better future. Even if he and his associates in the archival project were to die, he declares on June 26, 1942, they had managed to deal the Germans a severe blow by exposing the evil deeds of the Nazis for all the world to know:

> ... But one thing is clear to all of us. Our toils and tribulations, our devotion and constant terror, have not been in vain. We have struck the enemy a hard blow ... One thing we know — we have fulfilled our duty. We have overcome every obstacle to achieve our end. Nor will our deaths be meaningless, like the deaths of tens of thousands of Jews. We have struck the enemy a hard blow. We have revealed his Satanic plan to annihilate Polish Jewry, a plan he wished to complete in silence. We have run a line through his calculations and have exposed his cards ... [117]

Almost unbelievably in another entry from the same period, he discusses the reading preferences of the ghetto inmates. He notes that readers seem to concentrate on war literature from the Napoleonic era and particularly from the World War I period. He regards this phenomenon as added evidence of

155

Jewish determination not to despair. By reading about past wars that their forebears survived, the inmates of the Warsaw ghetto sought to remind themselves that their sufferings of the present, too, would eventually come to an end:

> ... Let it be said that though we have been sentenced to death and know it, we have not lost our human features: our minds are as active as they were before the war. The earnest Jewish reader is avidly interested in war literature. They read Lloyd George's memoirs and World War I fiction ... particularly pages that deal with the German defeat in 1918. They seek parallels to their time. They read with great satisfaction about the capitulation at Compeigne and visualize a like occurrence in their time ... [118]

In describing the morale-building activities that were carried on by the ghetto community, he singles out and lauds the women of the ghetto who managed to scrape together the necessities of life in order to keep their families united. [119] He acknowledges the work of the socialist *haShomer haTzair*, [120] as well as the endeavors of the Orthodox groups and their spiritual leaders, particularly the communal observances of Passover, Hanukkah, and Purim. [121]

Ringelblum makes several comments about *Kiddush Hashem* (martyrdom) as practiced in the ghetto. In two entries, he deals with this from the perspective of Warsaw's Orthodox Jews. One of the notations discusses rabbis who were forced to desecrate Torah Scrolls by trampling on them. He observed that this act could be justified by some on the basis that if they refused the whole community might be liable to punishment. [122] In another entry he notes:

> ... There is a lack of sense of *Kiddush Hashem*. We see Orthodox Jews trampling on Torah Scrolls and other similar scenes in order not to endanger life through opposition. *Kiddush Hashem* is today sublimated to the goal of maintaining the Jewish community intact ... [123]

In these terms he recognizes that there is an operative priority in the ghetto, namely the priority of human survival.

The ghetto diaries and other forms of ghetto first person reportage that have come down to us reveal the hunger of ghetto Jews for human dignity. These records document the resolve of significant numbers of ghetto inhabitants to confront death with a yearning for life and humiliation with a striving after sanctity. These materials represent but a small portion of the diaries that were meticulously kept, many anonymously. Each of these graphically document the trauma of the time and the will to survive. They portray the technique of survival, through the effort of building a viable pattern of life, to overcome through the heroism of daily living. It is also to maintain a modicum of human dignity and self-respect without which the individual could not survive. Des Pres's conclusions concerning human dignity and self-respect in concentration camps apply also to ghettos.

156

By passing through the degradation of the camps, survivors discovered that in extremity a sense of dignity is something which men and women cannot afford to lose. Great damage has to be borne, much humiliation suffered. But at some point a steady resistance to their obliteration as human beings must be made. They learned, furthermore, that when conditions of filth are enforced, befoulment of the body is experienced as befoulment of the soul. An they came to recognize, finally, that when this particular feeling — of something inwardly untouchable — is ruined beyond repair, the will to live dies. To care for one's appearance thus becomes an act of resistance and a necessary moment in the larger structure of survival. Life itself depends on keeping dignity intact, and this, in turn, depends on the daily, never finished battle to remain *visibly* human [124] (author's emphasis).

One might summarize the mood of the ghetto in the words of an unknown Lodz diarist. The writer was a woman who at first echoes the despair reflected in Joshua Perle's story *4580* but then turns back to renewed courage and determination:

> ... On the day they tied the number around your neck, you felt in all your senses that by doing so, they had reduced the stature which the designation of "personhood" affords the individual ... And then you wondered whether it was worth while fighting for the designation of "human being" if that category included corrupt creatures such as these. Yet, deep within your soul there flows an inner strength which enables you to understand the meaning of this designation despite the number. Humanity is not dormant. On the contrary, it is revealed in all its warmth and brightness as it takes form and bears witness to the struggle between (impersonal) number and (personal) name ... In its own manner, your soul bears witness to the eternal, never-to-be-vanquished victor who is called "human being." [125]

Chapter Twelve

Art In The Ghetto

Latvian-born Esther Lurie emigrated to Palestine during the period between the two World Wars. She happened to be in Kovno on a visit when
World War II broke out. Eventually, she was moved into the ghetto with the
rest of the Jewish population. There, she became well-known as one of the
artists who recorded ghetto life for posterity. She was to survive the war and she
returned to Israel, settling in Jerusalem. Her *Sketches from a Women's Labour
Camp* were published in Tel Aviv, with an introduction by the Israeli critic
Aryeh Lerner. Entitled "Art in the Valley of Death," Lerner's essay attempts to
assess the meaning of Lurie's work as well as that of all other artistic creativity
in the ghettos during the Holocaust period. Underlining the fact that such
creativity existed not only in the ghettos but even in the concentration camps,
Lerner seeks to interpret the basic human values which this creativity
reflects.

Was art of any kind possible in the ghetto, in the concentration
camp? It was. The flame of artistic creativity flared and flickered
in the Valley of the Shadow through the dark of the
Catastrophe...

Indeed, this is one of the mysteries of the human spirit. Even in
that hell on earth... a hell against which all the fires in Dante's
Inferno burn pallidly — the tormented masses, whose humanity
had been eradicated with Teutonic ferocity and obliterated with
German "thoroughness," still included a rare handful who clung
to culture and creativity. With the last of their strength they were
resolved to preserve the Divine likeness, writing poems and
books; playing music, drawing and arranging shows openly, secretly or underground, often doing so with the clear awareness that
they were risking their lives at the hands of the murderers who
wished to destroy the spirit before slaying the body.

... Was it the blazing Will-to-Live which cannot be extinguished
until the last breath and which obeys that awesome behest, 'Live

in thy blood!' (Ezekiel 16:6) from which some drew such a wealth of power and the strength to withstand anything, to avoid despair and keep wits and sanity despite the horrors? Or was it possibly a demonstration of the superiority of man and a decisive proof that he can be maltreated, his flesh may be shredded with iron combs and he can be physically exterminated, yet it is beyond all human power to destroy the spirit? [126]

It was through individual creativity in various artistic forms that the ghetto community was able to maintain a perspective and an understanding of the meaning of human worth. Creativity helped some people cope with the conditions to which they were exposed every day. This conviction was dramatized by Mark Dworzetsky in his assessment of life in the Vilna ghetto. He describes an evening devoted to an illustrated lecture on the art of Marc Chagall. In the midst of the proceedings, the air raid sirens began to wail outside but those who participated in the discussion refused to break up the meeting and seek shelter:

> ... It is better to die in an air raid while talking about art than to take shelter from death raining down from the sky and wait to be killed at the hands of men.

> Not one of us went down to the shelter. Sirens wailed, bombers roared over Vilna, and everyone else in the city ran to take cover. Meanwhile, in the ghetto, we remained in our places and calmly listened to a lecture on art ... [127]

The group listening to the lecture in the Vilna ghetto felt that life had a meaning deeper than mere physical survival. To them, the pursuit of art was a manifestation of worthwile living.

The viewing of art exhibits arranged either by the ghetto leadership or by the underground was a popular pastime in the ghettos. There are reports of many such exhibits in Kovno, [128] Vilna [129] and Lodz. [130] A most interesting report of an art exhibit in a Warsaw ghetto school is found in the diary of Mary Berg, the teen-age American girl who was caught in Warsaw at the outbreak of the war. In a diary entry dated September 28, 1941, she describes the works of her young fellow students in great detail, then concludes with an evaluation of the mood of the viewers:

> ... People seem to leave the exhibition full of impressions, and even on the street continue to discuss the various pictures and projects for a long time. Everyone simply refuses to believe that such works could be produced within the walls of the ghetto, especially under the present conditions of constant manhunts, hunger, epidemic and terror. And yet it is a fact! Our youth has given tangible proof of its spiritual strength, power of resistance, courage and faith in a new and juster world.

> Many visitors had radiant faces, shining with pride when they

left. Others were serious and absorbed . . . [131]

The late Tzvee Shner, who survived the Warsaw ghetto and became director of the museum at Kibbutz Lohame HaGetaot, the kibbutz founded by ghetto survivors after the war, reports an art exhibit arranged in the ghetto of Lodz, featuring the works of the artists Yosef Kovner and Yitzhak Brauner. The exhibit, which ran for six weeks, attracted no less than 12,000 viewers from all walks of life and caused Brauner to express his amazement at the enthusiastic response:

> When I entered the hall I was amazed to see that it was filled, and at the crowd gathered around the guide who was explaining the exhibits . . . This recurred every day . . . One must consider the conditions under which these people lived. It wasn't easy for them to find the money for the admission fee . . . It was the porters, the cobblers, the peddlers . . . of whom it used to be said that they and the arts were worlds apart, who showed particular interest in this exhibit. [132]

Lurie in her memoirs, and the artists Hersz Szylis and Alexander Bogen in interviews, provide an idea of the conditions under which the ghetto artists worked. In some instances, fortuitous circumstances provided them with an official cover of sorts. They might be working for the *Judenrat* on such various art projects as stage backdrops for theatrical performances or even for the German authorities, preparing posters, copying works of art, counterfeiting Allied documents and currency, painting portraits of German officers as gifts to be sent home to Germany, or decorating German army barracks and rest camps. [133] The artists' reward took the form of cigarettes or extra food rations or such privileges as curfew exemptions and private rooms in which they could work undisturbed. [134]

Szylis, who was born in Lodz and survived the Warsaw ghetto (he eventually settled in Safed, which is known for its artists' colony) notes that in Lodz he was hired by Mordecai Rumkovski, the ghetto leader, to make sketches of ghetto life and to paint portraits of Rumkovski himself. Lurie was employed for similar tasks by the *Judenrat* in Kovno. Alexander Bogen, who settled in Israel in 1951, did the same type of work for the official leadership of the Vilna ghetto. After joining the partisan movement, he broadened his artistic activities to include sketches of partisan life in the woods around Vilna.

Another artist, Halina Olomuzcka, began her artistic career as a ghetto teenager. Her artistic ability saved her. In return for sketching the portraits of Nazi officials and soldiers, as well as illustrating postcards for them, she was given leftover food. Halina survived the Warsaw ghetto uprising and miraculously lived through imprisonment in Maideneck, Auschwitz, and Ravensbruck. Today she lives in Holon, Israel where she continues her artistic work. Less fortunate are those artists who did not survive the Holocaust. They are known only through the few examples of their art that survived them. Among these are Amos Szwarc, who perished in Auschwitz; Nathan Spigel, who died in the Lodz ghetto; Jacob Lifschitz, who lived in the Kovno ghetto until he was shipped to Dachau where he died, and Szyman Szerman of Lodz, who worked in the ghetto adminstration's statistical section only to succumb.

The artists had to make do with crude materials. Szylis reports that he painted on scraps of paper, on cardboard sheets from old cartons and on sacks. He created his colors from textile dyes and, in effect, devised a new artistic technique which he still occasionally employs in his present work. [137] Bogen made his own charcoal from branches he gathered up and burned in the woods. [138]

In the Warsaw ghetto a group of 20 artists organized a cooperative to improve their working conditions and, incidentally, to improve their own and their families' chances for survival. [139] The artists realized that as long as the German authorities could use and exploit their talents, they would be spared deportation.

Of the art that was created and survived in the ghettos under review, only a small sampling will be discussed here. No attempt has been made to evaluate the sketches and paintings from the artistic viewpoint, although they do show considerable talent. They are presented solely in terms of their significance as responses to the ghetto situation. These works of art are evidence of the artists' determination to remain creative as long as humanly possible.

The paintings, sketches, and other forms of artistic expressions which come to us from the ghettos reveal not only the physical surroundings but also the emotions and the mood of the people. Through these media we view the streets, the marketplaces, the workplaces and the warrenlike courtyards where the inmates lived. They also capture events in ghetto life. The artist captures the mood of the people, expressing through his work their feelings and emotions as they struggle to survive. The artist conveys the anguish of deportation, the torment of hunger, and the agony of forced labor. Yet the very fact that the artist sketches or paints under ghetto conditions is in and of itself an act of hope, affirmation, and defiance. By continuing to practice their art, these individuals expressed their determination to lead a normal life if at all possible. Through their artistic endeavours they refused to be engulfed and spiritually destroyed.

The paintings, sketches, and other objects of art that are reviewed and re-produced here come from the collections found in The Archives of *Yad Vashem* and the Ghetto Fighters Museum. They were viewed and photographed by this writer. They represent the works of Hersz Szylis, Sara Glicksman-Fajtlowicz, and Szymon Szerman of Lodz; Esther Lurie and Jacob Lipschutz of Kovno, and Alexander Bogen of Vilna, as well as various art objects that were created anonymously. [140]

We turn first to two paintings by Sara Glicksman-Fajtlowicz. The earlier of the two, entitled *Driven into the Ghetto*, [141] is dated 1940. The second, *Bridge Connecting the Two Parts of the Ghetto*, [142] is dated three years later. The first depicts the Jews being herded into the ghetto. The street scene does not show individuals so much as a mass being driven in one direction. The painting conveys a sense of urgency, of movement and haste. Some of the people are carrying the meager remains of their possessions on their backs; others are struggling to push sleds through the snow. There also appears to be one horse-drawn wagon. The houses that line the street seem shrouded in a thick wintry mist. The picture leaves the viewer with an acute sense of dejection, harassment and confusion. Glicksman-Fajtlowicz's second painting portrays one of the wooden overpasses that bridged the "Aryan" streets which divided the Lodz ghetto into two sections. Unlike a number of other artists who painted the same scene,[143] Glicksman-Fajtlowicz depicted not only the bridge but the surrounding area. If one did not know the significance of the scene she portrays here, this picture would convey an almost serene mood: green grass, a tree in bloom, and houses in pastel shades. The people crossing the bridge do not convey a sense of urgency. Except for the soldier standing on guard, it is difficult to determine where the ghetto ends and the "Aryan" highway begins.

The marketplace in the Lodz ghetto is depicted in two rather descriptive works by Szymon Szerman. There is little to differentiate these pictures from paintings showing slums or blighted areas anywhere else in the world. In these two pictures Szerman seems to have portrayed the tragedy of poverty in general rather that the terrors of the Holocaust in particular. [144]

But some of his other works deal clearly with ghetto themes. In a gouache, he depicts in vivid colors two slave laborers yoked to what looks like a wagon filled either with garbage or construction materials. [145] He also executed several works in sepia tones, showing women toiling in ghetto workshops. [146]

Other artists, too, treated life within the ghetto with all its grimness and agony. There are pen-and-ink sketches as well as full color renditions of such subjects as hunger, illness, starvation, beatings, deportation, and forced labor. No tragic aspect of ghetto life is neglected. Some of these items are stark, clear evidence of hurried and harried execution; others convey painstaking labor. One quick sketch, the work of an unknown artist apparently executed in the Warsaw ghetto, portrays a tragic moment in ghetto life, the round-up of Jews on the streets. They are being loaded onto the back of an open truck, destined for deportation. These sketches record actual ghetto happenings left for future generations to agonize over. Amos Szwarc's *The Peddler*, Nathan Spigel's *Woman of the Ghetto*, and Halina Olomuzcki's grim *Mother and Children*, as well as her depiction of a youngster selling yellow badges, all capture the reality of ghetto life. [147]

Perhaps one of the most sensitive and revealing artistic expressions of ghetto emotions is the work of Hersz Szylis. One singular painting juxtaposes life and death within the ghetto as the artist himself witnessed them. Dated 1943, it is a courtyard scene painted in somber tones. In the center of the courtyard a child is sitting at a well; he seems to be reading a book. Nearby are two other children carrying a water bucket. In the foreground a horse-drawn wagon converted into a hearse is waiting in front of one of the dwellings from which members of the burial society are carrying out the dead. Two women are talking to one another, but seem to be watching the action. In this picture, we see the continuous paradox of ghetto existence, the determination to survive even in the midst of death. Even the children appear to have become inured to death and oblivious to its closeness. They do not interrupt their activities to watch the hearse. [148]

Other artists sought to portray some of the activities organized by the ghetto inmates to make their lives a little brighter. Examples of this type of work are two sketches by the Kovno artist Jacob Lipschutz. The first, [149] dated 1942, is a sketch of young people gathered in the building which once housed the Kovno Yeshiva. A speaker is addressing the group, which was either a class or an informal discussion group. Realistic and somber in tone, this sketch reflects a spirit of intensity, quiet determination, and the Jewish penchant for study under all circumstances.

Another Lipschutz sketch expressing the mood of ghetto youth in Kovno, dated 1943, [150] depicts three Jewish lads on guard duty in a vegetable patch. It must be remembered that there was very little space for plant life in the ghettos. In the Kovno ghetto an attempt was made to use every available open space for productive purposes. In a number of these spaces, the ghetto inmates planted vegetable gardens which were guarded by children and teenage volunteers. The youngsters in the sketch appear relatively clean-cut and healthy. The boy in the foreground is barefoot, but the clothing of all three is fairly neat. The faces of the boys reflect not despair, but serious attention to the guard duty for which they have volunteered.

In some of their sketches and paintings, the ghetto artists convey the moods of ghetto life through their use of color tones. At times the utter dejection of ghetto existence was relieved for a moment by a ray of hope; the artists capture these transient reprieves by means of contrasts between bright and dark. This is particularly notable in three paintings by Hersz Szylis. In the first of the paintings[151] we view a courtyard scene with men, women, and children. In the left foreground some of the youngsters are pushing and pulling a cart. The other people are not engaged in any particular activity, but their attention is focused on an itinerant musician in the center, who is playing his musical instrument. The musician and the space immediately surrounding him are brightened by a glimmer of light color, contrasting with the dark tones and symbolizing the ray of hope that can appear even in the midst of dark despair.

A similar mood is expressed in even more dramatic manner in Szylis' painting of another ghetto courtyard at dusk. [152] There are four children in this scene; three fair-haired girls dressed in white, and one boy. The boy and one of the little girls are carrying a water bucket, while the other two girls are running, dancing and frolicking in typical childlike fashion. Szylis uses dark and somber tones for the courtyard and the dwellings that surround it, but light is caught by the white dresses and the fair, tousled heads of the little girls at play.

Here again is a brief ray of hope in the midst of despair.

Szylis expresses the same feeling and mood in another undated sketch. This quickly executed work accentuates and suggests lighthearted childhood against the background of a somber ghetto courtyard. Here in subtle pastels he depicts a group of children dancing with abandon. They seem to be oblivious to their surroundings. In contrast, Halina Olomuzcki's pencil sketch of two gaunt women hovering over a child conveys the anguish of ghetto life.

Yet another view of ghetto life is conveyed by an earlier Szylis work dated 1940. This is a portrait of Chaim Rumkovski, Altester of the Lizmanstadt Ghetto, executed against the backdrop of the ghetto's barbed wire enclosure. In the foreground a burial party with a group of ghetto inhabitants (men, women and children) are clustered together. Their faces are turned to him for help and encouragement. His clothing, like theirs, is marked with the Star of David linking the commonality of their fate. [154]

The sketches made by Alexander Bogen during his Vilna ghetto period are not so much symbolic of a mood as they were meant to record Jewish resistance in and around Vilna. Bogen, who himself was one of the organizers of the resistance movement in the Vilna ghetto and helped 300 young people escape from the ghetto to a partisan unit in the woods beyond the city, made charcoal sketches of partisan fighters individually and in group settings. They are clearly primitive sketches executed hurriedly in the field under the most adverse conditions. [155]

Two unique objets d'art have survived from the Lodz ghetto. The first is a silver bracelet executed by an unknown craftsman in 1942. Its five links or panels depict ghetto scenes in vivid detail: ghetto inmates at various tasks and the wooden bridge that linked the two sections of the ghetto. The second is a hooked rug, also by an unknown craftsman, depicting two men at a loom in one of the ghetto workshops. [155]

Perhaps the most symbolic work in the collection of ghetto art is a black and white sketch which appears to have been executed by an unknown artist. It is futuristic, prophetic, and apocalyptic in character. [157] In bold strokes the artist depicts a vision of a new day dawning after the forces of darkness have been drowned by the forces of light. His message is conveyed by volcanic eruptions which cause the sea to break through a restraining dam in a floodtide. In the distance a ship is sailing away into the bright sunshine, thus expressing a vision of ultimate hope rather than despair.

There can hardly be a better recapitulation of this chapter than the words from an introductory brochure prepared for an exhibit of Holocaust art held in Haifa in 1952:

> All these pictures are important not only because they are living testimony of the shattering Hitler era but also because they reveal the inner spiritual strength of man, the life-giving quality hidden deep within our people. Even when the Holocaust was at its height, these artists found the fortitude to take pen or pencil in

hand and to set down for posterity the horrors they saw around them. [158]

This mood of defiance and hope is vividly caught in a woodcut which became a poster. It was executed by an unknown artist in the Warsaw ghetto, its caption *Mir Velen Leben* — *"We Shall Live"*. It depicts a group breaking out of the confines of the ghetto. It serves as a fitting climax, underscoring the will of the Jewish people ground into the dust by Hitler and Nazism if not to survive at least to live with hope and to die with dignity.

---

1. *See* Appendix XI.

2. Moshe Prager, ed., *Min Hametzar Karati* ("I Call from out of the Depth") (Jerusalem: Hotza-at Mosad Harav Kuk, 1954) p. 13.

3. From an interview with the artist Alexander Bogen in New York City on May 5, 1975. Tape I, no. 525.

4. Nachman Blumenthal, *Shemu-esen vegn der Yiddisher Literature unter der Nazi Occupatzyah* ("Conversations about Yiddish Literature During the Nazi Occupation") (Buenos Aires: Central Farband Polish Jews in Argentina, 1966) p. 113.

5. Prager, *Op. Cit.*, p. 9.

6. Moshe Prager, *"Shirey Am Govaya"* ("Poetry of A Dying People") *Davar Annual* (1946-1947) p. 298.

7. *Ibid.*, p. 299.

8. Dawidowicz, *Op. Cit.*, pp. 342-343.

9. Nachman Blumenthal, "Songs and Melodies in the Ghettos and Camps," *Yediot Yad Vashem*, II (28 Tamuz 5714) p. 2.

10. Leib Garfunkel, *Kovno Hayehudit B'Churbanah* ("Jewish Kovno Destroyed") (Jerusalem: Yad Vashem, 1959) Literary supplement, p. 301, "Lichvod der Grammen Fabrikatzie in Getto."

11. Blumenthal, *Op. Cit.*, p. 135.

12. *Ibid.*, p. 35.

13. *Supra.*, pp. 69-80.

14. Shmerke Katcherginsky, *Leider fun Gettos un Lagern* ("Songs from Ghettos and Camps") (New York: CyCo Books, 1949) p. 314. Translated from Yiddish.

15. Abraham Sutzkever, *Poetishe Werk* 2 vols., (Tel-Aviv: Private printing,

1963) Vol 2. p. 253. "Glust Zich Mir tzu ton a Tfillah" ("I Feel the Need to Pray,').

16. *Ibid.*, p. 285. "Unter Dieneh Vayseh Shtern ("Beneath your White Stars") Translated from the Yiddish by Gertrude Hirschler.

17. Yitzchak Katzenelson, *Al Naharot Bavel* ("By the Rivers of Babylon") (Beit Lochamai Hageta-ot, Israel: Katzenelson Ghetto Fighters' Institute, 1966) p. 38.

18. "Getto Dirot" ("Ghetto Dwellings") Unzer Lieder Zamlung. *Fun Letzen Churban* (September 1946) p. 76.

19. Yitzchak Katzenelson, *Ketavim Acharonim* ("Last Writings") (Beit Lochamai Hageta-ot, Israel: Katzenelson Ghetto Fighters' Institute, 1968–1969) p. 42. "Shfoch Hamathka" ("Pour Forth Thy Wrath").

20. Katcherginsky, *Op. Cit.*, p. 121.

21. Prager, *Op. Cit.*, p. 221. Anon., "Tateh Derbarem Dich . . ." ("Have pity, O Father . . ."). Translated from the Yiddish by Gertrude Hirschler.

22. Katcherginsky, *Op. Cit.*, p. 357, Leib Rosenthal, "Mir Lebn Aybik" ("We'll Live Forever"). Translated from the Yiddish by Gertrude Hirschler.

23. Katzenelson, *Op. Cit.*, pp. 59–64, "Avoy Lecha," ("Woe to You").

24. Katcherginsky, *Op. Cit.*, p. 103. Diskant, "Mein Klryner Martyrer" ("My Little Martyr").

25. Katzenelson, *Al Naharot Bavel, Op. Cit.*, pp. 89–90. *See* Ezekiel, chapter 34.

26. Katcherginsky, *Op. Cit.*, p. 19, Katriel Broido, "Mir Zenen Oich fun Fleysh un Blut" ("We, Too, Are Made of Flesh and Blood").

27. *Ibid.*, p. 300.

28. Garfunkel, *Op. Cit.*, pp. 271-273.

29. Katzenelson, *Ketavim Achronim, Op. Cit.*, pp. 52ff., "Hashir Shel Shelomo Zalechowski." ("Shelomo Zalechowski's Song"). The incident it describes was reported in the underground weekly newspaper *Yediot*, June 7, 1942.

30. Katcherginsky, *Op. Cit.*, pp. 34–35. Katriel Broido, "Es Shlogt di Sha-ah" ("The Hour Approaches,').

31. Shmerke Katcherginsky, *Dos Gesang fun Vilner Ghetto*, ("Vilner Ghetto Song") (Paris: Farband or Vilna Jews in France, 1947) p. 44. Katriel Broido, "Tzum Bessern Morgen" ("Towards a Better Tommorrow").

167

32. Garfunkel, *Op. Cit.*, p. 269. Abraham Axelrod, "Hafort Hatshe-ee" ("The Ninth Fort").

33. *Ibid.*, p. 317. Abraham Chipkin, "Hoffenung" (Hope).

34. Y. Kaplan, ed., *Fun Letzten Hurban*, Journal of the Historical Commission of the Central Committee of Liberated Jews in the American Zone, 1948, p. 26. Abraham Chipkin, "Unzer Lebn" (Our Life).

35. Prager, *Op. Cit.*, p. 96. Shmerke Katcherginsky, "Shtiller, Shtiller" ("Quietly, Quietly").

36. Muki Tzur, ed., The Holocaust (New York: American Zionist Youth Foundation, n.d.) p. 59. "Zog Nisht Kein Mol" (Never Say That This is the Last Road). Glick (1922-1944) who lived in Vilna wrote initially in Hebrew and later in Yiddish. On the eve of World War II he edited *Yungvald*, the organ of young Yiddish poets. He was interned in Vilna and subsequently at various labor camps. En route to the Goldfeld camp in Estonia, he escaped and was never heard from again.

37. *Erev Freihling, 1942* ("A Spring Eve, 1942") (Givat Haviva, Israel: Moreshet Archives, D2, 981).

38. Prager, *Op. Cit.*, p. 191. Shmerke Katcherginsky. "Shtay Oif Zum Kampf" ("Stand Up and Fight").

39. Knesset Bialik (Tel-Aviv: Hotza-at Dvir, 1945) pp. 29-30.

40. Katzenelson, *Al Naharot Bavel, Op. Cit.*, pp. 24-25.

41. The Hebrew title is taken from the opening verse of Chapter 12 of the book of Genesis. "The Lord said to Abraham: Go thou forth from thy native land and from thy father's house . . ."

42. S. Shayevitch, *Lekh Lekha* (Lodz: Central Jewish Historical Committee of Polish Jews, 1946) pp. 31-45. The word *Echad* refers to the Jewish affirmation of faith, "Hear O Israel, the Lord Our God, the Lord is One".

43. Katcherginsky, *Op. Cit.*, pp. 328-329. Diskant, "Genug Tzu Tzittern" ("Enough of Trembling').

    See also: Prager, *Op. Cit.*, p. 46. Anon., "Zei Freylich" ("Rejoice!"); p. 91. Abraham Sutzkever, "Es Shtayt der Toyt far di Oygen" ("Death Stares Us in the Face").

44. Bleicher, untitled poem (Givat Haviva, Israel, Moreshet Archives D-2-44). *See also*: Katcherginsky, *Op. Cit.*, p. 269. Adam Singer, "Kop Hoych" ("With Head Held High").

45. *Op. Cit.* Katcherginsky. p. 324. Frank is Hans Frank the Nazi Governor of the General

Governor of the General Government of Poland. Translated from the Yiddish by Gertrude Hirschler.

46. *Ibid.*, p. 118.

47. Hersh Glick, *Leider un Poemes* ("Songs and Poems") (New York: Ichuf Farlag, 1953) p. 54. Translated from the Yiddish by Gertrude Hirschler.

48. *Ibid.*, p. 60.

49. Meir Gutman *Farvolkente Teg ("Clouded Days")* (Bergen Belsen: Farlag Alin, 1949) pp. 71, 75.

50. Yeshayahu Spiegel, *Un Gevarn Iz Likht* ("It Became Light") (Warsaw: Farlag Yiddish Buch, 1949) p. 115.

51. Kaplan, *Op. Cit.*, p. 95. Abraham Axelrod, "Yiddishe Brigades" (Jewish Brigades).

52. Quoted in Berl Mark's introduction to the Polish version of Skalow's book, *Swastyka nad Gettem*, Warsaw 1954.

53. L. Olitzki, ed. *Tzvishn Lebn un Toyt* ("Between Life and Death") (Warsaw: Farlag Yiddish Buch, 1955) p. 5. Introduction by Berl Mark.

54. *Ibid.*, p. 17, *Vi A Bahaltener Vazzer Kval fun Unter der Erd* ("Like A Hidden Stream Beneath the Earth").
See also: Author's interview with Isaiah Spiegel, January 10, 1973, Tape I numbers 44-217, *passim*.

55. Olitzki, *Op. Cit.*, pp. 142-147 (the text of Yehoshua Perle's story *4580*) pp. 148-149.

56. *Ibid.*, pp. 143-145.

57. Rivkah Kviatkovsky-Pinchasik, "Shabbes" ("The Sabbath") in *Hent* ("Hands") (Haifa: n.n., 1957) p. 51.

58. Isaiah (Shaye) Spiegel, "Nokh Minha" ("After the Afternoon Prayers") in *Menshen in Tehom* ("People in the Depths") pp. 76-79. (Buenos Aires: Farlag Ikuf, 1949) p. 75.

59. *Ibid.*, p. 39. "Vedibarta Bom". The title of this story, "And thou shalt speak of them," refers to the first paragraph of the *Shema* prayer, "And these words which I command thee this day, shall be upon thy heart ... and thou shalt speak of them ... " (Deuteronomy 6:7).

60. *Ibid.*, p. 81.

61. Olitzki, *Op. Cit.*, pp. 30-34 (the text of Joseph Kirman's story, "Der Hessed fun a Shtillen Toyt" (The Mercy of a Peaceful Death") p. 30.

62. Spiegel, *Op. Cit.*, pp. 25-27.

63. Zalman Skalow, *Der Hakenkreitz* ("The Swastika") (Warsaw: Farlag Yiddish Buch, 1954) p. 52.

64. Olitzki, *Op. Cit.,* pp. 73-95, "A Shpatzir Ibber di Punkt," ("A Walk About Town"), p. 78.
See also: Ibid., Joseph Kirman "Ikh Red Tzu Dir Offen Meyn Kind," ("I Speak to you Openly My Child"), p. 35.

65. Skalow, *Der Hakenkreitz, Op. Cit.,* p. 125.

66. Olitzky, *Op. Cit.,* p. 38. Kirman's "Ikh Red Tzu Dir Offen Mein Kind".

67. *Ibid.,* pp. 100-141 (text of Yehoshua Perle's story "Churban Warsaw" — "The Destruction of Warsaw") p. 132.

68. Spiegel, "Mekle," *in Menshen in Tehom, Op. Cit.,* p. 63.

69. Isaiah Spiegel, "Der Himmel fun Onkel Teodor" ("Uncle Theodore's Heaven") in *Shtern Ibern Getto* ("Stars Over the Ghetto") (Paris: Biblioteck Organizatyah fun der Polishe Yidin in Frankreich, n.d.) pp. 55-64.

70. Rivkah Kviatkovsky-Pinchasik, "Hamesh Dakot L'shevah" ("5 to 7") trans. Y. Ben Elezer in *B'Yadayim Ne-emanot* ("Faithful Hands") (Haifa: Agudat Sofrei V'itonei Yiddish B'Haifa, 1964) p. 111.

71. *Ibid.,* p. 114.

72. *Ibid.,* pp. 25-26.

73. Isaiah Spiegel, "Halom" ("A Dream") in *Ohr Ma-amake Tehom,* ("Light From the Depths"). Trans., A. D. Shpir and Benjamin Teneh (Tel-Aviv: Y. L. Peretz, 1969) p. 193.

74. Spiegel, "Kinnah Al Bitte Hamaytah" ("Lament for My Dead Daughter") in *Ohr Ma-amake Tehom, Op. Cit.,* p. 125.

75. Kviatkovsky-Pinchasik, "Bayn Shte Halukot" ("Between Two Distributions of Food") *B'Yadayim Ne-emanot, Op. Cit.,* pp. 62-74.

76. Spiegel, "Goldene Yoch," in *Menshen in Tehom, Op. Cit.,* p. 76. The title refers to the soup customarily served to newlyweds as they break traditional fast immediately following the wedding ceremony.

77. Spiegel, "Yehudim" ("Jews") in *Ohr Ma-amake Tehom, Op. Cit.,* p. 14.

78. Yehuda Feld, "Gayrush PK," ("The Expulsion from P.K.") in *In Di Tzeiten fun Haman dem Tsveytem* ("In the Days of Haman the Second") (Warsaw: Farlag Yiddish Buch, 1954) p. 54. Before leaving the ghetto for the "Aryan" side, Feld advised a friend that he had buried his ghetto writings beneath a tree on Genshe St., 43. His writings, including this story, were included in the Ringelblum materials found in 1946.

79. Spiegel, "Di Mishpokhe Lifshitz Gayt in Ghetto," ("The Lipschutz Family goes to the Ghetto") in *Shtern Ibern Getto, Op. Cit.,* p. 5.

80. Isaiah Spiegel, *Malkut Hagetto* ("Ghetto Kingdom") (Tel Aviv: Hotza-at Hakibbutz Hameuchad, 1953) p. 9. Introduction by Dov Sadan.

81. Appendix XII. "Yomano Shel Almoni Mi-ghetto Lodz," ("Anonymous Ghetto Diary") (Diary from an Unknown in the Lodz Ghetto), facsimile (Jerusalem: Yediot Yad Vashem, 1970, No. 2) p. 8.

82. Appendix XIII.

83. Mordekhai Zar-Kavod, *"Yoman shel Menachem Oppenheim Mighetto Lodz,"* *Sinai,* Vol. 14, nos., 5-6, 1951, p. 272.

84. Kruk, *Op. Cit.,* pp. 195-197, *passim.*

85. Zelig Kalmanovitch, "Der Geist in Ghetto" ("The Spirit of the Ghetto") *Yivo Bleter,* Winter 1947, Vol. XXX, No. 2, pp. 170-171. The original Yiddish text includes the English words "Happy End."

86. Zelig Kalmanovitch, *Op. Cit.,* p. 52.

87. *Ibid.,* p. 44.

88. *Ibid.,* pp. 65-66.

89. *Ibid.,* p. 25.

90. *Ibid.,* p. 42.

91. *Ibid.,* pp. 24-25.

92. Yitzchak Rudashevski, *The Diary of the Vilna Ghetto,* trans., by Percy Matenko (Israel: Beyt Lohamai Haghetaot and Hakibbutz Hameuchad Publishing House, 1973) pp. 108-110.
See also: Appendix XIV.

93. See p. 67.

94. Rudashevski, *Op. Cit.,* p. 135.

95. *Ibid.,* pp. 99-100.

96. *Ibid.,* pp. 103-104.

97. *Ibid.,* pp. 104-105.

98. *Ibid.,* p. 121.

99. *Ibid.,* p. 121.

100. Kruk, *Op. Cit.,* pp. 45, 51-55, 191-193, 229-232, 252, 268, 308, 315, 328-329,

335, 424, 462, 466, 470.

101. *Ibid.*, pp. 179, 319-323, 329, 344-350, 368-369, 376-377, 412, 418-419, 421, 448, 464, 487.

102. *Ibid.*, pp. 108-110, *passim*.

103. Abraham Levin, "Keta Mitokh Yomano, ("A Chapter of our Lifetime") *Kovetz Mechkarim B'Farashat Hashoah V'hagvurah*, ("Collected Papers on the Holocaust and Heroism"), Vol. VI Yad Vashem, (1966) p. 284.

104. Abraham Levin, "Fun Ghetto Togbukh," ("From a Ghetto Daybook") *Bleter far Geshikte* ("Historical Paper") Jewish Historical Institute for Polish Jews, Vol. 5, No. 4, (1952), p. 67.

105. *Ibid.*, p. 67.

106. Chaim A. Kaplan, *Megilat Yesurim* trans., Joseph Rudavsky (Jerusalem: Hotza-at Am Oved and Yad Vashem, 1966) pp. 202-203.

107. *Ibid.*, pp. 513-514.

108. *Ibid.*, p. 324.

109. *Ibid.*, pp. 430-431.

110. *Ibid.*, pp. 432-433.

111. Peretz Opotinsky, *Reshimot* ("Reminiscences") (Kibbutz Lohamai Hageta-ot Beyt Lohamai Hagetaot al shem Yitzchak Katzenelson, 1970) pp. 243-244.

112. *Ibid.*, pp. 107-108.

113. *Ibid.*, p. 231.

114. Peretz Opotinsky, *Reportazhen fun Varshever Ghetto* ("Reportage From the Warsaw Ghetto") (Warsaw: Farlag Yiddish Buch, 1954) p. 87.

115. *Ibid.*, p. 137.

116. Emanuel Ringelblum, *Ketavim Fun Ghetto*, ("Ghetto Writings") 2 vols. (Warsaw: Farlag Yiddish Buch and Jewish Historical Institute, n.d.) Vol. I, p. 120.

117. *Ibid.*, p. 377.

118. *Ibid.*, p. 380.

119. *Ibid.*, p. 375.

120. *Ibid.*, p. 319.

121. *Ibid.*, pp. 128, 249, 324.

122. *Ibid.*, p. 263.

123. *Ibid.*, p. 234.

124. Terrence Des Pres, *The Survivors, An Autonomy of Life in The Death Camps* (New York: Oxford Press, 1976) p. 64.

125. Pesya Shereshevsky, *Karne Ohr B'makhskhe Hatofes* ("Beams of Light in the Darkness of Hell") (B'nai Brak: n. pub., 1968), p. 223.

126. Aryeh Lerner, "Art in the Valley of Death," introductory essay in Esther Lurie's portfolio, *Sketches from a Woman's Labour Camp* (Tel-Aviv: S. L. Peretz Publishing Co., 3rd ed., 1962) pp. 7-8.

127. Dworzetsky, *Op. Cit.*, p. 239.

128. Garfunkel, *Op. Cit.*, p. 236.
See also: Esther Lurie, "M'reshimoteha Shel Tzayeret" ("From an Artist's Notebook"), *Dapim L'chayker Hashoah V'hamered, Beyt Lochamai Hagetaot*, (February 1952) p. 163.

129. Dworzetsky, *Op. Cit.*, p. 245.

130. Shner, "Letoldot Hahayyim Hatarbutiyim B'geto Lodz," ("The Story of Cultural Life in the Lodz Ghetto") *Op. Cit.*, p. 98.

131. Berg, *Op. Cit.*, pp. 101-102.

132. Shner, *Op. Cit.*, p. 99.

133. Lurie, *Op. Cit.*, p. 96.
See also: Author's taped interview with Hersz Szylis at Safed, Israel, December 22, 1972, Tape I, No. 259.

134. *Ibid.*, numbers 388-485.

135. *Ibid.*, p. 306.

136. Lurie, *Op. Cit.*, pp. 93, 98.

137. Szylis, *Op. Cit.*, numbers 271-275.

138. Author's taped interview with Alexander Bogen in New York City, May 8, 1975, Tape I, Number 544.

139. Joseph Sandel, *Plastishe Kinst by Yidin in Polen* ("Plastic Arts of Polish Jews") (Warsaw: Yiddish Buch, 1964) p. 19.

140. See Appendix. All paintings, sketches and art objects discussed in the text will be referred to by plate number.

141. Appendix XV, plate 1.

142. Appendix XV, plate 2.

143. Appendix XV, plate 3.

144. Appendix XV, plates 4 and 5.

145. Appendix XV, plate 6.

146. Appendix XV, plate 7.

147. Appendix XV, plates 8, 9, 10, 11, 12 and 13.

148. Appendix XV, plate 14.

149. Appendix XV, plate 15.

150. Appendix XV, plate 16.

151. Appendix XV, plate 17.

152. Appendix XV, plate 18.

153. Appendix XV, plates 19 and 20.

154. Appendix XV, plate 21.

155. Appendix XV, plates 22, 23, 24, and 25.

156. Appendix XV, plates 26 and 27.

157. Appendix XV, plate 28.

158. Introductory statement in the program published in honor of exhibit of "Holocaust and Resistance in Literature and Art," Haifa, February 12 — March 22, 1952.

Chapter Thirteen

Kiddush Hahayyim, in the Concentration Camps and Death Camps

The human spirit is characterized by its resiliency as it responds to all circumstances to which it is exposed, even those that are most dire and dehumanizing. The human spirit is faced with the choice of either succumbing to such circumstances or to rise above them, even if only for a brief period. Judaism, as it understands the nature of human beings, reflects this basic approach to the reality of the human psyche. Judaism teaches *U'vacharta Vahayyim*—choose life. It also proclaims the concept of *Kiddush Hahayyim*—the sanctity of life. Both are operative as long as possible, no matter what the conditions. The Holocaust was the most recent circumstance that tested the resiliency of the spirit for the Jew.

Kiddush Hahayyim focuses on the inner strength of the hapless victims of the *Shoah*. It plumbs the depths of this inner fortitude as it confronts the unspeakable horror that despite all the research still defies critical analysis and understanding. *Kiddush Hahayyim* provides a theological basis for those who maintained their humanity as a challenge to Nazi inhumanity. Those who incorporated *Kiddush Hahayyim* in their lives had no illusions about the future. They were not motivated by false hope, either. They did not deny the realities of their time but rose about the savage persecution that they suffered. They clung to humanity when there was no humanity demonstrating the strength of the spirit.

As this spirit was evident in the ghettos, it was also evident in the concentration camps whether they were transit camps, labor camps, holding camps, or death camps. There is ample documentary *evidence* that Jews trapped in these camps were motivated to continue to live their tortured lives as human beings, as Jews. Many were committed to maintain authentic Jewish behavior patterns in defiance of the Nazis as long as possible. They would not succumb to dehumanization. They were humans created in the divine image, *B'Tzelem Elohim,* as Eliezer Berkowitz notes:

> The significance of what we have called authentic Jewish
> Behavior is that even in the ghettos and the death camps there

175

were numerous Jews who determined their own lifestyles. In the midst of the SS Kingdom they established their own realm of Jewish continuity, giving structure to the wilderness into which they were cast . . .

The camps had their own geographic pattern, designed to serve the goals of the extermination squads. But for these Jews, some of the roads were not paths of SS-prescribed misery, but were transformed by them into paths of daily renewal. The authentic Jewish lifestyles superimposed a space-structure of meaningfulness on the camp geography of humiliation and degradation . . .[1]

However, there was a difference that should be noted between those trapped in these camps and those who were earlier trapped in the ghettos.

As already noted, after the beginning of World War II, Poland consti-tuted the first step taken by the Nazis in the process of the liquidation of the Jews. As the Jews were concentrated in the ghettos and isolated from the surrounding population, they became a slave labor pool to be exploit-ed both within and outside the ghettos. In addition, the ghetto served as a mechanism employed to dehumanize and completely disenfranchise the Jews. The Nazis sought to break their spirit, prohibiting communal and personal religious practices and observances, closing schools, rifling and closing libraries, and prohibiting cultural events.

At the same time, the Nazis initiated steps to destroy the Jews physi-cally through starvation diets, slave labor, and unsanitary living condi-tions, which caused such illness as typhus. Such practices resulted in an ever increasing death toll.

The ghettos served the Nazis not only as a site where they would destroy the spirit of the Jew through a process of dehumanization but they also functioned as the first step in the ultimate physical decimation of the Jewish community. The next step in the evolving process was the further development of the concentration camps, which were introduced early in Germany as the Nazis took power. They were set up initially to incarcer-ate internal adversaries of the Nazi regime—leftists, liberals, Communists, and so on. The first such camp was established in Dachau on March 22, 1933, as a response to the Reichstag fire. Initially, Jews were interned as part of those who were considered politically undesir-able. After Kristallnacht, November 9 and 10, 1938, Jews began to be interned in the camps simply because they were Jews.

Following the beginning of World War II, concentration camps were set up in occupied areas, initially in Poland, where they operated side by side with the ghettos. For the Nazis they served a number of purposes. Actually they were forced labor camps, providing the Germans with a readily available cheap labor pool for the German government agencies and private German industrial concerns in munitions, road building, ditch digging, airport construction, quarrying, and so forth. Camp inmates were ill housed, ill clothed, ill fed. They were frozen, starved, worked to death, and became prime candidates for rampant illnesses, particularly typhus. Thus in practice, concentration camps became death camps, for in addition to supplying the Nazis with an inexpensive disposable labor force, they became a method by which to dispose of unwanted Jews.

In March of 1941, when plans were formulated by the Germans for the invasion of Russia, new plans for the total elimination of the Jews began to be developed, first through the operation of the Einsatzgruppen, four specially trained squadrons totaling 3,000 men. Their task after the invasion of Russia on June 22, 1941, was simple: follow the four invading German armies, killing off both Communists and Jews. Wipe out Russian Jewish communities behind the lines of advancing German armies. Though they massacred some 500,000 individuals by December 31, 1941, the Nazi hierarchy questioned the efficiency of this method. As a result, six death camps were established: Belzec, Chelmo, Majdanek, Treblinka, Auschwitz, and Sobibor. These camps were death factories, their mission to incarcerate and gas Jews as part of the Final Solution—the Endelösung orchestrated at Wannsee, a Berlin suburb, on January 22, 1942.

Obviously life in the concentration and death camps differed from life in the ghettos. In the ghettos there was a semblance of a community. There was an officially structured community which was established through the operation of the *Judenrat* mandated by the Nazis. In addition, a clandestine underground organizational structure was established by ghetto residents. In the ghetto, despite the formal and informal structure, there was chaos. Yet despite starvation, rampant disease, and slave labor, a pattern of spiritual life emerged.

In contrast, within the concentration camps and the death camps, there was no functioning, organizational structure. By way of comparison, the camps from the prisoner's viewpoint were a descent into purgatory. There were only individuals seeking to survive yet another day under the whiplash of the Nazis. Tormented, diseased, ravaged by hunger, there was neither the opportunity nor the inclination to create any semblance of community. This not withstanding, there is evidence that even within the camps a spiritual life continued on both an individual and group basis. There is documentation that trapped Jews were motivated to continue to live their tortured lives as Jews, as human beings. There were those who were committed to maintain a semblance of authentic Jewish behavior patterns as long as possible in defiance of the Nazis. They would not be dehumanized.

In the concentration and death camps, such individuals were determined to carry on with some semblance of human dignity as Jews. They were motivated by the same fundamental drives that were operative earlier in the ghettos. Some carried on their religious lives, others expressed their experiences and emotions through poetry, a few artists sketched, still others resorted to study, remembering fragments of text they had once known. A few attempted to develop clandestine cultural religious events. Some acted as individuals, while others were catalysts who succeeded in involving still others to share with them, particularly in the area of religious observances and cultural events. Most of such activities were one-time events clandestine in nature. If discovered by their Nazi captors, harsh punishment, even death, resulted.

The materials available to us reveal a complex picture of a struggle to maintain a sense of commitment to the maintenance of humanity through sporadic spiritual activity, clandestine religious improvisation, literary and artistic creativity.

Religious Activities:
Individual and Communal Ritual and Festival Observances

The power of religious bonds serves as an unequaled spiritual force that projects the image of the sanctity of the individual human being. It does so through the encounter with the Divine as well as in relationship to other human beings. For the Jew trapped in the concentration camps, even in the death camps, the will to live and to sanctify life reflected his affirmation of the Divine human encounter. It manifested itself in the determination to carry out Jewish religious practices as fully as possible in the given dire circumstances. Through such practices, the Jew substantiated his commitment not to lose the Divine human image, the *Tzelem Elohim,* which was an integral part of his being, as well as to affirm his relationship with God.

Despite the harsh circumstances that prevailed in the camps, the drive to fulfill one's religious obligations became the catalyst, particularly for the observant Jew. His life revolved around them. He was prepared to endure any hardship to fulfill the demands of his faith as best as he could. This commitment often aroused the dormant, submerged, repressed feelings of those who were estranged from Judaism. This commitment even reached those who completely turned their backs on the Jewish heritage, its culture and faith.

> . . . Among prisoners not educated religiously or who did not pray or fulfill other religious rituals there were those who tried to the best of their ability to help others to pray. Often they would take part in *Minyanim* [quorums for prayers—ten men] that were organized to enable their mourning companions to repeat the Kaddish [memorial prayer] properly.[2]

These imprisoned Jews were motivated by their faith and its meaning for them. It is reported that in the Sakalat camp many of the camp's inmates sought consolation and strength through faith and worship. Faith, inner strength and prayer could sometimes set aside evil decrees. Hasidic young men like Michael Klein, Asher Netter, Nissin Miting and others secretly prayed, observed *yarziet* [annual memorial prayers commemorating a death] and Kaddish. They achieved some beautiful moments in a life so sad. Even religious rebels gained inner strength, which led to moments of liberation and redemption, if not of the body, at least of soul.[3]

Such individuals, admittedly relatively few in number, who tried to carry on some form—better still, any form—of observance, personally or with others, were hampered by many things. Among them it is important to list the almost impossible rigorous living and working conditions in the concentration camps, conditions that sapped the strength of hapless internees and allowed little time for anything but work. The continuous shadow of death hung over them, resulting from perpetual all-consuming illness and ravenous hunger, which eroded the will to live. Add to this the ever present haunting fear of discovery by their Nazi captors. Such discovery brought with it severe punishment and often death.

In addition, there were problems of a different nature that had to be confronted, such as a lack of Jewish calendars by which they could chart their religious lives. There were those who painstakingly reconstructed by memory calendars to guide their lives. They lacked prayer books, Bibles, and other religious texts. Yet they reconstructed prayers in their proper sequence, Biblical passages both short and long remembered by heart, selections from the Mishnah and the Talmud that were recalled. They scrawled them on scraps of paper and fragments of cardboard. They recalled the words of study; they remembered the words of prayer.

Lacking the religious objects of Judaism they improvised, making Sabbath candles, fabricating Hanukkah menorahs, secretly baking *Matzah* (unleavened bread) for Passover, setting up a camouflaged *Sukkah*, or passing one phylactery from hand to hand.

The religious objects they managed to assemble were more than physical things. They represented the triumph of the spirit. They recalled the inner meaning of the object in question. Sabbath candles were no more than bits of tallow or drops of oil that they managed to save or find. For a brief moment it brought with it Sabbath tranquillity and the proximity of God. The *ersatz Matzah* that they somehow baked rekindled hope. Building a makeshift *Sukkah* secreted away in some hidden concentration camp corner linked them again to their people's past and gave them something to cling to.

We share a telling passage describing the meaning of *Shabbat*—the Sabbath day. Its observance represented a wellspring of faith, consolation, and hope for Jews in normal circumstances. How much more so in camps! The feelings that it expresses about the Sabbath can be applied also to other festivals.

> Despite the persecution and the attacks, the Jews gathered strength; clandestinely, though their lives were endangered, they continued to observe the Sabbath and the Holidays. . . . The children of Israel diligently and enthusiastically fulfilled the Sabbath and Festival requirements to the best of their ability. In this way they expressed the will to live which resonated in them as well as their hope that they will yet see the defeat of their oppressor enabling them to again observe their festivals properly. Even those who prior to the Holocaust did not carefully observe now grasped at every opportunity to join observant Jews and sought ways to return to their wellspring.

> Though faced by the terrible reality that their lives hung in the balance, the Jews found a measure of consolation and strength in the Sanctity of the Sabbath: "On the Sabbath we feel a joyous, extra soul in our innermost being." Kindled Sabbath candles filled them with faith and trust in the most difficult of moments: "A new soul filled the individual— nobler, better and purer."[4]

Under the most terrible of circumstances, Jewish women labored unceasingly to fulfill the commandment to kindle Sabbath candles. We note a telling incident of a woman leading the death march holding burning Sabbath candles. In Auschwitz, when their tormentors tried to destroy the Divine image, Jewish women kindled Sabbath candles.[5]

Attempts were made to observe every holiday in one fashion or another, to fulfill every religious requirement with the same devotion and conviction with which the Sabbath was observed. Surviving materials and survivors' memoirs, written or verbal, shed light on these practices. We do not know how many carried out these observances, but regardless of the numbers, these activities strengthened the morale of the victims who did so.

Passover was particularly significant. Its message of the liberation of ancient Israelites from Egyptian slavery resonated with meaning for them. It was more than a reminder of an ancient moment in history. It was replete with contemporary relevance. Typical of the mood that prevailed was a report of a Passover seder conducted in Auschwitz, entitled "The Song *Chad Gadyah* in Auschwitz."

> . . . Of all the melodies that he sang to us he was most moved when he sang "*Chad Gadyah*," then all of us thought that we were overpowering and defeating the Kapos, the Blockelester and the destroying Satan himself.

Izzi-Motel sang "*Chad Gadyah*" softly and sweetly as though he wanted us to understand its hidden message. Who was "*Chad Gadyah*" that father bought, and what was its fate? When he came to the end of the song he raised his trembling voice, shaking up all of us: "And the Holy One, Blessed Be He, appeared and slaughtered the slaughterer" . . . he repeated with emphasis, "And the Holy One, Blessed Be He, slaughtered the slaughter." We awoke with a shiver, for each of us understood exactly who the slaughterer was and that soon his end, brought about by the Holy One, Blessed Be He, would engulf him.[6]

There were numerous attempts to conduct seders in the camps. Of course they were clandestine, with few, if any, of the normal Passover symbols such as *Matzah* (unleavened bread) *maror* (bitter herbs) Wine, *Hagadot* (the narrative retelling the story of Passover). Attempts were made to provide the necessary symbols. From scraps of grain begged, bartered, or stolen, *Matzah* was baked in storage sheds, barracks, or warehouses. As for bitter herbs, *Maror*, their living conditions reflected the real bitterness of actual slavery and was its ample symbol. With such symbols the prisoners found it possible to conduct something resembling a seder in a ritual sense.[7]

Other holy days were equally significant and were observed in one way or another in the camps. The ten-day period that begins with Rosh Hashanah (the New Year) and concludes with Yom Kippur (the Day of Atonement) marked a period of critical personal spiritual meaning. These were days of introspection, self-reassessment, and reconciliation for the individual, rebuilding one's relationship with God and restoring one's faith. It was also a time when the individual pondered his relations with other human beings, his future, and his life in the days to come. Traditionally, one's life or death was determined during this period. The tenth day, Yom Kippur, the Day of Atonement, the great white fast, was a day of prayer and reflection. Its mood was set a sunset with the solemn chanting of the *Kol Nidre* prayer, the age-old prayer filled with haunting words chanted to a heartfelt melody. Next to the *Shema*, the Jewish affirmation of faith, *Kol Nidre* is perhaps the most meaningful and moving Jewish prayer.

For the Jews trapped in the camps, the reflections of women in the Stutthof camp defines and describes the feeling of the day.

> Silence, holy silence. Yom Kippur! Thousands of Jewish women lay row on row on boards covered with naked straw. Not one was angry, not one bothered her neighbor. This was *Kol Nidre* night. Suddenly we heard a ringing voice, the voice of the woman whom we called the camp head: "My sisters,

today is Yom Kippur, the ancient holiday of love and for-
giveness. But it is also the day when we are inscribed either
in the book of life or the book of death. My sisters, even
though few of us doubt that we will be inscribed in the book
of death, we must believe and hope nevertheless . . . with this
faith, with this hope we pray that next Yom Kippur will find
us returned to health united with our families in our own
homes."[8]

To better understand the mood of Jews trapped in the camps, it is
important to note that joyous holidays contrasting sharply with their tragic lives were not neglected. Holidays such as Hanukkah, Tisha Asar
Bishvat, and Sukkot were observed. The gaiety these holidays required,
the affirmation of life they signified, the commitment to Jewish survival
they called for, stood in stark contrast to the reality of life and death in the
camps. Yet ways and means were found to observe these holy days in this
way to dispel a little of the gloom and despair the prisoners encountered.
Such observances helped to lift their spirits and distilled hope when hopelessness abounded.

On Purim, for example, there were those who through memory con-
trived to recall the *Megillah*, the Biblical scroll that recalls in part the story
of Haman, an ancient historic tormentor of the Jews. His fate forecast the
fate of Adolf Hitler, their contemporary tormentor. We have a typical
memoir of Purim observed in the Buchenwald concentration camp:

Actually, for several days with my remaining strength I
gathered scraps of paper in the camp's courtyard—bits and
pieces of Nazi interoffice memos; pieces of heavy bags used
for concrete or empty borders of salvageable pages from
illustrated Nazi newspapers. I gathered them very carefully,
for I was determined to write the scroll of Esther from memory on them.

We distributed the scraps of paper to several members of our
group. We had one pencil, that is to say not a pencil but a bit
of lead from some pencil fragments that workers and carpenters discarded. It passed from hand to hand. Each wrote a passage of the Megillah that he remembered . . . at the end of the
'Fast of Esther' all of us assembled at the appointed hour on
the barracks' highest bunk. The reading itself took place with
an elevated mood and an enthusiastic spirit: Most important,
when we completed the *Megillah* reading we began to sing
Shoshanat Yaacov aloud. Our song burst forth from our lips
with fury. It seemed to us that the whole of Buchenwald held
its breath and listened to us trembling—'Cursed is Haman

182

who sought my destruction, blessed is Mordecia, Mordecia
the Jew!'

Next morning we awoke and dragged our feet as usual.
Nevertheless something changed in the camp's atmosphere,
since we dared to call out aloud 'Arur Haman'—'Cursed is
Haman!' It was clear to all who the 'Haman' was. As a result,
our terrible depression was eased a bit.[9]

On other holidays prisoners developed similar stratagems to avoid
their captors and to commemorate other meaningful religious occasions,
serving as their response to Nazi premeditated dehumanization.
Hanukkah, the festival of light marking the victory of ancient Israel over
the Syrian-Greeks and the restoration of the Jewish Commonwealth, was
another such moment. That ancient victory served as a goad and a catalyst, yielding hope and faith. The Jews maximized their efforts to
observe it with its proper and appropriate ritual. Rabbi Sinia Adler
recalls:

In our barracks, the youth barracks in Auschwitz, there were
young people from Greece . . . daily we would pray together
in a corner. Praying together and observing other mitzvot
[commandments] bound us together closer . . . at Hanukkah
time we were able to procure a candle. On the first night of
Hanukkah we gathered near the lowest bunk and lit the candle.

This burning candle kindled new hope in our hearts for a better future and strengthened our faith in the 'Rock of our salvation . . .' longings for the past were aroused in us, a past
when each observed Hanukkah in our parents' houses joyously. But that past has disappeared. There awoke within us
a persistent plea. It burst forth from the depths of our hearts
for the still distant future when our prayers that we chant will
be fulfilled, particularly the prayer "May our house of prayer
be restored, there will we offer thanks as we celebrate with
joy the dedication of the altar."[10]

It is obvious that religious observances and rituals played an important morale-sustaining role for those trapped in the camps. Attempts
were made to observe every ritual, every practice in one form or another. No holiday was neglected or abandoned. In addition to the holidays
already discussed, we note that Sukkot, which shares both agricultural
and historical meanings, was observed. The Sukkah—booth (symbolic of
both farmer's and Sinai Desert huts) was improvised in camp storage
sheds or barracks' overhanging roofs. Palm branches, Aravim (willow)
and Hadasin (myrtle), which make up the Lulav and Essrog (citron), the

plants symbolizing the holiday, were somehow found—never all four as required, but they made do with even one.[11]

Then there were those individuals who persisted in fulfilling such religious obligations as daily morning prayers, few with the required pair of *tefillin* (phylacteries). Others would satisfy their prayers with one phylactery, fulfilling their obligations with either the phylactery for the head or for the arm. Still others secretly gathered together to form a *minyan*, a quorum of ten required for communal prayer.[12]

There were those who comprehended the spiritual implications of continued study of the sacred texts—Torah, Prophets, the Writing, Mishnah, and Talmud and their copious commentaries. They appreciated the meaning of the saying *Talmud Torah K'neged Kulam*, "The Study of the Torah is equal to all other things." The sound of Torah study was not stilled despite restraints, persecution, and mortal danger. For the believing individual, continued study became a source of solace and strength. A survivor from the Birkernau death camp notes in his oral testimony . . . "I can say that this study so lightened our suffering and torture considerably that many of our fellow sufferers were jealous of us. . . ."[13]

Study also meant verbal rendition of remembered passages of the Bible, the Mishnah, or Talmud with appropriate commentaries or reference to hidden copies of a text.

Some repeated the texts they remembered quietly in their barracks, studying by themselves or with fellow prisoners. Others reviewed the words recalled as they marched from their barracks to the workplaces. Still others, in order to help those who did not remember the words, wrote the passages they recalled on scraps of paper. These in turn were passed from hand to hand.

We have sampled religious practices and observances in the camps. Individuals improvised; Jews, observant and nonobservant, turned inward to their tradition. This seemed to sustain them in their hour of trial. They clung to hope, perhaps naively, in light of the realities of their time. Yet for them it was real, it was meaningful, it was sustaining, proving to them that they were still human beings.

Cultural Activities as Experienced in the Camps

Religious life in all its forms was not the only means by which the victims of Nazi depredations sought to express their humanity, foiling the Nazi plans to dehumanize them and affirming their determination to cling to life. In the camps they expressed their commitment in a variety of ways, employing the full spectrum of cultural possibilities. There were poets and artists. Some were celebrated and recognized, others novices and unknown. All were determined to share their feelings, describing their cruel and inhumane living conditions. They also expressed their faith, their hopes, their visions of liberation and their future despite the horrors that they were experiencing. In addition to individual creativity, communal cultural events took place secretly, conducted by groups of prisoners.

We possess fragmentary information about these activities. They are available as a result of discoveries of caches of materials hidden away in the ruins of the camps and other places. These contain diaries, eyewitness reports, poems, songs, drawings, and music written or drawn on scraps of paper. These included notations describing clandestine cultural activities in the barracks that escaped the watchful eyes of the Germans or their collaborators.

In addition to the materials that were found following the war, another significant source is the oral history testimonies provided by the survivors. In reviewing the materials from Auschwitz, Majdanek, and Estonian camps such as Kluga, we may conclude that cultural activities were conducted in the camps side by side with artistic and literary works as well as fragmentary eyewitness reports that were created.

It is legitimate to conclude from available sources that in the camps, Jewish literary and artistic life was sustained by both well-known and little-known figures—writers, composers, and artists who employed their talents. They did so despite the dangers that confronted them. They did so alone or within the setting of the group. Concerning Auschwitz, Daniel Frishberg recalls in his "Darkness Covers the Earth":

> Sunday, 1:00 a.m., soon after I was transferred to the barracks, I noticed abnormal preparations. People gathered in the eating area; "the prominent ones" sat near the tables, the others nervous, huddled, waiting for something. I asked about the preparations and was told, tonight an artistic-literary gathering is planned, a regular happening in this barrack once every few weeks on Sundays during the night . . . For me this was something new. Since September 1939 I did not participate in literary evenings. I also knew that any cultural or communal gatherings in the camp was forbidden, strongly forbidden . . . Guards were stationed around the barracks to warn the participants of danger. People from other barracks also arrived . . . Joseph Potoshinksy opened the gathering; he was once an actor in the "Vilna Troupe" . . . His material came from classic Yiddish sources as well as Russian literature.
>
> Others took part in the program . . . I remember especially the two Goldman brothers from Cracow, thirty–year–old twins, who sang their own songs set to their own melodies about the camp realities . . .

185

I stood there mesmerized, in another world. I shared an abnormal experience, especially in the Auschwitz death camp, with a thirst. I drank every word, every phrase. The words of Gebertig's *Es Brent* shook me to the depths of my soul, words that did not lose their meaning over the years. Again I enjoyed the beauty and the folkish wisdom of Manger's songs, which I always loved, as I enjoyed other songs and stories. I lay awake for a long time on my bunk after the end of the program, and as I lay I could not fall asleep from excitement.

This first evening was more than a passing experience for me. It shook me up and lit my way. I was jealous of those who organized the evening. When I listened to the Goldman brothers I asked myself: Am I unable to create such a thing? Isn't it my responsibility to contribute to the literary evenings? My decision to try provided me with a meaning for my life in Auschwitz.[14]

There are other such instances that have been documented describing comparable happenings in other camps. Such secretive gatherings responded to the deep psychological needs of the trapped prisoners. These were emotional and spiritual needs that helped them defy their captors. Such happenings enabled a number of individuals to endure. In this regard, it is important to state that though the numbers were relatively small, the very fact that these morale-building cultural and spiritual events occurred are significant in and of themselves. Not only did these events take place, but often they served as catalysts to poets, songsters, and artists to express themselves through their talents. Their works in turn were coopted and used as part of such happenings.[15]

Nathan Livneh, in his volume *Women's War: The Story of a Nazi Forced Labor Camp (AEG)*, insightfully reveals the effects of such happenings on women prisoners. The camp in question was Kaiserwald, on the outskirts of Riga. The volume is anecdotal. Several of the anecdotes tell of the activities of Flora Rom Eisman. In this camp, 800 to 1,000 women were incarcerated. From the reports, Flora, who in prewar days was an architect, emerged as the catalyst of cultural events in the camp.

Flora Rom Eisman, in her anecdote entitled "The Struggle for a Healthy Soul," observes, "Just as hunger engulfed us, weakening and enervating us physically, so the lack of any cultural activities threatened us with spiritual disintegration whose results could be no less destructive and terrible then the living conditions. . . ."[16]

As a result, Flora Eisman set about to organize a puppet theater, which involved a group of women with the task of making puppets, sewing costumes, and arranging performances. The puppet theater triggered other cultural events, including literary and musical evenings, birthday celebrations, and even a "Hebrew speaking group." These activities enabled the women to withstand the humiliation, the hunger, the beating, the lice that they encountered.[17]

Shulamit Avarmiski, one of the women involved, remembering her experiences in the camp, shared her memories with her daughter ". . . that she should know that the war against Hitler was carried not only with arms. The strength of the moral resistance—to remain human under inhuman circumstances without the hope of remaining alive—this was our victory."[18] Livneh, who gathered this anecdotal material, concludes his epilogue with the following observation:

> This group of women, some in Israel, others in the diaspora, since their liberation maintain strong friendly ties . . . again they see themselves as a group continuing to weave the cord of hope of those days—a cord that united them and helped to overcome all the difficulties and trials to reach this moment, the hope and the determination that if they survived, at any price, to remain with a healthy and strong spirit. This was their special teaching in the camp. An individual can remain alive broken in body as long as the soul, "the divine image within" remains; that individual does not lose one's humanity but remains whole and human in all circumstances, no matter the cost.[19]

Art and Literature in the Camps

In an unsigned, undated introduction to what appears to be an art catalog entitled *Suffering and Hope—Artistic Creations of Oswiecem Prisoners*, the anonymous editor makes the following observations:

> How could anyone in a Nazi death camp, a 20th century hell invented by people for people, create works of art?

> That is the question that puzzles everyone who has ever seen the artistic productions of the Auschwitz prisoners.

> The answer to this question leads to a further series of questions, reaching right to the very essence of human nature. Perhaps the instinct for life is something more than simply the struggle for biological survival. Could the wish to leave behind some trace of one's individual existence be equally strong as the will to live? (How can one combat death inflicted with premeditation?) How to overcome fear? (How to leave behind one's own traces in the sand?) Maybe that was

187

what they were trying to do—to save just a tiny part of their human dignity.

To create works of art illegally in Auschwitz concentration camp meant intentionally risking interrogation, torture, camp arrest, or being transferred to the punishment squad, which was not infrequently the same as being sentenced to death . . .

It would be impossible to use merely artistic criteria to evaluate these works, bearing in mind the specific camp conditions in which they were created and the people who made them and finally the role they played in the camp. And yet this artistic creativity, dictated by the inner needs of the artist-prisoners, is not only of indisputable documentary value but the greater part also has qualifications for being placed among genuine artistic achievements. Moreover, an outstanding feature of all these works is their poignant authenticity, reflecting both physical and moral sufferings, and the power of their accusation. . . .[20]

This assessment of the nature of artistic endeavors may well be applied to the works of Jewish artists and by extension to the creations of literary figures trapped not only in Auschwitz but to all those caught in other camps.

Art and literature are two modes of expression through which the individual captures and articulates his or her inner self. The one through the words he or she writes, the other through the works of his or her hands expresses the deepest inner feelings not only of the particular artist or poet, but also those of the extended community of which they are a part. This was particularly true during the Holocaust.

They were the voices of the world that they shared. The visions they saw, the dreams they dreamt, the feelings they felt were not theirs alone. They were not unique. Through their words, through the images they created, they gave meaning, form and substance. They were the voices that articulated and formulated an understanding of their world and their time. They were determined to bear witness to the indescribable horror to which they were subject. To call out in protest to the world beyond the confines of their prison walls. They sought to reach out to the world that was so distant, so divorced from their plight with the cry, you are your brothers keepers.

Yet in their anguish they shared more. They shared idealized and romanticized memories of a life that ceased to exist as a result of the Nazi onslaught. The shtetl that disappeared, the homes that were no more, the villages that were leveled in the fury of war, the cities that were decimated, the families that were torn asunder. They evoked not only the physical life that was destroyed, but also the spiritual life that was uprooted.

The houses of study—the Yeshivoth that were vandalized. The Synagogues that lay in ruins. The sacred texts that were desecrated. The sainted spiritual leaders that were humiliated and then murdered.

Some artists and poets did not only bemoan the past; some looked to a future, a future that would be bright with hope that would certainly arise out of the ashes. Even if they individually would not survive, yet a new day would dawn and with it rebirth for their people that could not be denied. Their spirit would not be overwhelmed.

Artists, poets, and other literary figures trapped in the camps used their talents in this way. They did not use their artistic and literary talents to beat a hasty retreat, burying themselves in their work to escape the reality of suffering that engulfed them. They cried out—cried out as human beings, cried out as Jews. They sought to distill some measure of sanity and human sanctity from the chaos and insanity that trapped them. They sought not only solace but the strength to carry on, to dare to hope to record for posterity the agony of their lives, to give some meaning to their suffering, to testify that the will of the human spirit was a flame that could not be extinguished.

A review of available literary and artistic works, murals, their pencil sketches, their drawings, their watercolors on scraps of paper, as well as the poems they wrote and the fragmented diaries they kept—these items found hidden after the war in caches behind double walls, buried or given to sympathizing gentiles, represent a much larger volume of works from the concentration and death camps. These were works from both known and unsung artists and literary figures, works they created as they used improvised brushes, paints, and scraps of scavenged paper.

Whether their efforts were great *pieces* of art or literature is insignificant. Their literary and artistic quality is unimportant. The fact that they sketched, painted, or wrote under such circumstances is significant.

Currently there is available an increasing number of collections of these works, such as the Yad Vashem collections in Jerusalem, the Lohamei Hagetaot Museum collection, the United States Holocaust Memorial Museum, Yivo, and private collections.

In addition to these collections, various published works and albums presenting art executed in the concentration and death camps have been published.[21] Among the camps represented in these works, we can list the following: Drancy, Gurs, Buchenwald, Terezin, Bergen-Belsen, Stutthoff, Leibitsch, Tost, Nisko, Auschwitz, Birkenau, and their various subcamps. While the list of artists, some who survived with samples of their work, others who became victims but a few fragments of their work remain to attest to them, include such names as Georg Jiri Jilovsky, Edith Links, Jacques Makiel,[22] Louis Ascher, David Olere, Halina Olomucki, Uri Kochba, Yehuda Bacon, and Hirsh Shilis, among many others.[23]

We turn to *literature*, the genre most often discovered and cited, poetry, and song. In addition, there is evidence that in various camps prisoners kept what amounts to fragmentary diary notations and eyewitness reports, which unfortunately did not survive. Dworzetski reports that Herman Kruk, Yisrael Dimantman, and Hirsh Gutshtalt kept such diaries in Kluga.[24]

In his work, Dworzetsky focuses on the poetry and songs of the Estonian camps written by well-known poets such as Hirsh Glick, Katriel Broido, and Leib Rosenthal, among others. There are numerous others who wrote poetry, among them Yitchak Kominkovski. In his volume entitled *Songs from the Camp*, he describes life in Bleichhammer, an Auschwitz subcamp. These works were read at clandestine prisoner gatherings, while Zamy Feder collected several poetic works from Kaiserwald, Buchenwald, and Bergen-Belsen.[25]

In his monograph dealing with prisoners in the Estonian camp, Dworzetsky presents seven Yiddish poems that reflect the conditions, the spirit, and the trauma experienced in the Kluga, Kivilli, and Vevekon camps. In these well-crafted poems, the basic themes of the period are interwoven. They include descriptions of sufferings, anguish, and fear, accompanied by faith and hope. The Yiddish poem entitled "We'll Be Silent, We'll Be Still Now" was attributed to either Hirsh Glick or Katriel Broido. Zev Dormashkin set it to music. It is a prayerful invocation on the part of the poet of his mother against the backdrop of the fences that surround him and the guards that trap him as he raises the question, will this be his end?

> We'll Be Silent, We'll Be Still Now
>
> We'll be silent, we'll be still now
> Quiet, not a word;
> we will close our eyes and whisper
> a prayer barely heard.
> The fences that surround us,
> the soldiers standing guard,
> cannot forbid weeping
> that remains inward.
>
> Oh wind, don't pass over us,
> as though we were silent trees.
> Won't you, please, oblige us
> and carry our prayerful pleas?
> Fly fast, fast, oh wind,
> fly and please be quick.
> Bring warmest wishes
> to my mother, aged, sick.

Thousands of eyes,
many different ones, I know,
but you will recognize
my mother's by their special glow.
Relentlessly, she cries.
No chance for tears to dry.
From the camp her sad soul flies
to her child somewhere outside.

I send regards to her with you—
wind that blows far and wide;
she will see her child again
with her own yearning eyes.
The wind laughs and maybe
that is no laughter but a lament.
Is it whispering its secret to me
that here I will find my end?

I have questions for the wind. I'd ask
but my tears are a heavy weight.
The wind moves on so fast
it is already late.
We'll be silent we'll be still now
Quiet, not a word;
we will close our eyes and whisper
a prayer barely heard.[26]

Golda Gordonovitz is represented by four Yiddish poems she composed while in Estonian camps. "Spring," written in Kivilli in the spring of 1944, is a poem full of encouragement, hope, and optimism. The spring, the season of rebirth of faith and hope, is contrasted to the prisoner's suffering and pain. Yet these traumatic experiences are mitigated by the vision of a better day, bringing with it victory and freedom.

Spring

In the big beautiful world
it is already spring,
rich with fragrance and flowering.
Nature is awake once more
alive with magical splendor.

. . . in these huts, where we are—
enclosed in iron bars,
the sun has still not appeared
nor is there laughter here.
So much anguish and pain,

our suffering so great.
No one knows how long we can live like this,
how long can we wait?

. . . Yet our spirit is strong
we push our despair away,
our roots our deep
and we see a future day
when a new generation will appear
valiant and free of fear.
We will look ahead and trust,
to God we'll silently call
and pray for our foe's swift downfall.

When spring comes again and brings
a world of glories on its wings
who will compare to us?
The sun in full view,
we in our ancient land, renewed—
Once again, the sun
will light every space
every corner, every face.
We'll no longer worry,
Courage will replace fears
our spirit will emerge undaunted
from those awful years.

Filled with hope and confident
we will then arrive
our hearts intent
on a new life
joyous and bright
a life of labor, freedom, light.

And the world—
the world will marvel,
will gaze up at us,
at our courage,
and bow down
to our spirit, newly found,
to our fortitude and pluck,
our talent, our wondrous luck . . .[27]

Another of her poems, "*Ami*," "My People," is a moving piece of
work. Its opening verses depict the poetess torn by the fate of children.
She visualizes them silently filing beneath her window and asks, "Why?"
They seem lost, as though never born, without a mother's loving caress.

She bemoans and lament's her people's misfortune—its villages torched, its communities razed—yet she does not give way to despair or surrender to resignation, for her people will be fully avenged.

My People

These places—here was the din of life.
Its flow brought joy and graced
both young and old,
as well as children all now erased.
My heart's blood is spilled,
pained is my soul
as I wait fervently to fulfill
my own vengeful goal.

Then my people will rise up,
its youth filled with pride—
so Jewish are their eyes
and opened wide;
into the world they will go,
determined and enraged,
judgment by mercy unassuaged.
Their fists tightly engaged
will unleash fierce blows,
striking the vile faces of our foes.

Persecutions and woes,
terror and slaughter,
suffered at their hand—
they will pay for all this on demand.
For murder, torture, pain
of innocents; for the millions slain.
Revenge will be sweet and sure—
for my mother's soul so pure
and the spilling of her blood.[28]

In a companion poem, "Camp Vivikon," the poetess expresses her longing, her memories, and her yearning after her childhood in Vilna, now but memories lost as a result of the slave labor to which she is assigned.

Camp Vivikon

Do you know my homeland, my origins
There I lived free, tender and strengthened
The forests, do you know the valleys the heights?
Now winter's blast—snow covered . . .
Those whose youth was spent there,
Those who experienced life there,

Those with tender childhood there! . . .
Strengthened, refreshed in heart
When I hear the beloved name, Vilna
From whence they brought me here
To Vitikin from Vilna my City,
Here in camp, immediately imprisoning me,
At once they numbered me,
In my hand a pickax, an iron rod they placed
Then to the earth bowels for slaved labor they led me.[29]

The last of her poems in this grouping, entitled "Prisoners of War," is of a different nature. It blends the sufferings of the poetess with that of others, Russian prisoners of war trapped in the same camp. The poetess feels their pain as she labors in the kitchen with the starving Russian prisoners camped nearby. She, with the aid of some coworkers and the acquiescence of a German guard, provides the prisoners with some soup. She links her hopes to theirs and offers them words of hope and encouragement.

Prisoners of War

Fate wished to bring us both to this place,
you, native of a land great in space,
its courage and power widely praised,
and I, daughter of a people
poor, tortured, driven.
Though you are unknown to me and foreign
your hand I will firmly clutch
for we have both suffered too much
and one cruel fate to us both is given.

But be brave, my brother, be alert, take heart,
don't think too much of the mountain's dark.
A beautiful new world will be here before long,
once again we will hear freedom's song.
Violence will end,
fists and boots no longer reign.
And you will live to see your home again.
Our brother, at your gate
your dear ones will wait—
your two children and your wife so dear.
Beside them, standing near,
your aging mother will appear.[30]

The materials originating in the concentration camps that have been reviewed suggests that although the Nazis sought to obliterate the Jews, destroying them as human beings, they resisted physically and spiritually. Through religious observance, through cultural activities, through artistic and literary creativity, Jews defied their tormentors. As individuals and as proud members of their faith and their people, broken in body, there were those who refused to succumb. They struggled to maintain their humanity, their sanctity. They refused to give up their human persona. Among the Jewish victims of Nazi atrocities, there were those who lived with hope and when hope failed them as Jews, they died with dignity.

1. Eliezer Berkovitz, *With God in Hell* (New York: Sanhedrin Press, 1979), *passim*, pp. 63–65.

2. Mordecai Dworzetsky, *Estonian Jewish Camps 1942–1944* (Jerusalem: Yad Vashem, 1970), p. 299, p. 201 n. 27.

3. Yehoshua Eibshutz, *Concerning Unleavened Bread and Bitter Herbs*, A Documentary Collection (Kiryat Atta, n.d.), p. 6.

4. Mordecai Eliav, *Op. Cit.*, p. 165.

5. *Ibid.*, pp. 165, 173.

6. *Ibid.*, p. 227.

7. Eibshutz, *Op. Cit.*, p. 190. *See also* Eliav, *Op. Cit.*, pps. 217–226 *passim*.

8. Eliav, *Op. Cit.*, p. 190. See also Menashe Ungar, *Der Giestiecher Widerstand Fun Yiden In Getos Un Lageren* (Tel Aviv: Farlag Menorah, 1970), pp. 157, 192–211 *passim*.

9. *Ibid.*, pp. 216–217 *passim*.

10. *Ibid.*, p. 209. *See also* Berkowitz, *Op. Cit.*, p. 118.

11. *Ibid.*, pp. 202–203.

12. Ungar, *Op. Cit.*, p. 79. *See also* Eliav, *Op. Cit.*, pp. 115–116.

13. Yad Vashem, Oral Testimonies 03/739, January 17, 1958. *See also* Eliav, *Op. Cit.*, pp. 156–169 *passim*.

14. Daniel Frishberg, *Choshech Kisah Aretz* (Beit Lohamai Hagetaot: Kibbutz Hameuchad, 5730 [1970]), p. 247.

15. Dworzetsky, *Op. Cit.*, pp. 261–262.

16. Nathan Livneh, ed., *The Womens War: The Story of AEG, A Nazi Forced Labor Camp* (Tel Aviv: The Association of Vilnaites and the Surrounding Areas, n.d.), p. 64.

17. *Ibid.*, p. 123.

18. *Ibid.*, p. 104.

19. *Ibid.*, pp. 118–119.

20. Jerzy Datek and Teresa Swieboka (eds.) and Irena Szymanska, *Hope and Suffering, Artistic Creations of Oswiecem Prisoners* (Poland: 1989).

21. List of Art Albums as follows:
    Richard Fister and Nora Levin, eds., *The Living Witness: Art in the Concentration Camps* (Philadelphia: Museum of American Jewish History, Oct. 18, 1978–November 19, 1978).
    Janet Blatter and Sybil Milton, eds., *Art of the Holocaust: A Layla Production Book* (New York: Rutledge Press, W.H. Smith Publishers, 1981).
    Leonard A. Schoolman, ed., *Spiritual Resistance: Art in the Concentration Camps 1940–1945* (New York: Union of American Hebrew Congregations, 1981).

22. *Hope and Suffering, Op. Cit.*, pp. 20, 22, 23.

23. *Spiritual Resistance, Op. Cit.*, pp. 42; 48; 110; 146–152; 154–158.

24. Dworzetsky, *Op. Cit.*, p. 265.

25. See Yitzchak Kominkovski, *Leider Fun Katzet* (Tel Aviv: Chedekel Press, 1969).

    Zami Feder, ed., *Katzet Un Geto Leider* (Jerusalem: Central Jewish Committee in Bergen-Belsen, Yad Vashem Archives, n.d.), number 2^0–67–184, *Op. Cit.*, p. 267.

26. Dworzetsky, *Op. Cit.*, p. 267.

27. *Ibid.*, p. 274.

28. *Ibid.*, p. 271.

29. *Ibid.*, p. 269.

30. *Ibid.*, p. 272.

Part Five

Epilogue

Epilogue

Prior to the outbreak of World War II, Viktor Frankl was a psychiatrist in Vienna. The Nazis put him, along with 1,500 other Jews, aboard a train of boxcars bound for "points east." He survived to tell his story. His own experiences in German concentration camps, including Auschwitz, his observations of fellow inmates and the general quest for the meaning of human existence "after Auschwitz" inspired Dr. Frankl to develop a new school of psychotherapy which he named logotherapy.

Logotherapy is based on human spiritual values rather than on a system of immutable psycho-biological laws. Accordingly, environment, heredity and instinct are not the sole determinants and the inexorable factors in the formation of the human psyche. They do not in and of themselves determine human behavior patterns and responses. Logotherapy postulates that the human being, in contrast to other forms of life, is endowed with free choice, an attribute molded by spiritual values. In the process of treating disturbed individuals, logotherapy emphasizes the search for meaning in human life, maintaining that the human being has a fundamental "will to meaning." Hence one of the main causes for frustration and thus of much mental and emotional disorders today, is the lack of assurance that there is indeed some meaning to human existence. For Frankl, meaning is pivotal for human survival.

In his widely cited book *Man's Search for Meaning*, Dr. Frankl asserts that even under such unspeakable conditions as those found in ghettos and concentration camps man is not stripped of his ability to decide what is to become of him, both mentally and spiritually. Frankl writes:

> . . . even a man who finds himself in the greatest distress, in which neither activity nor creativity can bring value to life, nor experience give meaning to it — even such a man can still give his life a meaning by the way he faces his fate, his distress. By taking his unavoidable suffering upon himself, he may yet realize values.

199

Thus life has a meaning to the last breath. For the possibility of realizing values by the very attitude with which we face our unchangeable suffering — is the highest achievement that has been granted to man. [1]

Applying this thought to the Holocaust and the suffering, trials, and tribulations it brought with it, Frankl notes:

... Fundamentally, therefore, any man can, even under such circumstances, decide what shall become of him — mentally and spiritually. He may retain his human dignity even in a concentration camp ... There is also purpose in that life which is almost barren of both creation and enjoyment and which admits of but only one possibility of high moral behavior: namely, in man's attitude to his existence, an existence restricted by external forces. A creative life and a life of enjoyment are banned to him. But not only creativeness and enjoyment are meaningful. If there is a meaning in life at all, then there must be meaning in suffering ... [2]

In Frankl's view, the sanctity of human life is expressed in man's search for meaning and his commitment to a meaningful human existence even *in extremis*. Frankl reflects authentic Jewish thought which focuses on innate human worth and sanctity. Even in the Holocaust period it is clear that life is not an act of denial, resignation, or despair. Life is an act of hope, an act of faith. It directs man to work towards the sanctification of life as he faces its realities, even its indescribable horrors, meeting them with meaningful living. This is universally true for all human beings. Even during the Holocaust tragedy, man was not helpless or meaningless. On the contrary, the human potentiality was expressed in the movement towards sanctity and human worth even in the most desperate conditions. We have identified this as a characteristic of Judaism dealing with the quality of life which has come to be called *Kiddush Hahayyim*.

This concept was certainly expressed in heroic terms by human beings who though segregated, enslaved, starved, and murdered by the Nazis for no other reason but that they were Jews, sought to give their lives meaning. Seen from the perspective of *Kiddush Hahayyim*, the Jews trapped in the Holocaust ghettos did not suffer in vain. The memory of their sufferings had meaning for those who succumbed as well as those who survived and for future generations. This significance emerges not merely because they were martyrs, but because of the spirit that they demonstrated as they lived with hope and died with dignity. Confronted by martyrdom imposed by a brutal enemy, they struggled to create schools for their children and institutions of higher learning for themselves. Many practiced their faith at the risk of death. Actors performed on the underground stage. Publicists published clandestine periodicals. Zionists conducted *hachsharah* centers. Poets, short-story writers, biographers, painters, sketchers plied their crafts. Each in his own way expressed the determination to maintain the image of his humanity, to demonstrate the meaning and to affirm the integrity of the human being.

These singular spirits were motivated also by what the historian of the Holocaust, the late Philip Freidman (1901-1960) terms the "Judeocentric" impetus for ghetto activities.[3] This attitude called for maintaining the integrity of the image of the Jews as one expressed one's Jewishness against all who questioned its validity. The struggle to live a life of Jewish quality served as a counterfoil to German Nazism, whose intention was to destroy the Jew both physically and spiritually. Through a viable Jewish life, they would be denied their ultimate victory over Judaism. The cry heard in the ghetto was "be Jewish". The structure of activities and creative works reflected this attitude, which sought to build inner Jewish defenses.[4]

It is in this attitude that one may sense the deeper meaning of the conflict between Judaism and Nazism and the vindication of the former. In the face of overwhelming Nazi power, there was a commitment that both Jews as a people and Judaism as a way of life would survive and outlive the oppressors. The ultimate victory of the human spirit lay in their continued existence. Such existence would foil the Nazis and rob them of their ultimate triumph. This feeling was articulated again and again by the Yiddish term *Iberleybn*,[5] to survive, to remain alive. *Kiddush Hahayyim*, sanctifying life by living as Jews, became both a challenge and a *Mitzvah*, a commandment. To live and to create despite the Nazi represented the final triumph and the vindication of Judaism in the eyes of the world.[6] It was in fact a victory of the spirit for those who fought the Nazi onslaught with spiritual resistance.[7]

Evaluating the ghetto experience from the perspective of *Kiddush Hahayyim*, it is possible to conclude that as tragic as this experience was, it did not constitute a period of absolute hopelessness, disorientation, and total immorality. There were positive elements and directions that evolved even in the time of a tragedy unparalleled and unmatched in human history. A pattern of activities emerged; a body of literature and art was created that did not allow the victims to be dehumanized by becoming obsessed only with their own physical survival. Life was raised above and beyond that survival. The very fact that religious, educational, cultural, and Zionist activities were structured and carried on, no matter what the level of such activities, is evidence of the meaningfulness of life in spiritual terms. The fact that poems were composed; short stories and biographies were written; diaries were kept; paintings; sketches and drawings were executed; craftsmen plied their trade, all served as evidence of the commitment of Jews to live meaningful lives. As they reinforced the spiritual stance of the ghetto population, those trapped by the ghetto walls were able to better cope with the existential problems of physical survival.

The effect of ghetto activity and ghetto creativity was to elevate life, if even only temporarily, setting a premium on positive values, on meaningfulness. It is this drive that we have termed *Kiddush Hahayyim*, a value implicit and integral to Judaism. Thus we may conclude with Yosef Gottfarstein that *Kid-*

dush Hahayyim was an operative frame of reference accounting for the Jewish response in the ghettos to Nazism.

> This spirit of devotion and self-sacrifice was fittingly expressed in the motto, Sanctify Life, sanctify life out of the profound recognition that the precept of *Kiddush Hashem* — dying for the Sanctification of the Name — in the conditions of the ghettos and the horror camps was neither in substance nor in essence superior to the precept of sanctifying life; for all the precepts and commandments were given for the sole purpose of learning them, teaching them and observing them — none of which is possible except on this earth, for it is written, '... live by them' (Leviticus 18:5) and not 'die by them.' Everybody came to know that the ultimate Sanctification of the Name was in the sanctification of life.
>
> ... Moreover: any motto or slogan which proclaimed death to death and which called on both the sanctifiers of the Name and the sanctifiers of life to rebel against submission, prevented desecration of the Name, and saved not only the honor of the people of Israel, but also the honor of the God of Israel. [8]

It is in this manner that those imprisoned in the ghettos and camps transmuted acts of *Kiddush Hahayyim* into expressions of *Kiddush Hashem* as they lived and as they died.

---

1. Viktor E. Frankl, *The Doctor and the Soul* (New York: Alfred E. Knopf, 1965). Introduction, p. XIII.

2. Viktor E. Frankl, *Man's Search for Meaning* (Boston: Beacon Press, 1966) pp. 66-67.

3. Yad Vashem Studies III (1959) p. 33.

4. Dworzetsky, *Op. Cit.,* p. 127.

5. Esh, *Op. Cit.,* p. 107.

6. Eck, *Op. Cit.,* p. 244.

7. Irving Halperin, *"Hahitnagduth Haruchanith B'Sifrut Hashoah,"* ("Spiritual Resistance on Holocaust Literature") Yad Vashem Studies VII (1968) p. 70.

8. Yosef Gottfarstein, *"Kiddush Hashem over the Ages and its uniqueness in the Holocaust,"* Proceedings of the Conference on Manifestations of Jewish Resistance, April 7-11, 1968, Yad Vashem, Jerusalem, p. 477.

Appendices

Appendix I

Map of Kovno Ghetto

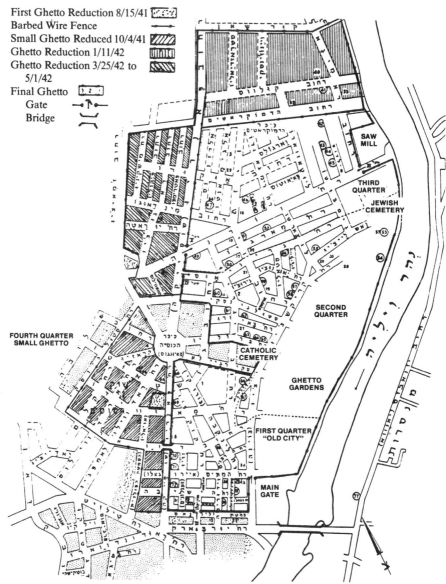

Zvi A. Baron and Dov Levin, *Toldotheha Shel Makhteret* (Jerusalem: Yad Vashem, 1962) p. 422.

Appendix II

Map of Lodz Ghetto

1. Central Secretariat
2. General Welfare Department
3. Kitchens
4. Jewish Police Command
5. Fire Brigade
6. School
7. Children's Colony
8. Rabbinate
9. Department for Social Welfare
10. Secretariat of *Hakhsharah* Groups
11. Central Jail
12. Jewish Cemetery
13. Public Works Office (Arbeitsamt)
14. Ghetto Factories
15. Statistics Bureau and Archives
16. Hospitals
17. Post Department

J. I. Trunk — Lodzer Ghetto
Source: Encyclopedia Judaica, Volume II, p. 427.

Appendix III

Map of Vilna Ghetto

תכנית של גיטו ווילנה

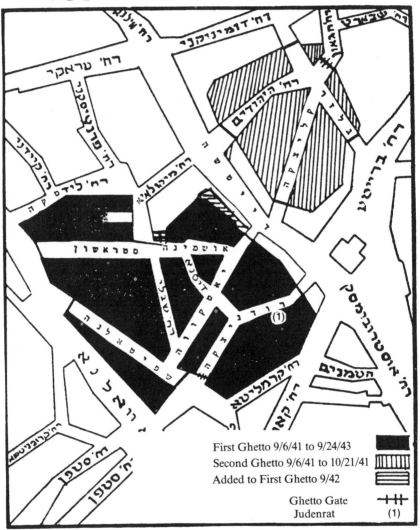

First Ghetto 9/6/41 to 9/24/43
Second Ghetto 9/6/41 to 10/21/41
Added to First Ghetto 9/42

Ghetto Gate
Judenrat   (1)

Yitzchak Arad, *Vilna Hayehudith B'Ma-avak U'Vkilyonah* (Jewish Vilna, Its Struggle, Its Death) (Tel-Aviv: Yad Vashem and Tel-Aviv University, 1976.) p. 416.

Appendix IV

Map of Warsaw Ghetto

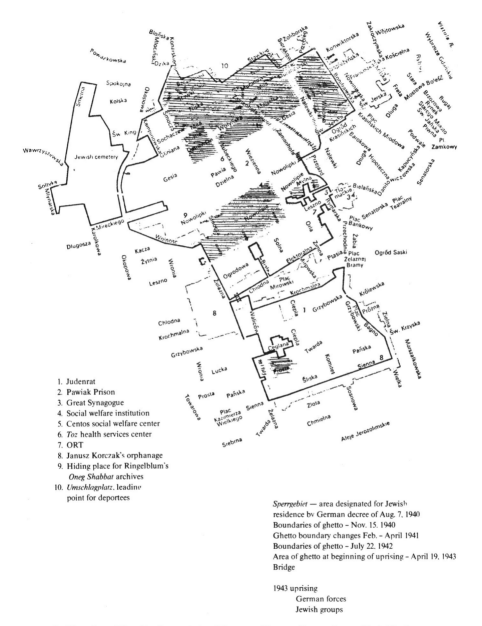

1. Judenrat
2. Pawiak Prison
3. Great Synagogue
4. Social welfare institution
5. Centos social welfare center
6. *Toz* health services center
7. ORT
8. Janusz Korczak's orphanage
9. Hiding place for Ringelblum's
   Oneg Shabbat archives
10. *Umschlagplatz*, leading
    point for deportees

Sperrgebiet — area designated for Jewish
residence bv German decree of Aug. 7, 1940
Boundaries of ghetto - Nov. 15, 1940
Ghetto boundary changes Feb. - April 1941
Boundaries of ghetto - July 22, 1942
Area of ghetto at beginning of uprising - April 19, 1943
Bridge

1943 uprising
    German forces
    Jewish groups

J. Ziemian, *The Borders of the Warsaw Ghetto*, (Jerusalem: Yad Vashem,
1971.) Reproduced in: Encyclopedia Judaica, Volume 16, p. 347.

Appendix V

Announcement of a lecture on "Judaism and Hellenism" given by Eliezer
Goldberg in the Vilna Ghetto in the summer of 1942.

Sutzkever-Katcherginsky Archives (New York: Yiddish Scientific Institute)
Document A-8506.

Appendix VI

Eliezer Goldberg's lecture manuscript.

Sutzkever-Katcherginsky Archives (New York: Yiddish Scientific Institute) Document A1-512.

Appendix VII

Minutes

Minutes of the Judges meeting held on February 13, 1943 concerning the Musical Contest.

Present: A. Slipes, chairman, S. Gershowitz, S. Kaickin, deputized for G. Yanowsky, director of the Cultural Department.

The Panel evaluated the works of the composers who participated in the Contest. They have decided to award prizes to all four entries, dividing the prizes as follows:

1. 250 Marks for *Elegy for Full Orchestra* ("Elegy"). Workmanlike but not entirely original.

2. 200 Marks for *Mozartiade* ("Fermata"). Except for a small part in the middle of the work, this work is modeled on the style of Mozart.

3. 100 Marks *Valse* ("Allegro"). An old-style waltz, very primitive but melodious.

4. 50 Marks for *Ghetto Song* and *Melody with Five Variations*, both by the same author ("Fena"). The composer is a beginner (there are several grammatical errors) but shows creative ability.

Sutzkever-Katcherginsky Archives (New York: Yiddish Scientific Institute) Document 458.

Appendix VIII

פּראָגראַם
פֿון בעטהאָווען=אָוונט
I טייל:

1) פֿראַגמענטן פֿון דער אָפּערע „פֿידעליאָ"
שפּילט דער אָרהעסטער

2) פֿידל=קאָנצערט (ד-דור)
א) אַלעגרע, ב) לאַרגעטאָ, ג) ראָנדאָ

3) טערקישער מארש
שפּילט ב. ראָטשטאַט מיט אָרהעסטער=באַגלייטונג

II טייל:

4) לאַרגעטאָ פֿונדער II סימפֿאָניע
5) צווייטער זאַץ פֿונדער I סימפֿאָניע
6) אָווערטיר „עגמאָנט"
שפּילט דער אָרהעסטער.
דיר. טעאָדאָר רידער

ליצמאַנשטאַט, 7-V, 1941-

PROGRAM OF A BEETHOVEN EVENING

Part I

1. Excerpts from the Opera *Fidelio* . . . . Orchestra

2. Violin Concerto in D Major
   (a) Allegro (b) Larghetto (c) Rondo

3. Turkish March . . . . B. Rotshtat and
   Orchestra

Part II

4. Larghetto, from Second Symphony

5. Second Movement of First Symphony

6. Overture to *Egmont*

Performed by
the Orchestra
Dr. Theodor Rieder

Lizmanstadt, 7 May 1941

Yad Vashem Archives, Jerusalem, Document 043/10

אַ י נ ל אַ ד ו נ ג

דערמים האָבן מיר יעב כבוד אײַך אינצוּלאַדען צו דער ערעפעני
פֿון אונזער מאַריאַנעטען טעאַטער „ה . אַ . ד . ג . אַ . י . אַ",
דער ערעפענינגס פּראָגראַם הײסט :

„ צ אָ ל ז ש ע ... "

פֿון יצחק ברוינער.

די פּרעמיערע װעט פֿאָר קומען י' מיטװאָך אין כראַװעצ־אַ
אין דער קראַװיעצקי גאַס 3 , אָנהייב 5½ אַ זייגער נאָכב
נאָ פֿאַהרייך ביי בילעטן קויב מעג אין געזונב־הייסט
אָבטיילונג לאַגיענניצא 34 36 פֿון 4 ביז 7 נאָכם.
אין טאָג פֿון דער פֿאָרשטעלונג פֿון 11 פֿרי אַ ביי די קאַסע.

(אַלע פּלעצער זענען נומערירט)

INVITATION

We are pleased to invite you
to the opening performance
of our Marionette Theatre
"HAD GADYA"

The opening program
is entitled:

"WHY BE DISTRESSED ....."
by Yitzhak Brojner

The premiere will take place on
Wednesday, the eleventh in the theatre
hall at Krawiecka 3, beginning at 5:30 p.m.

Purchase tickets at the Health Department,
Lagiennicka 3436 from 4 to 7 p.m. on the day of the
performance from 11:00 a.m. in the box office.

(All Seats are Reserved)

Sutzkever Katchevginsky Archives (New York, Yiddidh Scientific Institute) Document 043.

שעה של סופר יהודי ואומן יהודי

(קונצרט מיוחד במינו ומקורי)

ידידנו הנכבד !

אנו מתכבדים להזמינך לשעה מוסיקה וספרות
יהודית (שירה, סיפור, ואסיי), שתתקיים ביום
שבת הקרוב, 15 בפברואר ,1941 בשעה שחיים
בצהריים, באולם "מאז" (TOZ), רח' גנשא 43.

הקונצרט יצטיין במקוריותו גם בשל כך, שתוכלו
להאזין למוסיקה יהודית, נגינה בכינור, פסנתר,
זימרה, דיקלום, ריקוד-באלט, שירה, סיפור, אסיי,
ולא תכביד עליכם הרב-גוניות של הצדה זו.

שלוש דקות לכל יצירה. הוכן הכל בטוב טעם
ובצורה אסטטית, במידה ובנימוס, כדי לא להעמיס
יתר על המידה על מצב רוחכם הקשה בזמנים אלה
וכן כדי לאפשר לכם להינתק מהסובב אתכם ולהכניס
את המאזינים לאווירה ולמצב רוח נוח ואינטימי.

ואם תחשבו, שבהשתתפותכם במסיבה אומנותית זו,
תסייעו גם לסופר ולאומן יהודי להתפרנס בכבוד,
בוודאי תואילו להופיע ולהשתתף בהצגה מקורית זו.

התוכנית הצפוייה:

מוסיקה יהודית

כינור – עוא קאזטיידאג – בוגרת הקונסרבטוריון
פסנתר – מינא מאטלאנטסקא – בוגרת הקונסרבטוריון
ריקוד-באלט – סולה קאמינסקא – בוגרת הבאלט של
פרושיצקי
זימרה – יופיע הזמר העממי הערשעלע סטערן

ספרות יהודית

דיקלום – שירה יהודית וספרות קלה ומיוחדת
המינה – ידוקלם האומן ז. שקלאר
שירה – ש. גילבערט, ש. וויילנאד, י. לערער,
יצחק קאצענעלסאן
סיפור – יוסף סטאלאטש, י. קורמאן, ז. סקאלאוו,
יהודה פעלד
אסיי – ישראל סטערן, י. בערנסטיין, נ.שטערנבערג,
רחל אוייערבאך
דברי פתיחה – ד"ר יצחק לייפונער
הוועד המארגן

ווארשא, 9 בפברואר 1941
המכתב הזה משמש ככרטיס כניסה,
יש להחליפו בקופה ביום הקונצרט.

Appendix X

Joseph Kermish, "Al Itonut Hamachateret Shel Geto Varshe," (The Warsaw Ghetto Underground Press"), Yad Vashem Mechkarim I, 1967, following p. 80, documents.

Appendix XI

Example of the condition of materials found in Ghetto rubble, a poem by Yitzchak Katzenelson.

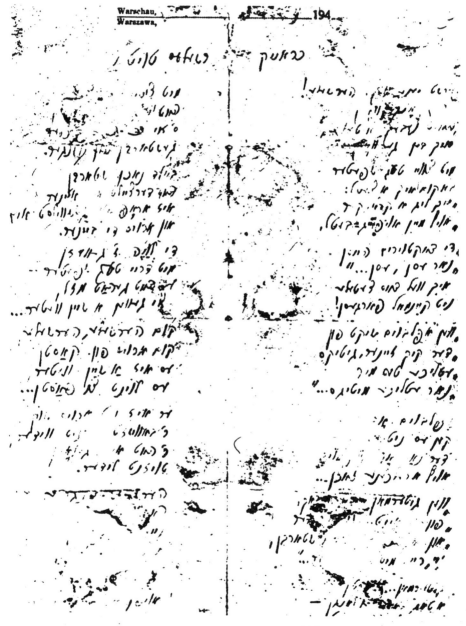

Ghetto Fighters House Archives, Document KI 1033

216

Appendix XII

Multilingual segment of a Lodz Ghetto Diary by an anonymous author.

"Yomano Shel Almoni M'Geto Lodz," Yediot Yad Vashem, No. 2, 1970, p8, Document D33/1032.

L'HONNÊTE CRIMINEL

Nom d'un chien, qu'il faisait froid !
Un brouillard à couper au couteau, un
vrai brouillard de veille de Noël, où les
becs de gaz qu'on venait d'allumer, bien
qu'il fût à peine quatre heures de l'après-
midi, ne jetaient que des halos jaunâtres,
et où les passants — silhouettes fantasti-
ques — se hâtaient sur les trottoirs, les

"Yomano Shel Almoni M'Geto Lodz," *Yediot Yad Vashem*, No. 2, 1970, p. 9.

Appendix XIV

A page from the Diary of Yitzchak Rudashevski.

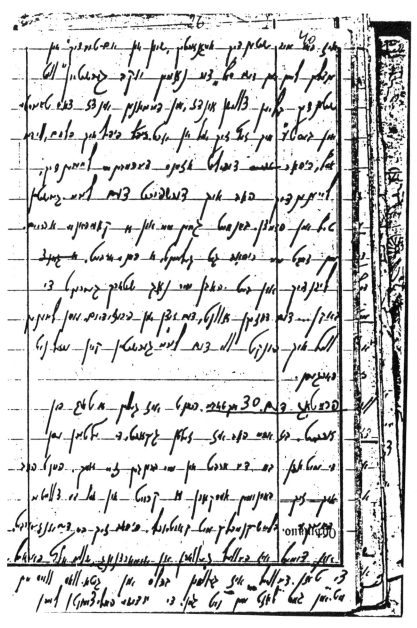

Sutzkever-Katcherginsky Archives (New York: Yiddish Scientific Institute) file 10.

Appendix
XV

Plate 1. Sara Glicksman-Fajlowicz. Entitled: Driven Into The Ghetto. Dated: 1940, Lodz. Oil on Cardboard. 24" × 30". Courtesy Yad Vashem Art Museum, Jerusalem, Israel.

Plate 2. Sara Glicksman-Fajlowicz. Entitled: The Bridge. Dated: 1943. Courtesy Yad Vashem Art Museum, Jerusalem, Israel.

221

Plate 3. Esthur Lurie. Entitled: A Wooden Bridge In Kovno. Dated: 1941. Courtesy Yad Vashem Art Museum, Jerusalem, Israel.

222

Plate 4. Szymon Szerman. Dated: 1940, Lodz. Gouache, 10" × 13". Courtesy Ghetto Fighters Art Museum, Kibbutz Lohamai Hagetaot, Israel.

Plate 5. Szymon Szerman. Undated. Courtesy Ghetto Fighters Art Museum, Kibbutz Lohamai Hagetaot, Israel.

Plate 6. Szymon Szerman. Undated. Courtesy Ghetto Fighters Art Museum, Kibbutz Lohamai Hagetaot, Israel.

Plate 7. Szymon Szerman. Undated. Courtesy Ghetto Fighters Art Museum, Kibbutz Lohamai Hagetaot, Israel.

226

Plate 8. Artist Unknown. Life in the Warsaw Ghetto. Courtesy Ghetto Fighters Art Museum, Kibbutz Lohamai Hagetaot, Israel.

227

Plate 9. Artist Unknown. Life in the Warsaw Ghetto. Courtesy Ghetto Fighters Art Museum, Kibbutz Lohamai Hagetaot, Israel

228

Plate 10. Artist Unknown. Life in the Warsaw Ghetto. Courtesy Ghetto Fighters Art Museum, Kibbutz Lohamai Hagetaot, Israel.

Plate 11. Amos Szwarc. Entitled: The Peddler In The Ghetto. Dated: 1944, Lodz. Watercolor, 7½" × 5". Courtesy Ghetto Fighters Art Museum, Kibbutz Lohamai Hagetaot, Israel.

Plate 12. Nathan Spigel. Entitled: Woman In The Ghetto. Undated, Lodz. Red
pencil. 11½" × 9". Courtesy Ghetto Fighters Art Museum, Kibbutz
Lohamai Hagetaot, Israel.

231

Plate 13. Halina Olomucki. Entitled: Peddler With Yellow Star. Warsaw, 1941-3. Pencil on yellowed paper. 7" X 5". Courtesy Artist.

Plate 14. Hersz Szylis. Undated. Oil on cardboard. Courtesy Artist.

233

Plate 15. Jacob Lipshutz. Undated. Courtesy Yad Vashem Art Museum, Jerusalem, Israel.

Plate 16. Jacob Lipshutz. Undated. Courtesy Yad Vashem Art Museum, Jerusalem, Israel.

Plate 17.   Hersz Szylis. Undated. Courtesy Artist.

Plate 18. Hersz Szylis. Undated. Courtesy Artist.

237

Plate 19.   Hersz Szylis. Undated. Courtesy Artist.

Plate 20. Halina Olomucki. Dated: 1945.
 Courtesy Artist.

Plate 21. Hersz Szylis. Dated: 1940, Lodz Ghetto. Courtesy Yad Vashem Art Museum, Jerusalem, Israel.

Plates 22, 23, 24, 25.   Alexander Bogen. Entitled: Revolt (Jerusalem: Yad Vashem, 1974)

Plate 23. Alexander Bogen. Entitled: Friendly Chat. Charcoal. (Jerusalem: Yad Vashem, 1974)

Plate 24. Alexander Bogen. Dated: 1943. Entitled: At Rest. India Ink. (Jerusalem: Yad Vashem, 1974)

Plate 25. Alexander Bogen. Dated: 1943. Entitled: Rescue. India Ink. (Jerusalem: Yad Vashem, 1974)

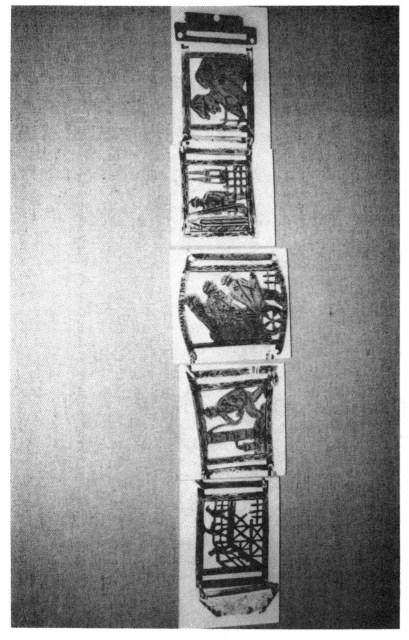

Plate 26. Craftsman Unknown. Silver bracelet. Courtesy Yad Vashem Art Museum, Jerusalem, Israel.

245

Plate 27. Craftsman Unknown. Ghetto weavers. Courtesy Yad Vashem Art Museum, Jerusalem, Israel.

246

Plate 28. Artist Unknown. Courtesy Yad Vashem Art Museum, Jerusalem, Israel.

Bibliography

Primary Sources
English

Adler, Cyrus, ed. *American Jewish Yearbook 5664 (1903-1904)*. Philadelphia: The Jewish Publication Society of America, 1903.

Berg, Mary. *Warsaw Ghetto Diary*. New York: L. B. Fischer Co., 1945.

Bialer, Tosha. "Behind the Walls," *Colliers Magazine*, February 20, 1943.

Bogan, Alexander. *Revolt*. Jerusalem: Yad Vashem, 1974.

Goldstein, Bernard. *The Stars Bear Witness*. New York: Viking Press, 1949.

International Military Tribunal Sitting at Nuremberg, Germany. *The Trial of Major War Criminals*, Part II from transcripts of H. M. Attorney General, H. M. Stationery office, Document 22330-PS Exhibit USA 281 Identified CV 1941; Document 1919 PS Exhibit USA 170; Document 2738-PS Exhibit USA 296, 1946. London: third December 1945 to fourteenth December 1945.

Kalmanovitch, Zelig. A Diary of the Nazi Ghetto in Vilna. *YIVO Annual of Jewish Social Studies*, Vol. III. New York: Yiddish Scientific Institute, 1953.

Lauterbach, J. Z., ed. *Mekilta de Rabbi Ishmael*, 3 Vols. Philadelphia; The Jewish Publication Society of America, 1935.

Lurie, Esther. *Sketches from a Woman's Labour Camp*. 8th ed. Tel Aviv: J. L. Peretz Publishing House, 1962.

Pinsker, Leon. *Road to Freedom*. New York: Scopus Publishing Co., 1944.

Ringelblum, Emanuel. "Underground Cultural Work." *YIVO* Bleter, Vol. XXIV. New York: Yiddish Scientific Institute, September-October 1944.

Ringelblum, Emanuel. *Notes from the Warsaw Ghetto*. Translated by Jacob Sloan. New York McGraw-Hill, 1958.

Rudashevski, Yitzchak, *The Diary of the Vilna Ghetto, June 1941-April 1943*. Translated by Percy Matenko, Kibbutz Lohamei Hagetaot: Beyt Lohamei Hagetoat and Hakibbutz Hameuchad Publishing House, 1973.

Simon, Leon, ed. *Ahad Ha-am, Essays, Letters, Memoirs*. Oxford: East West Library, MCMXLVI.

Shub, Boris, ed. *Jewish Religion in Axis Europe*. Institute of Jewish Affairs, Vol. 1, Nos. 11-13. New York: American Jewish Congress, June-August 1942.

Weizman, Chaim. *Trial and Error*. New York: Harper Brothers, 1949.

Yahil, Leni. *Readings on the History of the Holocaust*. Jerusalem: Hebrew University, 5731.

Yad Vashem Exhibitions. Jerusalem: Yad Vashem, Martyrs and Heroes Memorial Authority, January-March 1960.

Zylberberg, Michael. *A Warsaw Diary, 1939-1945*. London: Vallentine, Mitchell and Co., Ltd., 1969.

Interviews by Rabbi Joseph Rudavsky

Adler, Rabbi Sinia. Private interview, Ashdod, Israel, January 22, 1973.

Arnon, Joseph. Author and Biographer of Janusz Korczak. Taped interview, Tel-Aviv, Israel, July 23, 1973.

Auerbach, Rachel. Warsaw Ghetto survivor and partisan leader and writer on Aryan side. Taped interview, Tel-Aviv, Israel, January 10, 1973.

Bacon, Yehuda. Terezin ghetto survivor and artist. Taped interview, Stamford, Connecticut, March 21, 1973.

Blumenthal, Nachman. Ghetto literary critic. Taped interview, Tel-Aviv, Israel, January 25, 1973.

Bogen, Alexander. Vilna Ghetto artist and partisan. Taped interview, New York, New York, May 6, 1975.

Bryks, Rachmil. Ghetto survivor and writer. Taped interview, New York, New York, March 15, 1972.

Dworzetsky, Dr. Mark. Vilna Ghetto historian. Private interview, Jerusalem, Israel, July 20, 1973.

Donat, Alexander. Ghetto survivor, writer and publisher. Interview, New York, New York, May, 1942.

Eck, Dr. Nathan. Warsaw Ghetto survivor, Holocaust historian. Taped interview, Neve Avivim, Israel, July 25, 1976.

Fackenheim, Emil. Three lectures on the Holocaust. Taped Jerusalem: Hebrew University, July 24-26, 1974.

Garfunkel, Leib. Survivor, community leader and historian of Kovno Ghetto. Taped interview, Jerusalem, Israel, July 19, 1973.

Goldfarb, Zvi. Survivor Warsaw Ghetto. Taped interview, Kibbutz Parod, Israel, August 10, 1973.

Groak, Trude. Terezin Ghetto art teacher. Taped interview, Tivon, Israel, July 29, 1973.

Groak, Dr. Willi. Terezin Ghetto youth worker. Taped interview, Kibbutz Ma-anit, Israel, July 29, 1973.

Kermish, Dr. Joseph. Warsaw Ghetto survivor, historian, Holocaust researcher, Yad Vashem archivist. Interviews, September, 1972; January, 1973; and July, 1975.

Kominkovsky, Yitchak. Ghetto and concentration camp poet. Taped interview, Givatayim, Israel, January 10, 1973.

Kwiatkovsky, Rivkah Pinchasik. Survivor and short story writer. Interview, Kiryat Haim, Israel, December 27, 1972.

Lurie, Esther. Kovno Ghetto artist. Interview, Jerusalem, Israel, January, 1973.

Meed, Vladka. Ghetto survivor and writer. Interview, New York, New York, May, 1975.

Novich, Miriam. Warsaw Ghetto survivor, art curator. Interview, Kibbutz Lochamai Hagetaot, July, 1972.

Oleiski, Jacob. Kovno Ghetto survivor, Director ORT School, Kovno Ghetto. Taped interview, Tel-Aviv, Israel, November 29, 1972.

Prager, Moshe. Ghetto survivor, literary critic and ghetto anthologist. Taped interview — Hebrew University, Dept. of Comtemporary History, Testimonies and interviews tape #2049, B'nai Brak, Israel, January 24, 1973.

Schapiro, Yisrael. Secretary to Rabbi Isaac Nissenbaum. Taped interview, Jerusalem, Israel, July, 1976.

Shazar, Shelomo. Archivist, Moreshet Archives. Interview Givat Haviva, Israel, December 15, 1972.

Szyllis, Hersz. Lodz Ghetto survivor and artist. Taped interview, Safed, Israel, December 25, 1972.

Shner, Zvi. Warsaw Ghetto survivor, Director of Museum Kibbutz Lochamai Hagetaot. Interview, Kibbutz Lochamai Hagetaot, Israel, July, 1972.

Spiegel, Isaiah. Lodz Ghetto survivor, poet and short story writer. Taped interviews for Hebrew University Department of Contemporary Jewish History, Testimonies and interviews tape #2024, Givatayim, Israel, November 29, 1972 and January 10, 1973.

Stern, Hana. Youth leader and survivor of Terezin and Auschwitz Family Camps. Taped interview, Jerusalem, Israel, July 21, 1973.

Sternbach, Dr. Kalman. Historian. Taped interview, Jerusalem, Israel, August 5, 1973.

Sutzkever, Abraham. Vilna Ghetto survivor, poet and community leader. Taped interview for Hebrew University Department of Contemporary

Jewish History, testimonials tape #2049, Tel-Aviv, Israel, January 25, 1973.

Trunk, Isaiah. Lodz Ghetto survivor, historian and Holocaust researcher. Taped interview, New York, New York, April 27, 1971.

Yahel, Leni. Ghetto researcher and historian at Hebrew University. Interview, Jerusalem, Israel, January 23, 1973.

Wells, Dr. Leo. Ghetto and concentration camp survivor and writer. Author of *The Janowski Road*. Interview, Closter, New Jersey, April 15, 1973.

Zuckerman, Isaac. Warsaw Ghetto partisan leader, Deputy Commander of ZOB, Associate Director Beit Lohamai Hagetaot. Interview, Kibbutz Lochamai Hagetaot, Israel, July 1972.

Primary Sources
Hebrew

אבנון, אריה . <u>עתונות גורדוניה במחתרת גיטו ורשה</u>. חולדה :
הוצאת ארכיון גורדוניה מכבי-הצעיר, 5726.

אברמוביץ, חיים יצחק. <u>וחי בהם, פיקוח נפש בהלכה</u>. ירושלים:
הוצאת אורות, 1957.

אהרונסון, יהושע. <u>זכרונות</u>. ירושלים: יד-ושם רשות הזכרון
לשואה ולגבורה, מחלקת עידויות, כסלו חש"ט.

אוירבך, רחל . <u>בחוצות ורשה 1941-1939</u>. תל-אביב:עם עובד,
5714.

אופוצ׳ינסקי, פרץ. <u>רשימות</u>. קיבוץ לוחמי הגיסאות:בית לוחמי
הגיסאות ע"ש יצחק קצנלסון והוצאת קיבוץ מאוחד,
תש"ל.

אורבך, סרה. <u>מבעד לחלון ביתי , זכרונות מגיטו לודז׳</u>.ירושלים:
יד-ושם, תשכ"ד.

אליאב, מרדכי. <u>אני מאמין , עדויות על חייהם ומותם של אנשי
אמונה בימי השואה</u>. ירושלים: הוצאת מוסד הרב
קוק, תשכ"ט.

אפרתי, שמעון. <u>מגיא ההריגה , כפר שאלות ותשובות</u>. ירושלים:
יד-ושם רשות הזכרון לשואה ולגבורה, תשכ"א.

ארגעלברנד, שמואל, חיים, (עורך). <u>מדרש רבה</u>, שני כרכים ורשה:
תרל"ח.

ארד, יצחק. <u>וילנה היהודה במאבק ובכליון</u>. תל-אביב: יד-ושם
רשות הזכרון לשואה ולגבורה ואוניברסיטת
תל-אביב, המכון לחקר התפוצה, 1976.

ארני, יהודה. <u>לקט שירים ופרוזה</u>. ירושלים: יד-ושם רשות
הזכרון לשואה ולגבורה. 1971.

253

אש, שאול. "קידוש השם בתוך ההרבן - על ההגדרה של תקופה הטואה",
ירושלים: ירחון מולד, כרך י"ס חוברת 154-153.

אשרי, אפרים. חידושי הלכות וביאורי סוגיות בש"ס ונספח קונטרס
מעמק הבכא שאלות מקאוונא. ניו-יורק: תש"ס.

אשרי, אפרים. ממאמקים, ספר שאלות ותשובות, שלשה כרכים,
ניו-יורק: הוצאת דפוס אחים גרוים, תשכ"ס.

אשרי, אפרים. "בית יעקב בגיטו קובנה". ירושלים: בית יעקב,
ירחון לעניני הינוך ספרות ומחשבה. מספר יג,
סיון תש"ך.

באנער, שלמה (עורך). מדרש המיוחס לרבי תנחומא ברבי אבא על
חמשה חומשי תורה, שני כרכים. ירושלים: צולם מחדש
ע"ו אורצל, חשכ"ד.

באומינגר, אריה ; בלומנסל, נחמן; וקרמיש, יוסף. הילד והנוער
בשואה ובגבורה. ירושלים: הוצאת קריה ספר, 1965.

ביאליק, ח.נ. כל כתבי. תל-אביב : הוצאת דביר, מהדורה שניה,
הרצ"ס.

בובר, מ. אור הגנוז-סיפורי חסידים. תל-אביב, ירושלים:
הוצאת שוקן, תשכ"ס.

בלומנסל, נחמן. "החנוך בימי השואה, הילד והנוער בשואה ובגבורה"
ירושלים: קרית ספר בע"מ, 1965.

בלומנסל, נחמן; וקרמיש , יוסף. הטרי והמרד בגיטו וארשא, ספר
מסמכים. ירושלים: יד-ושם, הטכ"ה.

בלומנסל, נחמן; וקרמיש, יוסף (עורכים). הרב טמעון הוברבאנד.
קידוש השם. תל-אביב: הוצאת זכור מיסודו של שמחה
הולצברג, תשכ"ס.

בן מימון, משה (רבינו) . מטנה תורה, הוא היד החזקה, שבעה
כרכים. ירושלים: הוצאת אל המקורות, הוצאה חדשה,
ה' תשי"ד.

ברגמן, הוגו שמואל. קידוש השם. ירושלים: אגודת סטודנטים
ציוניים "בר-כוכבא" הוצאה חדשה מטעם מוסד ביאליק
של הסתדרות הציונית העולמיה, דפוס מרכז, כסלו תשכ"ג.

גלברד, חנה, והלפגרס, ירחמיאל. מיומני, חלוצים במחתרת תורגם
מאידיש ע"י מטה בוסק. הוצאת הקיבוץ המאוחד.

254

גנחובסקי, משה (עורך). כתבים נבחרים מאמרי יסוד בציונות וביהדות מאת הרב יצחק ניסנבוים. ירושלים; הוצאת האחים לוין-אפשטיין, תש"ח.

גירונדי, יונה בן אברהם (רבנו). שערי תשובה. ירושלים: הוצאת קריה-נאמנה, יעקב פלדהיים , תשכ"ז.

גרפונגל, ל. קובנה היהודית בחורבנה. ירושלים; יד-ושם, תשי"ט.

גרובשטיין, מאיר (עורך). העמידה היהודית בתקופת השואה, דיונים בכינוס חוקרי השואה ט-י"ג ניסן תשכ"ח. ירושלים: יד-ושם, תש"ל.

יחיל, לני. "העמידה היהודית-אספקלריה לקיום היהודי לצורותיה הפעילות והסבילות בתקופת השואה".

דבוריצקי , מאיר. "העמידה בחיי יום-יום בגיטאות ובמחנות ".

גוטרפשטיין, יוסף. "קידוש החיים במהלך הדורות וייחודו בתקופת השואה".

דבוריצקי, מ. "החיים הדתיים בגיטו וילנא." ישראל: ירחון ירחון סיני, אייר תש"ך.

דינור, בן-ציון. זכור, דברים על השואה ועל לקחה. ירושלים: יד-ושם תשי"ח.

דפים לחקר השואה והמרד. קיבוץ לוחמי הגיטאות: בית לוחמי הגיטאות ע"י יצחק קצנלסון למורשת השואה והמרד.

מאסף ראשון, בלומנסל, נחמן (עורך). אפריל 1951.

סנר, צבי. "לתולדות החיים התרבותיים בגיטו לודז".
מעודות "מן המיצר".
"החלוץ הלוחם מספר 29".
"קורספונדנציה פנימית".

מאסף שני, בלומנסל, נחמן, (עורך), פברואר, 1952.

לוריא, אסתר, "מרשימותיה של ציירת"
תעודות, "המספר" שנה שלישית.

סידרה שניה מאסף א', שנר, צבי ודרך שלמה (עורכים).

מאהלר, רפאל.   "מכתביו של עמנואל רינגלבום
                 מגיטו וארשה".

סורקוב, יונס.   "על הצלח ילדים מגיטו וארשה".

ברמן, אדולף אברהם. "שירה מן התהום".

דרור, לוי (עורך). ספר השומר הצעיר, שלשה כרכים.
מרחביה: הוצאת ספרית פועלים, 1961.

הורביץ, מן המיצר. תל-אביב: הסתדרות כללית של עובדים
עברים בארץ ישראל, 1944.

הודעה הארצית להנצחה קהילות. לקט שירה ופרוזה.ירושלים:
יד-ושם רשות הזכרון לשואה ולגבורה, 2 פברואר,1971.

הערץ, יוסף צבי (מוהר"ר). ספר תפלות לכל השנה במנהג פולין.
ניו-יורק: הוצאת בלוך פובלישינג קומפאני, תש"ך.

הרב רבינו שמעון. ילקוט שמעוני, שני כרכים. ירושלים:
הוצאת כפרים לוין-אפשטיין בע"מ, תשכ"ז.

זילברמן-קיכלר, לנה. אנו מאשימים עדויות ילדים מן השואה.
מרחביה: ספרים פועלים, הוצאת הקיבוץ הארצי השומר
הצעיר, מהדורה חמישית, 1969.

זרטל, מטה. אמנים יהודים-חיים יהודים. מרחביה : ספרית
פועלים, תש"ל.

זר כבוד, מרדכי. "יומנו של מנחם אפפנהיים מגיטו לודז'.
ירושלים: הדפסה מיוחדת מ"סיני", כרך כ"ה תשי"א.

סורקוב, יוניס. היה היתה וארשה היהודית. תל-אביב:
חרבות וחינוך, 1969.

יומנו של אלמוני מגיטו לודז'. ירושלים : ידיעות יד-ושם,
מספר ב', תש"ל.

יומנו של רופא מגיטו וילנא. ירושלים : ידיעות יד-ושם,
מספר ד', תשל"ג.

--ילדי השואה מספרים. ירושלים: משרד ההינוך והתרבות,
תשכ"ו.

כהן, מנחם (עורך) מַחֲנַיִם, מסכת לחייל לשמונת ימי חנוכה, לקידוש השם בישראל, צבא הגנה לישראל. הרבנות הראשית, חנוכה תש"ך.

דינור בן-ציון.   "קידוש השם וחילול השם".

גורן, שלמה (רב)   "מצוות קידוש השם לאור ההלכה".

לנדוי, בצלאל.   "קידוש השם בתורת החסידות".

ברגמן, הוגו שמואל.   "קידוש השם".

לוין, אברהם. מִפִּנְקָסוֹ שֶׁל מוֹרֶה מִ"יהודיה" בְּגִיטוֹ וַארְשָׁה. אפריל 1942-ינואר 1943. קיבוץ לוחמי הגיטאות: בית לוחמי הגיטאות, קבוץ המאוחד, תשכ"ט.

לוצאטו, משה היים רבנו. מְסִלַּת יְשָׁרִים. ירושלים: הוצאת יעקב פלדהיים, הוצאה חדשה, תש"ל.

לוריא, אסהר. יהודיות בשעבוד, אוסף ציורים. מרחביה: ספרית פועלים, 1945.

לוריא, אסהר. עִידוּת חיה, גיטו קובנה עם ציורים. תל-אביב: דבר עם סיוע יד-ושם, תשי"ח.

מאירוביץ, אהרון (עורך). הם עמדו על נפשם. תל-אביב: יד ושם ביה לוחמי הגיטאות, ומורשת, תשכ"ד.

מאירוביץ, אהרון (עורך). מן הדליקה ההיא. קיבוץ לוחמי הגיטאות: בית לוחמי הגיטאות ע"י יצחק הצנלסון הוצאת הקיבוץ המאוחד, תשכ"א.

---מה מליל. תל-אביב: הוצאה יבנה, 1944.

מייזליש, צבי-הירש. שאלות ותשובות. שיקגו: שער המד זר זהב מקדשי שם, חשס"ו.

משנה עם פירוש רבינו עובדיה מברטינורה. ניו - יורק: הוצאה הורב, ה' תרפ"ו.

ניסנבוים, יצחק (רב). הגות הלב דרושים ונאומים קצרים. ורשה פולין : הוצאה שניה, 1911.

ניסנבוים, יצחק . <u>היהדות הלאומית</u>. ורשה : דפוס הצפירה,
הרצ"פ.

נשמית, שרה. <u>מאבקו של הגיטו</u>. קיבוץ לוחמי הגיטאות : בית
לוחמי הגיטאות ע"ש יצחק קצנלסון והוצאת קיבוץ המאוחד ,
תשל"ב.

נשמית, שרה. <u>לתולדות השואה והמרד</u>. קיבוץ לוחמי הגיטאות:
בית לוחמי הגיטאות ע"ש יצחק קצנלסון, תשכ"א.

נשר, צ. <u>שירים מקריח המות</u>, תרגום בני ציון בנשלום.
תל-אביב : הוצאת גזית, תש"ה.

סגלוביץ, זיסמאן. <u>בנתיב הלהבות</u>. ירושלים: הוצאה ראובן
מכ אור לעד, 1946.

סמולנסקסין , פרץ בן משה. <u>מאמרים</u>.ארבעה כרכים. ירושלים:
הוצאת קרן סמולנסקים, תרפ"ה.

<u>כפר ארחות צדיקים, או ספר המידות</u>. ירושלם: הוצאת פלדהיים,
הוצאה חדשה, תש"ל.

סוצקבר, אברהם. <u>חרות עלי רוח, שירים</u>. מרחביה : ספרית פועלים,
1949.

סוצקבר, אברהם. <u>גיטו וילנה</u>, תרגום מאידיש ע"י נתן לבנה.
תל-אביב : שכבי 5707.

עק, נתן. <u>התועים בדרכי המות</u>. ירושלים: יד – ושם, תש"ך.

פראנק, כלמה. <u>טאגבוך פון לאדזשער געטא</u>. תל-אביב: פארלאג
מנורה, תשי"ח.

פלנטובסקי, נח. <u>על פתחי תהום</u>. ירושלים: קרית ספר, תש"ז.

פרגר, משה (עורך) <u>מן המצר קראתי, שירי הגיטאות, מחנות
עבודה, וחצרות המות</u>. ירושלים: הוצאה מוסד הרב קוק,
תשם"ו.

פרגר, משה. <u>שירי עם גווע</u>. תל-אביב: חדפים מצנתון "דבר",
תש"ג.

צ'רניאקוב, אדם. <u>יומן גיטו וארשא</u>. ירושלים: יד-ושם, מהדורה
שניה, תש"ל.

258

קוויאטקאווסק פינחסיק, רבקה. <u>נשים מאחורי הגדר</u>. תל-אביב:
הוצאת י.ל. פרץ, 1961.

קוויאטקובסקי-פנחסיק, רבקה. <u>בידים נאמנות</u>, תרגום י.ב.
אליעזר. חיפה: הוצאת ספרים ליד אגודת סופרי
ועתונאי יידיש, 1964.

קוק, אברהם יצחק הכהן (הרב). <u>אורות הקדש</u> , שני כרכים.
ירושלים: האגודה להוצאת ספרי הרב אברהם יצחק
הכהן קוק ז"ל תרצ"ח.

קלמיש, קולונימוס. <u>אש קדוש, אמרות טהורות בשנות השואה
ת"ש-תש"א-תש"ג, שנאמרו בשבתות וי"ט בגיטו ורשה
הדוויה</u>. ירושלים: יוצא לאור ע"י חסידי פיאסצנה, תש"ך.

קצנלסון, יצחק. <u>כתבים אחרונים ת"ש-תש"ד</u>. קיבוץ לוחמי הגיטאות :
בית לוחמי הגיטאות ע"ש יצחק קצנלסון הוצאת הקיבוץ
המאוחד, מהדורה הדשה, מורהבה. 1969.

קורצ'ק, רוז'קה. <u>להבות באבר</u>. מרחביה : מורשת בית עידות ע"ש
מרדכי אניליביץ וספרית פועלים הוצאה הקיבוץ הארצי
השומר הצעיר, 1965.

--<u>קידוש השם בדורות תערוכה ספרותית קסלוג תשכ"ס 1969-1968</u>,
ירושלים: מחלקה לתרבות תורנית. משרד החינוך ובית ספרים הלאומי.

קפלן, ח.א. <u>מגילת יסורין, יומן גיטו ורשה 39, 9, 1-42:8,4</u>.
ירושלים: הוצאת עם עובד ויד-ושם רשות הזכרון לשואה
ולגבורה, השכ"ו.

רבנו בחיי ב"ר יוסף זצ"ל. <u>ספר תורת חובות הלבבות</u>, שני כרכים.
ירושלים: הוצאת קריה נאמנה, תשכ"ה.

רוסקירון ליוויה (עורכת) <u>קובץ מחקים בפרשיות השואה והגבורה</u>.
תשעה כרכים, ירושלים, יד-ושם.

קרמיש, יוסף. "על עיתונות המחתרת של גיטו וארשה"
כרך א'.

דבורז'צקי, מארק. "הכתגלות העצירים לחיי הגטאות
והמחנות והכתגלותם החדשה לחיי החופש'. כרך ה'.

שוינקידנר, ש. "מיומנו" כרך ה'.

הלפירן, ארווינג. "ההתנגדות הרוחנית בספרות השואה"
כרך ה'.

לוין, אברהם. "קטע מתוך יומנו" כרך ו'.

רוח, ליבליך ז"ל. <u>יומנה של נערה</u>. ירושלים: יד ושם זכרון
לשואה ולגבורה , מחלקת לגבית עידות 03/3442.

--תערוכה, השואה והמרד בספרות ובאמנות. חיפה; 21 פברואר-
22 מרס 1952.

סיינטון, יחאל. <u>כתבי שפיגל, קצנלסון וסוצקבר</u>. ירושלים:
דסטציה אונברסיטה עברית, לא נדפס עדיין.

סניאורסון, פישל. <u>אני מאמין, מכפוריו של יוסלה אוסטרובצר</u>.
פליט סגיכו ווארשה. תל-אביב: הוצאה אל-דמי, תש"ד.

סנר, צבי. <u>הפחרון הסופי, תעודות על השמדת יהודי אירופה בידי
גרמניה הנאצית</u>. קיבוץ לוחמי הגיסאות, בית לוחמי
הגטאות למורשת השואה והמרד הוצאת הקיבוץ המאוחד, תשכ"א.

ספירא, ישראל (עורך) <u>מועדים, דרשות נבחרות לחגים ולמועדים
מאת הרב יצחק ניסנבוים</u>. ירושלים: הוצאת ראובן מס, 1967.

ספירא ישראל (עורך). <u>עלי-חלד תרכ"ט-תרפ"ט מאת יצחק ניסנבוים</u>.
ירושלים: הוצאה ראובן מס, מהדורה שניה, תשכ"ט.

ספירא, ישראל, (עורך). <u>אגרות הרב ניסנבוים</u>. ירושלים: דפוס
אחות. תשס"ז.

שפיגל, ישעיה. <u>אור מעמקי תהום</u>. תל-אביב: הוצאת י.ל. פרץ,
1969.

שרשבסקי, פסיה. <u>קרני עור במחשכי התופת</u>. בני ברק : חשכ"ח.

רפאל, יצחק (עורך) <u>תורה שבעל-פה</u>, ירושלים: הוצאה מוסד
הרב-קוק, תשל"ב.

רובינשטיין, שמואל תנחום (רב), "הצלת נפשות ע"י
גילוי עריות-בהלכה".

פרידמן, נתן, (רב). מצוות קידוש-השם בקום ועשה
או בשב ולא תעשה".

260

תורה, נביאים, כתובים. ירושלים: הוצאת קורן, בחסות החברה
העולמית לתנ"ך החברה לחקר המקרא בישראל.

תלמוד בבלי, 16 כרכים. ניו-יורק: הוצאת בית מסדר ספרים
פרדס.

תלמוד ירושלמי. ניו-יורק: הוצאת יד התלמוד האחים שולסינגר.

Yiddish

אונגר, מנשה. דער גייסטיקער ווידערשטאנד פון ייִדן אין
לאגערן. תל-אביב: פארלאג מנורה, תש"ל.

אויליקי, ל. (רעדאקטר). צווישן לעבן און טויט. ווארשא:
פארלאג ייִדיש בוך, 1955.

גרויל (ז.סקאלאוו). "א שפאציר איבער די פונקט".
פערלע, יהודה "4580".
קירמאן, יוסף. "דער הסד פון אסטילן סויט".
קירמאן, יוסף. "כ׳ רעד צו דיר אפן מיין קינד".

אייזענבאך, א. בערענשטיין, ט.;מארק, ב.;און רוסקאווסקי,
א. (רעדאקטאן). רינגעלבלום, עמנואל, כתבים פון געטא
צוויי בענד. ווארשא: ייִדישער היסטארישער אינכטיטוט
און פארלאג ייִדיש בוך, 1963.

אייזמאן, יהודה. ממעמקים 1944–1939. פאלקסלידער פון לאגערס
און געטאס אין פוילין. בוקארעסט: ביבליאטעק החלוץ, 1945.

אונדזער געזאנג. ווארשא : צענטראל קאמיטעט פון די ייִדין אין
פוילין אנטיילינג פון קולטור, 1947.

אפאטשינסקי, פרץ. רעפארטאזשן פון ווארשעווער געטא. ווארשע:
פארלאג ייִדיש בוך, 1954.

אשרי, אפרים. חרבן ליטע. ניו-יורק; הרב אשרי בוך קאמיטעט,
1951.

באלבעריסקי, מאג. <u>סטרקה פון אַיזן</u>. תל-אביב: פֿאַרלאַג מנורה.

בלומענטאל, נחמן. <u>שמועסן וועגן דער יידישער ליטעראטור</u>
<u>אונטער דער די נסער אָקופּאַציע</u>. בוענאָס-איירעס:
צענטראַל פֿאַרבאַנד פון פוילישע יידין אין אַרגענטינע,
1966.

<u>בלעטער פֿאר געשיכטע</u>. ווארשע יידישער היסטאַרישער אינסטיטוט
בײַם צ"ק פון יידין אין פּוילין.

בלומענטאל, נחמן. "די יידישע שפּראַד און דער קאַמפּף
קעגן נאַצי רעזשים. "באַנד א, העפֿט ג-ד.

אײַזענבאַך, אהרון. "ווירטשאַפֿטלעכער פֿאַרשוינגן אין
ווארשעוער געטאָ" באַנד א , העפֿט א-ב; באַנד ד,
העפֿט א.

---אַנקעטע פון צונג שבת". באַנד א, העפֿט ג-ד.

לעווין, אברהם. "פֿונעם געטע-טאָאגבוך" באַנד ה, העפֿט ד.

גאָטליב, מלכה און מלאַסעק, חנה. (רעדאַקטאָרן) <u>געטאָ לידער</u>.
ניו-יורק: בילדינגס-קאָמיטעט פון אַרבעטער-רינג,1968.

גליק, הירש. <u>לידער און פּאָעמס</u>. ניו-יורק: איקוף פֿאַרלאַג, 1953.

גרינהויז, סמואל. <u>דאָס קולטור לעבן אין קאָוונער געטאָ</u>. ניו-יורק:
קובץ ליטא קולטור געזעלשאַפֿט פון ליטווישע יידין, 1951.

דווארזעצקי, מאַרק. <u>ירושלים דליטא אין קאַמף און אומקום</u>.
פּאַריס: יידישן נאציאָנאַלן אַרבעטער פֿאַרבאַנד אין אַמעריקע
און יידישן פֿאָלקספֿאַרבאַנד אין פֿראַנקרייך, 1948.

<u>דורך פֿײַער און בלוט, געטאָ בלעטער</u>. ווארשע; נאַציאָנאַלן
קאָמיטעט און דער יידישע קעמפּערס אַרגאַניזאַציע, 1944.

דיכסער, אַבבאַקאַנט. <u>געטאָ דירות</u>, אונדזער לידער זאַמלינג פון
לעצטן חורבן, כעפֿטעמבר, 1946.

---<u>נוען פּוילין איז געפֿאַלן</u>. ניו-יורק פֿאַרלאַג ציק"א, 1943.

262

ייווא בלעטער שריפט פון ייִדישן וויסנשאפטלעכן אינסטיטוט. ניו-יורק; ייווא.

לייקן, כימא. "סטראשון גאס 12 אין ווילנער געטא", באנד ניצער 2.

נאסאנבלום, אנא, "די סולן אין ווארשעווער געטא", באנד נומער 2.

קלמאנאוביץ, זעליג. " א סאגבוך אין ווילנער געטא", באנד נומער 2.

קלמאנאוויסט, זעליג. "דער גייסט אין געטא". באנד נומער 2.

טרונק, ישעיה. לאדזשער געטא. ניו-יורק, ייִדישער וויסנשאפטלעכער אינסטיטוט, 1962.

יאסני, וואלף. די געשיכטע פון ייִדין אין לודזׁ אין די יארן פון דיישער אוסההארג. צווי בענד, ישראל: י.ל. פרץ, 1960.

מארק, בערל. דער אומגעקומענעז שרייבער. ווארשע: פארלאג ייִדיש בוך, 1954.

ניגער, ש. קידוש השם. ניו-יורק: צׁ קא ביכער פארלאג, חש"ז.

ניישאטס, מלך (רעדאקטער). חורבן און אויפשטאנד פון ייִדין אין ווארשע. צווי בענד. תל-אביב: קידות בלעטער און הזכרה, 1948.

סאנדעל, יוסף. אויסטעלונג, ווערק פון ייִדיש קינסטלער פלאסטיקער קדושים אומגעקומנס אין צייט פון דער דיוטשע אקופציע 1945-1939. ווארשע: ייִדישע געזעלשאפט צו פארמעריטן קינסט און יודישע הקטאורישע אינסטיטוט, אפריל - מאי 1948.

סאנדעל, יוסף. פלאסטישע קינסט ביי ייִדין אין פולין. ווארשע: ייִדיש בוך, 1964.

סאנדעל, יוסף. אומגעקומענע ייִדישע קינסטלער. צווי בענד. ווארשע: פארלאג ייִדיש בוך, 1957.

סוצקעווער, אברהם. פאעטישע ווערק. צוויי בענד. תל-אביב:
1963.

סוצקעווער, אברהם. פון ווילנער געטא. מאסקווע: מעלוכע-
פארלאג דער עמעס, 1946.

סוצקעווער, אברהם יידישע גאס. ניו-יורק: פארלאג מחנות ביים
שלום-עליכם פאלק אינסטיטוט.

סוצקעווער, א. די פעסטונג, לידער און פאעמס געשריבן אין
ווילנער געטא און אין וואלד 1944-1941. ניו-יורק:
איקוף פארלאג.

סוצקעווער, אברהם . לידער פון געטא. ניו-יורק: איקוף פארלאג.
1946.

סקאלאוו, זלמן. דער האקאקרויץ-די האק אן קרייץ. ווארשע;
פארלאג יידיש בוך, 1954.

פומס, רוסע (רעדאקטער) . דאס ליד פון געטא וווארשא: פארלאג
יידיש בוך, 1962.

פירסטון,אלחנן. "פון לעצטן חורבן" מוניך. צייטשריפט, סעפטעמבער,
1948.

פולאווער, משה. געווען איז א געטא בילדער געצייכנט פון
וואלף אדלער. תל-אביב : י. ל. פרץ, 1963.

פעלד, יהודה. אין די צייטן פון המן דעם צווייטן. ווארשע:
פארלאג יידיש בוך, 1954.

קאסטערגינסקי   סמארקע, דאס געזאנג פון ווילנער געטא.
פאריס: פארבאנד פון ווילנער יידין אין פארנקרייך,
1947.

קאסטערגינסקי, סמארקא. לידער פון געטאס און לאגערן. ניו-יורק:
ציק"א ביכער פארלאג, 1948.

קאפלאן, י. (רעדאקטאר). פון לעצטן חורבן, צייט טרריפט פאר
געשיכטע פון יידישע לעבן בעתן נאצי-רעזשים : מינכען :
הסטארישע קאמיסיע ביים זענטראל קאמיטעט דער באפרייטע
יידין אין דער אמעריקאנער זאנע, 1946-דעצמבר 1948.

264

אונדזער לידער זאמלונג. קפלן י. "קאוונער סול און
לערערשאפט אין אושקום".
אלוזקי, י. א. פאכסול אין קאוונער געטא.
"דער רעליגיזע לעבן אין קאוונער געטא"
גורעוויטש, י. "קאוונער געטא ארקעסט".

קאצענעלסון, יצחק. דאס ליד פונעם אוסגעהרגעטן יידישער פלאק.
ניו-יורק: פארלאג פון הקיבוץ המאוחד, 1948.

קאצענעלסאן, יצחק. על נהרות בבל. קיבוץ לוחמי הגיטאות: בית
לוחמי הגיטאוה ע"י יצרק קאצענעלסון, תשכ"ז.

קוויאטקאוווסקי-קנחסיק, רבקה. הענט. חיפה; ארגון אסירי
הנאצים לשעבר, תשי"ז.

קרוק, הערמאן. מאגבוך פון ווילנער געטא. ניו-יורק:
יידישער וויסנשאפטלעכער אינסטיטוט, 1961.

ראלניק, מאשע. איך מוז דערציילן. וואראשא : יידיש בוך: 1965.

ראן לייעזר, און קאריסקי (רעדאקטאר). בלעכער ווענן ווילנא;
זמאלבוך. לאדזש: פארבאנד פון ווילנער יידין אין פולין
ביי דאר צענטראלער יידישער היסטורישער קאמיסיע, 1947.

טאיעוויטש, ש. לך לך. לאדזש' : צענטראל יידישער היסטארישע
קאמיסע פון פוליטע יידין, 1946.

בלומענטאל, נחמן. דער אריינפיר – "דאס ליסער אריכע
לעבן אין ליצמאנסטאט-געטא". "פרילינג, חש"ב".

שפיגל, ישעיהו. און געווארן איז ליכט. ורשה: פארלאג יידיש
בור, 1949.

שפיגל, שאיע, מענטשן אין סהאוום. בוענעס-איירעס: פארלאג
איקוף, 1949.

שפיגל, ישעיה. ליכט פונעם אפגרונט. ניו-יורק: ציק"א ביכער
פארלאג, 1952.

שפיגל ישעיה. מלכות געטא . לאדזש' : פארלאג דאס נייע לעבן
קליינע ביבליאטעק, 1947.

שפיגל ישעיה. טרערן איבערן געטא. פאריס:יידישעפאלקס-ביביל-
אטעק, ארגאניצאציע פון דער פולישע יידין אין פראנקריר.

שפייזמאן, ל. די יידין אין נאצי-פולין, ניו-יורק: פארלאג
יידישער קעמפער, 1942.

265

עדויות

האוניברסיטה העברית, המכון ליהדות זמננו, המדור לתיעוד בעל-פה.

סרט 1651: המרואיין : ירחמיאל בריקס
המראיין : יחיאל שיינסון
סרט 1991: המרואיין : רבקה פנחסיק
המראיין : יחיאל שיינסון
סרט 2024: המרואיין : ישעיהו שפיגל
המראיינים : הרב יוסף רודבסקי, יחיאל שינסון
סרט 2049: המרואיין : אברהם סוצקבר
המראיינים : הרב יוסף רודבסקי, יחיאל שינסון

ארכיונים

ארכיון יד-ושם, רשות הזכרון לשואה ולגבורה, ירושלים
אוסף, ארכיון רונגלבלום חלקא דמותו של תלמיד בבית
ספר יסוד.
לבעית החינוך בתקופה המלחמה
שעה של סופר יהודי ואומן יהודי
תיאור בית מחסה לפליטים
גטאו דיקטער אי אנאנימע, אומבאקאנטע

ארכיון יד-ושם רשות הזכרון לשואה ולגבורה, גבית עידות
שמואל בלומנפלד; ישראל סגל; אהרון גפנר; יצחק רסנר;
פרדי דיאמנט; חוה רוזנברב; רות רייכר; שמאי רוזנבלום;
י. בילקינד; ויעקב גרינבערג.

ארכיון יד-ושם, רשות הזכרון לשואה ולגבורה, ירושלים. מכמכים
שונים:
אוסף נזונאבנד, חעודות מגיטו לודז'
דער ווערקער 12 אפריל, 1942
דאס פריי ווערט 23 מאי 1942
בולעטין ידיעות פון לאנד ינואר 1942
הלל צייטלין שירים (מיקרופילם)
יונגע גוארדיע נומער 1, יולי 1941
געטא-צייטונג, דער עלטסטער פון די ייידין אין ליצמאנסטאט
געטא 7 מערץ 1941; 21 מערץ 1941; 4 אפריל 1941;
25 אפריל 1941; 2 מאי 1941; 18 מאי 1941.
געטא ידיעות: וואיכנבלאט, דערשיינט יידער זונטאג אין
ווילנער געטא. 30 נובמבר 1942; 3 מערץ 1943;
14 מערץ 1943; 21 אפריל 1943; 7 יולי 1943;
1 אויגוסט 1943.

ארכיון, יידישן וויסנשאפטלעכן אינסטיטוט, ניו יורק
סוצקעווער - קטסרגינסקי קאלעקציע
זאנעבענס - קאלעקציע
וואסער - קאלעקציע

ארכיון מורשת ע"ש מרדכי אנילביץ, גבעת חביבה

266

Art

Works of the following ghetto artists were viewed and photographed.

Yad-Vashem Archives:

Esther Lurie
Yaacov Lipshutz
Sara Fajlowicz Glicksman
Friedrich Bloch
Peter Ginz
Hilda Zadikow
David Labkowvski

Museum and Archives of Kibbutz Lohamai Hageta-ot:

Chana Bursova
Alexander Szerman
Israel Lejzerowicz

Safed, Israel Art Colony:

Hersz Szyllis

Secondary Sources
English

Agus, Jacob B. *The Evolution of Jewish Thought*. New York: Abelard-Schuman, 1959.

Agus, Jacob B. *Banner of Jerusalem*. New York: Bloch Publishing Company, 1946.

Ainzstein, Reuben. *Jewish Resistance in Nazi-Occupied Eastern Europe*. London: P. Elek, 1974.

Arnon, Joseph. "The Passion of Janusz Korczak," *Midstream Review*, Volume XIX, No. 5, May 1973.

Bauer, Yehuda. *They Chose Life*. New York: American Jewish Committee and Institute of Contemporary Judaism, Hebrew University, 1973.

Belkin, Samuel. *In His Image*. New York: Abelard-Schuman, 1960.

Buber, Martin. *Hassidism*. New York: Philosophical Library, 1948.

Davitt, Michael. *Within the Pale*. Philadelphia: The Jewish Publication Society of America, 1903.

Dawidowicz, Lucy S. *The War Against the Jews*. New York: Holt, Rinehart and Winston, 1975.

Des Pres, Terrence. *The Survivors, An Anatomy of Life in the Death Camps*. New York: Oxford Press, 1976.

Dubnow, Simon B. *The History of the Jews in Russia and Poland*, 3 vols., Philadelphia: The Jewish Publication Society of America, 1920.

Esh, Saul. "The Dignity of the Destroyed: Towards a Definition of the Period of the Holocaust," *Judaism Magazine*, Volume XI, No. 2, Spring 1962.

Fackenheim, Emil L. *God's Presence in History*. New York: Harper and Row, 1972.

Fackenheim, Emil L. *The Human Condition after Auschwitz*. Syracuse: B. G. Rudolph Lectures in Jewish Studies, Syracuse University, April 1971.

Feldman, David. *Birth Control in Jewish Law*. New York: New York University Press, 1968.

Finkelstein, Louis. *The Jews*, 2 volumes. Harper Brothers, 1949.

Frankel, Viktor E. *Man's Search for Meaning: An Introduction to Logotherapy*. Boston: Beacon Press, 1962.

Frankel, Viktor E. *The Doctor and the Soul*. New York: Alfred A. Knopf, 1965.

Graetz, Heinrich. *The History of the Jews*, 6 volumes. Philadelphia: The Jewish Publication Society of America, 1945.

Halperin, Irving. *Messengers from the Dead*. Philadelphia: The Westminster Press, 1970.

Hertzberg, Arthur, ed. *The Zionist Idea*. New York: Harper and Row, 1959.

Heschel, Abraham J. *Man is Not Alone*. New York: Farrar, Strauss and Young, Inc., 1951.

Heschel, Abraham J. *The Insecurity of Freedom*. New York: Noonday Press, Division of Farrar, Strauss and Giroux, 1967.

Hilberg, Raul. *Documents of Destruction, Germany and Jewry*. Chicago: Quadrangle Books, 1971.

Hilberg, Raul. *The Destruction of the Jews in Europe*. Chicago: Quadrangle Books, 1961.

Hitler, Adolf. *Mein Kampf*. Translated by Ralph Manheim. London: Hutchinson of London, 1969.

Hitler, Adolf. *Secret Conversations, 1941-1944*. New York: Farrar and Strauss, 1953.

The Jewish Encyclopedia, 12 volumes. New York: Funk and Wagnalls Co., 1904.

Kadushin, Max. *Organic Thinking*. New York: Jewish Theological Seminary, 1938.

Leftwich, Joseph. *Abraham Sutzkever, Partisan Poet*. New York: Thomas Yoseloff Publisher, 1971.

Levin, Nora. *The Holocaust*. New York: Thomas E. Crowell Company, 1968.

Louvish, Misha, ed. *Facts About Israel 1970*. Israel: Information Division of the Ministry of Foreign Affairs, Government of Israel, 1970.

Marcus, Jacob R. *The Jew in the Medieval World*. New York: Harper Torah Books, 1965.

Martin, Bernard. *A History of Judaism*, 2 volumes. New York: Basic Books, 1974.

Montefoire, C. G., and Loewe, H. *The Rabbinic Anthology*. Philadelphia: The Jewish Publication Society of America, 1960.

Moore, George Foote, *Judaism*, 2 volumes. Cambridge: Harvard University Press, 1932.

Nahon, S., ed. *Theodore Herzl, Fifty Years After His Death*, Jerusalem. Executive of the World Zionist Organization, 1954.

Poliakov, Leon. *Harvest of Hate*. Westport, Connecticut: Greenwood Publishers, 1951.

Prager, Moshe. *Sparks of Glory*. Translated by Mordecai Schreiber. New York: Sheingold Publishers, Inc., 1974.

Reitlinger, Gerald. *The Final Solution*. New York: A. S. Barnes & Company, Inc., 1961.

Robinson, Jacob, ed. "The Holocaust." *Encyclopedia Judaica*, 16 volumes. Jerusalem: The McMillan Co., 1971. Volume 8.

Rosenbaum, Irving J. *The Holocaust and Halakhah*. New York: Ktav Publishing House, Inc., 1976.

Rudavsky, David. *Emancipation and Adjustment*. New York: Diplomatic Press, 1967.

Schleunes, Karl A. *The Twisted Road to Auschwitz*. Urbana, Illinois: University of Illinois Press, 1970.

Scholem, Gershon. *Major Trends in Jewish Mysticism*. New York: Schocken Books, 1941.

Silver, Abba Hillel. *Vision and Victory*. New York: The Zionist Organization of America, 1949.

Syrkin, Marie. *Blessed is the Match*. New York: Alfred A. Knopf, 1947.

Trunk, Isaiah. *Judenrat*. New York: The McMillan Co., 1972.

Uffenheimer, Rivkah-Shatz. *Quietistic Elements in Eighteenth Century Hassidic Thought*. Jerusalem: Hebrew University, 1969.

Ury, Zalman. *Studies in Torah Judaism, The Musar Movement*. New York: Yeshiva University Press, 1970.

Secondary Sources
Hebrew

אבן-שושן, שלמה. <u>יצחק קצנלסון מקונן השואה</u>. ירושלים: המשרד הדיווך וההרבות עם בית לוהמי הגיטאות ע"ש יצחק קצנלסון, ניסן תשכ"ב.

אייגיס, יעקב. "ההידוש שבתורה הבעל שם טוב" <u>שבועון הדואר</u>, כרך כ"ה מספר ל , ד' תמוז תש"ה.

אונגר מנשה. <u>אדמו"רים שנספו בשואה</u>. ירושלים: הוצאה מוסד הרב קוק , תשכ"ס.

אש, שאול. <u>עיונים בחקר הכואה ויהדות זמננו</u>. ירושלים: האוניברסיטה העברית המכון ליהדות זמננו יד-ושם ומכון ליאו בק, תשל"ז.

בלומנטל, נחמן. "בתי <u>ספר בגיטו</u>" ירושלים: אינציקלופדיה של גלויות, 1959.

בראון, צבי: וליין, דב. <u>תולדותיה של מחתרת ארגון הלוחם של יהודי קובנה במלחמה עולם השני</u>. ירושלים: יד-ושם, חשכ"ב.

ברט, אהרון. <u>טוב ורע בספרו "דורנו מול שאלות הנצח" קוים להשקפה עולם</u> , ירושלים: הוצאה המדור הדתי במחלקת לעניני הנוער וההלוץ חשט"ו.

ברקאי, דפנה. <u>יהדות קובנה בשואה</u>. תל-אביב: סבת תשכ"ט.

גוטמן, ישראל: ורוטקירכן, ליוויה (עורכים) <u>שואת יהודי אירופה</u>. רקע - קורות-משמעות. ירושלים: יד-ושם, תשל"ג.

גוטמן, ישראל. <u>הנועח הנוער במחתרת ובמרד הגיטאות, העמידה היהדוה בשואה</u>. ישראל: יד-ושם, תש"ל.

גוטספורכט, דוד; הדרי, חיים; וריכמן אהרון; (עורכים) <u>ספר דרור</u>. עין -חרוד: ההכהדרות דרור החלוץ-הצעיר הוצאת קיבוץ-המאוהד, תש"ז.

גרינבוים, יצחק. <u>אינציקלופדיה של גלויות, ספר זיכרון לארצות הגולה ועידותיה</u>. שחים עשרה כרכים, ירושלים-תל-אביב: הוצאת אנציקלופדיה של גלויות, 1953.

273

גרפונקל, ליב (עורך). יהדות ליטה ירושלים: כתב סכונת
כתיבה, בלי האריך.

כולל מאמרים :
הרב אלחנן פרסון, "חיי הדת בגיטו קובנה".
"מוסיקה בגיטו קובנה".
יעקב אולייסקי, "בית ספר מקצועי בגיטו קובנה".
סוניה סגל-ורהבסקי ז"ל, "ילדי בית סר העברי בגיטו קובנה".
ד"ר ש. גרריינהויז, "חיי תרבות בגיטו קובנה".
ליב גרפונקל, "הגיטו ותדמיתו".

דובנוב, שמעון, תולדות החסידות. תל-אביב: הוצאת דביר, הדפסה
שלישית, תהכ"ז.

הכסקוף ה. וארשה 24 ציורים מגיטו וארשה וסביבותיו. תל-אביב :
מגנזי יד-ושם, 1961.

וולפסברג, ישעיה, "היהדות הנאמנה במלחמה". ירושלים: ארשח
ספר הכנה של איגוד הסופרים הדתיים, תשי"ד.

ויס, שבתי. מאוצר המחשבה של החסידות. תל-אביב: הוצאת
מחברות לספרות, תשכ"א.

זולקיס, גניה."מגילת פורים בגיטו ורשה" ניו-יורק: שבועון
הדואר , ח' אדר חשל"א.

סברסקי, יוחנן,לפסיכולוגיה של ההסדות" ניו-יורק: שבועון
הדואר, כרך כ"ה, מספר ל. ד' תמוז הש"ה.

ידיעות בית לוחמי הגטאות, הוצאה בית לוחמי הגטאות:
אפריל 1958
רשימות גיטו ורשה.

מאי 1959
מקורות המרד.
רשימות מגיטו ורשא.
ילדים מספרים.
לפרשת החינוך.

אפריל 1960
עיתונו של דרור במחתרת גיטו ורשה.
לפרשת התנגדותם.
בן י"ד הייהי.

ידיעות יד-ושם, אירועים, פעולות, פרסומים, ירושלים:הוצאת
יד-ושם.
חוברת 11/10 אלול השט"ז
קרמיש,יוסף, "אנשי הגות בגיטו וארשה על תופעות
מיוחדות בחיי קהילתם".

חוברת ב' תמוז חשי"ד.
בלומנטל, נחמן, "שירים ומנגינות בגיטאות ובמחנות".

274

כ"ץ, דב. <u>תנועת המוסר</u>. חמשה כרכים. ירושלים: הוצאת וייס, חש"ל.

כשר, משה שלמה. <u>פרקים במשנת החסידות</u>. ירושלים: מכון תורה שלמה, חש"ל.

כשר, משה שלמה. <u>פרקים במחשבת הרסידות</u>. ירושלים: הוצאת מכון תורה שלמה, חשל"ב.

כשר, משה שלמה. <u>פרקים בתורת החסידות</u>. ירושלים: מכון תורה שלמה, חשכ"ח.

כשר, משה שלמה. <u>עיונים במחשבת ההסידות</u>. ירושלים: הוצאת מכון תורה שלמה, חשל"ד.

לחובר, פ. <u>ביאליק חייו ויצירותיו</u>, שני כרכים, תל-אביב: דביר מהדורה רביעית, חשכ"ד.

לסקר, עמוס, <u>גיטו וארשה החיים, המאבק והמרד</u>. ירושלים: יד-ושם, חשכ"ט.

נשמית, שרה. "לפרשת החנוך המאורגן בגיטו ורשה" קיבוץ לוחמי הגיטאות; <u>ידיעות בית לוחמי הגיטאות</u>, כ"ז ניסן תשי"ט.

סביב, אהרון, <u>"ערכי אדם ואומה לאור השואה"</u> ניו יורק: <u>שבועון הדואר</u>, ש' שבט חשל"ג.

פראגר, משה אלא שלא נכנעו, <u>קורות תנועת המרי החסידית בגטאות</u>, שני כרכים. בני-ברק: הוצאת נצח, 1963.

קלוזנר, יוסף, <u>ח.נ. ביאליק שירתו וחייו</u>, תל-אביב: הוצאת דביר, חשי"א.

צינדר, ראובן, "בסוד הבעש"ם וחסידיו". ניו-יורק: <u>שבועון הדואר</u> כרך כ"ב, מספר ל, ד' תמוז חש"ה.

ריבולוב, מנחם. "שבחי חסידות" ניו-יורק: <u>שבועון הדואר</u> כרך כ"ה, מספר ל', ד' תמוז חש"ה.

שורר, ה ; קורן, י. ויניצקי, ד. <u>הפגרם בקישונייב ניסן תרס"ג</u>. תל-אביב: אגודה עולמים יהודי בסרברביה, 1963.

סטיינמן, אליעזר. <u>כהבי רבי נחמן</u>. תל-אביב: הוצאת כנסת, תשי"א.

סלהב, יעקב. "קידוש חיי היהודי בתקופת השואה" תל-אביב: <u>ידיעות</u> בליכוז הנוער האקדמי הדתי, גליון יט', אביב חשכ"ב.

שפירא, ז. <u>ביאליק ביצירותי</u>. תל-אביב: דוד שמעוני, חש"א.

Credits

Every effort has been made to locate the owners of copyrights for the selections used in this volume and to secure permission to reprint the copyrighted passages. The author expresses his gratitude for the use of the passages by those whose names appear below. In the future, the author will gladly correct any error or omission that may be pointed out.

Auschwitz-Birkenau State Museum from Hopes and Suffering by Jerzy Datek and Teresa Swiebocka (eds.) and Irena Szymanska. © 1989. Reprinted by permission of Auschwitz-Birkenau State Museum.

Am Oved, from "Megilat Yesurim, Yomano Shel Geto Varshe" by Chaim Kaplan, © 1966. Reprinted by permission of Am Oved.

ACUM, Society of Authors, Composers, and Music Editors in Israel. "Poetishe Werke" by Abraham Sustzkever, © 1963. "Unter Dyne Vyse Stern." Reprinted by permission of Abraham Sustzever and ACUM.

Beit Lochamai Hagehtaot and Hakibbutz Hameuchad, from "The Diary of the Vilna Ghetto" by Yitskhok Rudashevski. Translated by Percy Matenko, © 1973. Reprinted by permission of Beit Lochamai Hagehtaot.

Beit Lochamai Hagehtaot, from "Dapim L'Chayker Hashoah V'hamered," Nachman Blumenthal, editor, © April, 1951. Reprinted by permission of Beit Lochamai Haghetaot.

Beit Lochamai Hagehtaot, from the Archives item KII 1033. Reprinted by permission of Beit Lochamai Haghetaot.

Beit Lochamai Hagehtaot and Hakibbutz Hameuchad, from Sefer Dror, Gottesfurcht, Hadari and Reichman (eds.), © 1967. Reprinted by permission of Beit Lochamai Hagehtaot.

Beit Lochamai Hagehtaot, from "Al Naharot Bavel" by Yithak Katzenelson. © 1961. Reprinted by permission of Beit Lochamai Hagehtaot.

Beit Lochamai Hagehtaot and Hakibbutz Hameuchad from "Ketavim Acharonim" by Yithak Katzenelson. © 1969. Reprinted by permission of Beit Lochamai Hagehtaot. "The Song of Zelig Zelkovski."

277

Beit Lochamai Hagehtaot Museum, Collection of Holocaust Art. Anonymous. Appendix plates 8, 9, 10; Szymon Szerman, Appendix plates 4, 5, 6, 7; Amos Szwarc, Appendix plate 11; Nathan Spigel, Appendix plate 12. Reprinted by permission of Beit Lochamai Hagehtaot.

Bogen, Alexander, Revolt (Art Portfolio), © 1971. Appendix plates 22, 23, 24, 25. Reprinted by permission of Alexander Bogen.

Cyco Books from Leider Fun Getos Un Lagern by Shmerke Katsherginsky. © 1949. Reprinted by permission of Cyco Books. "Es Shlogt de Sha-ah;" "Mein Klayner Martyrer;" "Oy Habet Mishamayim U'e'eh;" "If I Have No Faith;" "Why Should We Weep;" "Mir Leben Aybik;" and "Genug Tzu Tzittern."

Central Jewish Committee of Polish Jews, from "Lech Lechna" by Shayevitch. © 1946.

Chief Rabbinate of Israel Defense Forces, Machanayim, Hanukkah Issue, from "Kiddush Hashem" by Samuel Hugo Bergman. © 1970. Reprinted by permission of Defense Department IDF.

Dvir Publishing House from Kitvey Hayyim Nachman Bialik the poem "Ir Haharegah." © 1939. Reprinted by permission of Dvir Publishing House.

American Zionist Youth Foundation, from "The Partisan Hymn." No Date. This organization has ceased to exist. There is no successor organization.

Farband of Vilna Jews in France from "Dos Gesang fun Vilner Ghetto," by Smerke Katcherginsky. © 1947. "Katriel Broido Tzum Bessern Morgen;" "Rubinstein Let Them Go To Hell;" and "Anonymous Why Should We Weep." Reprinted by permission of Vilner Association of France.

Givat Haviva Archives item D-2-44 from Moreshet, an untitled and undated poem. Reprinted by permission of Givat Haviva Archives.

Ickuf Farlag from Leider Un Poemes, © 1953. Poems by Hersh Glick, "Sunlight On The Beach;" "Flaxen Hair Like an Ear of Corn." Reprinted by permission of Ickuf Farlag.

Journal of the Historical Commission Liberated Jews in the American Zone Issue September © 1946. From "Unser Lieder Zamlung fun Letzten Churban;" "Unser Lebn by Abraham Chipkin;" "Geto Dirot;" and "Yiddishe Brigades" by Abraham Axelrod.

Keter Publishing House and Encyclopedia Judaica, volume 11, Map of Lodz Ghetto. Reprinted by permission of Keter Publishing House.

Labor Zionist Alliance, from "Yerushalayim D'Lita In Kampf Un Umkum," by Mark Dworzetski. © 1948. Reprinted by permission of Labor Zionist Alliance.

Lurie, Esther, Sketches From a Women's Labour Camp from the Introduction, Art In The Valley of Death by Aryeh Lerner. © 1962. Reprinted by permission of Esther Lurie.

Mossad Harav Kuk, from Ani Ma-amin by Mordiecai Eliav. © 1965.

Mossad Harav Kuk from Min Mamatzar Karatee, by Moshe Prager. © 1954, the poem, "Tateh Derbarem Dich."

Olomucki, Halina, Artist. Wartime Sketches—Plate 13, Peddler With Yellow Star, Plate 20 untitled. Reprinted by permission of Halina Olomucki.

Sifriat Poalim, from "The Struggle and Destruction of The Jews of Vilna," by Yitzchak Arad. © 1976. Appendix III Map of Vilna Ghetto. Reprinted by permission of Sifriat Poalim.

Szylis, Hersz, Artist. Wartime Sketches. Undated. Plates 14, 17, 18, 19, 21. Reprinted by permission of Hersz Szylis.

Yiddish Scientific Institute. Yivo Annual of Social Services, volume VIII. From A Diary of The Nazi Ghetto in Vilna by Zelig Kalmanovitch. © 1953. Reprinted by permission of Yiddish Scientific Institute.

Yiddish Scientific Institute from Sutskever Katcherginsky Archives, Appendix V document A-8506; Appendix VI document A1-512; Appendix VII document 458; Appendices VII and IX document 043. Reprinted by permission of Yiddish Scientific Institute.

Yad Vashem, Martyrs' and Heros' Remembrance Authority, from Jewish Camps in Estonia 1942–1944 by Dr. M. Dworzecki. © 1970. The poems: "We'll Be Silent, We'll Be Still;" "Spring;" "My People;" and "Camp Vivikon." Reprinted by permission of Yad Vashem.

Yad Vashem, Martyrs' and Heros' Remembrance Authority, from Kiddush Hashem Over The Ages and Its Uniqueness In the Holocaust Period by Yosef Gottfarstein in Proceedings Of The Conference On The Manifestations of Jewish Resistance, April 7–11, 1968. © 1971. Reprinted by permission of Yad Vashem.

Yad Vashem Martyrs' and Heros' Remembrance Authority, from The Destruction of Kovno's Jewry by Lieb Garfunkel. © 1959. The Poems "Der Ninter Fort by Axelrod;" and "Hoffening by Chipkin." Reprinted by permission of Yad Vashem.

ABOUT THE AUTHOR

Dr. Joseph Rudavsky was the founder-director of the Center of Holocaust and Genocide Studies at New Jersey's Ramapo College from 1979 until his retirement in 1996.

He has served as a Reform Rabbi in Ithaca, New York; Lawrence, Massachusetts, and River Edge, New Jersey, and has directed Hillel Foundations and Jewish studies at the Universities of Texas and Georgia. He currently teaches a Holocaust-oriented course at the Hebrew College—Jewish Institute of Religion.

Dr. Rudavsky served as an officer of the International Association of Holocaust Organizations as well as the boards of the Central Conference of American Rabbis, and the New Jersey Bergen County Federation. He was the founding President of Bergen County's Board of Rabbis and the President of the CCAR's New York Region.

The current volume is based on research at Yad Vashem and the Ghettos Fighters Archives and Museum, the basis for a Ph.D. awarded to him by New York University.